CONTENTS

Maps

ON THE ROAD WITH FODOR'S

WE'RE ALWAYS THRILLED to get letters from readers, especially one like this:

It took us an hour to decide what book to buy and we now know we picked the best one. Your book was wonderful, easy to follow, very accurate, and good on pointing out eating places, informal as well as formal. When we saw other people using your book, we would look at each other and smile.

Our editors and writers are deeply committed to making every Fodor's guide "the best one"—not only accurate but always charming, brimming with sound recommendations and solid ideas, right on the mark in describing restaurants and hotels, and full of fascinating facts that make you view what you've traveled to see in a rich new light.

About Our Writers

Our success in achieving our goals—and in helping to make your trip the best of all possible vacations—is a credit to the hard work of our extraordinary writers and editors.

While living in Sweden for 12 years, English journalist **Chris Mosey**—this book's original author—was correspondent for the London newspaper *The Times* and *The Observer*.

Since leaving SAS, where he was an information manager, Stockholm-based writer **Daniel Cooper** has specialized in travel journalism, reporting on Sweden's latest goings-on for Fodor's.

New This Year

We're proud to announce that the American Society of Travel Agents has endorsed Fodor's as its guidebook of choice. ASTA is the world's largest and most influential travel trade association, operating in more than 170 countries, with 27,000 members pledged to adhere to a strict code of ethics reflecting the Society's motto, "Integrity in Travel." ASTA shares Fodor's devotion to providing smart, honest travel information and advice to travelers, and we've long recommended that our read-ers consult ASTA member agents for the experience and professionalism they bring to the table.

On the Web, check out Fodor's site (www.fodors.com/) for information on major destinations around the world and travel-savvy interactive features. The Web site also lists the 85-plus radio stations nationwide that carry *Fodor's Travel Show,* a live call-in program that airs every weekend. Tune in to hear guests discuss their wonderful adventures—or call in to get answers for your most pressing travel questions.

Eric Sjogren's essay, **"Reflections of Stockholm,"** in our Portraits chapter, illuminates the ethereal city of Stockholm and its archipelago.

How to Use This Book

Organization

Up front is the **Gold Guide,** an easy-to-use section divided alphabetically by topic. Under each listing you'll find tips and information that will help you accomplish what you need to in Sweden. You'll also find addresses and telephone numbers of organizations and companies that offer destination-related services and detailed information and publications.

The first chapter in the guide, Destination: Sweden, helps get you in the mood for your trip. What's Where gets you oriented, Fodor's Choice showcases our top picks, and Festivals and Seasonal Events alerts you to special events you'll want to seek out.

Chapters in *Fodor's Sweden,* each dealing with a major region or city, contain recommended walking or driving tours. Within each city, sights are covered alphabetically. Within each region, towns are covered in logical geographical order, and attractive stretches of road and minor points of interest between them are indicated by the designation *En Route.* Off the Beaten Path sights appear after the places from which they are most easily accessible. Within town sections, all restaurants and lodgings are grouped together. The A-to-Z section at the end of each chapter covers getting to your destination, getting around, and helpful contacts and resources.

At the end of the book you'll find Portraits, with a chronology of the history of Sweden, followed by suggestions for any pretrip research you want to do, from recommended reading to movies on tape with Sweden as a backdrop.

Icons and Symbols

★   Our special recommendations
✕   Restaurant
🏠   Lodging establishment
✕🏠 Lodging establishment whose restaurant warrants a special trip
⚠   Campgrounds
🐥   Good for kids (rubber duckie)
☞   Sends you to another section of the guide for more information
✉   Address
☎   Telephone number
🕐   Opening and closing times
💵   Admission prices (those we give apply to adults; substantially reduced fees are almost always available for children, students, and senior citizens)

Numbers in white and black circles that appear on the maps, in the margins, and within the tours correspond to one another.

Dining and Lodging

The restaurants and lodgings we list are the cream of the crop in each price range. Price charts appear in the Pleasures and Pastimes section of Chapter 1.

Hotel Facilities

We always list the facilities that are available—but we don't specify whether they cost extra: When pricing accommodations, always ask what's included. Assume that all rooms have private baths unless otherwise noted. Breakfast is almost always included in the price of Swedish hotels.

Restaurant Reservations and Dress Codes

Reservations are always a good idea; we note only when they're essential or when they are not accepted. Book as far ahead as you can, and reconfirm when you get to town. Unless otherwise noted, the restaurants listed are open daily for lunch and dinner. We mention dress only when men are required to wear a jacket or a jacket and tie.

Credit Cards

The following abbreviations are used: **AE**, American Express; **D**, Discover; **DC**, Diners Club; **MC**, MasterCard; and **V**, Visa.

Don't Forget to Write

You can use this book in the confidence that all prices and opening times are based on information supplied to us at press time; Fodor's cannot accept responsibility for any errors. Time inevitably brings changes, so always confirm information when it matters—especially if you're making a detour to visit a specific place. In addition, when making reservations be sure to mention if you have a disability or are traveling with children, if you prefer a private bath or a certain type of bed, or if you have specific dietary needs or other concerns.

Were the restaurants we recommended as described? Did our hotel picks exceed your expectations? Did you find a museum we recommended a waste of time? If you have complaints, we'll look into them and revise our entries when the facts warrant it. If you've discovered a special place that we haven't included, we'll pass the information along to our correspondents and have them check it out. So send us your feedback, positive *and* negative: email us at editors@fodors.com (specifying the name of the book on the subject line) or write the Scandinavia editor at Fodor's, 201 East 50th Street, New York, New York 10022. Have a wonderful trip!

Karen Cure
Editorial Director

Sweden

Norwegian Sea

NORWAY

FINLAND

Gulf of Bothnia

Baltic Sea

Gulf of Finland

Gulf of Riga

ESTONIA

LATVIA

LITHUANIA

DENMARK

N

0   50 miles
0   75 km

Kiruna
Gällivare
Jokkmokk
Haparanda
Töre
Kalix
Arjeplog
Arvidsjaur
Luleå
Tärnaby
Sorsele
Piteå
Storuman
Lycksele
Skellefteå
Åsele
Umeå
Strömsund
Åre
Östersund
Tännäs
Sundsvall
Hudiksvall
Idre
Bollnäs
Mora
Söderhamn
Falun
Gävle
Borlänge
Avesta
Fagersta
Uppsala
Karlstad
Västerås
Stockholm
Mellerud
Örebro
Strömstad
Uddevalla
Trollhättan
Norrköping
Göteborg
Linköping
Borås
Jönköping
Visby
Nässjö
Oskarshamn
Värnamo
Gotland
Falkenberg
Halmstad
Växjö
Kalmar
Öland
Helsingborg
Karlskrona
Malmö
Kristianstad
Trelleborg
Ystad

Mälaren
Vänern
Vättern
Klarälven
Ljungan
Umeälven
Luleälven

Gotska Sandön

E10
400
E10
45
E12
95
342
45
90
92
E4
E14
84
45
70
62
80
E4
E18
E20
E20
E4
E22
40
23
E6/E20

Scandinavia

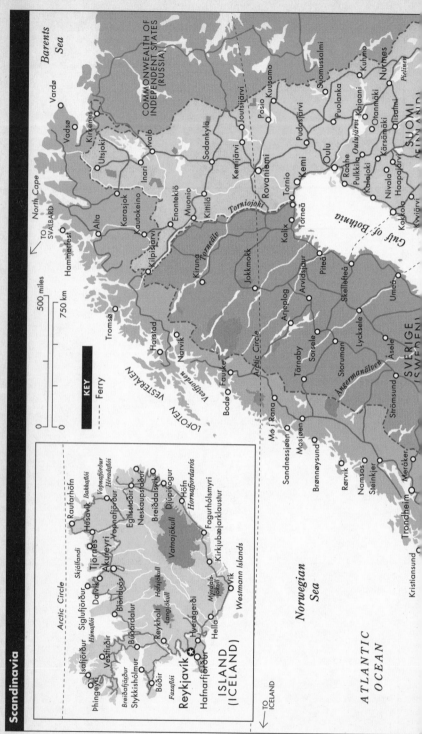

World Time Zones

Numbers below vertical bands relate each zone to Greenwich Mean Time (0 hrs.).
Local times frequently differ from these general indications,
as indicated by light-face numbers on map.

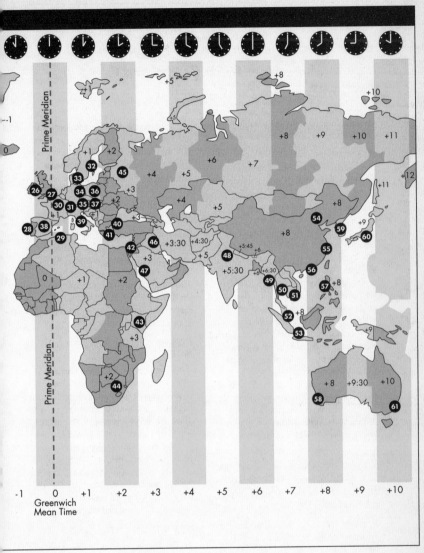

SMART TRAVEL TIPS A TO Z

Basic Information on Traveling in Sweden, Savvy Tips to Make Your Trip a Breeze, and Companies and Organizations to Contact

A

AIR TRAVEL

MAJOR AIRLINE OR LOW-COST CARRIER?

Most people choose a flight based on price. Yet there are other issues to consider. Major airlines offer the greatest number of departures; smaller airlines—including regional, low-cost, and no-frill airlines—usually have a more limited number of flights daily. Major airlines have frequent-flyer partners, which allow you to credit mileage earned on one airline to your account with another. Low-cost airlines offer a definite price advantage and fewer restrictions, such as advance-purchase requirements. Safety-wise, low-cost carriers as a group have a good history, but **check the safety record before booking** any low-cost carrier; call the Federal Aviation Administration's Consumer Hotline (☞ Airline Complaints, *below*).

➤ FROM THE U.S.: **American** (☎ 800/433–7300). **Finnair** (☎ 800/950–5000). **Scandinavian Airlines (SAS)** (☎ 800/221–2350).

➤ FROM THE U.K.: **Scandinavian Airlines (SAS)** (☎ 0171/734–4020). **British Airways** (☎ 0181/897–4000).

GET THE LOWEST FARE

The least-expensive airfares to Sweden are priced for round-trip travel. Major airlines usually require that you **book far in advance and stay at least seven days** and no more than 30 to get the lowest fares. Ask about "ultrasaver" fares, which are the cheapest; they must be booked 90 days in advance and are nonrefundable. A little more expensive are "supersaver" fares, which require only a 30-day advance purchase. Remember that penalties for refunds or scheduling changes are stiffer for international tickets, usually about $150. International flights are also sensitive to the season: **plan to fly in the off season** for the cheapest fares. If your destination or home city has more than one gateway, **compare prices to and from different airports.** Also price flights scheduled for off-peak hours, which may be significantly less expensive.

To save money on flights from the United Kingdom and back, **look into an APEX or Super-PEX ticket.** APEX tickets must be booked in advance and have certain restrictions. Super-PEX tickets can be purchased at the airport on the day of departure—subject to availability.

DON'T STOP UNLESS YOU MUST

When you book, **look for nonstop flights** and **remember that "direct" flights stop at least once.** International flights on a country's flag carrier are almost always nonstop; U.S. airlines often fly direct. Try to **avoid connecting flights,** which require a change of plane. Two airlines may jointly operate a connecting flight, so ask if your airline operates every segment—you may find that your preferred carrier flies you only part of the way.

USE AN AGENT

Travel agents, especially those who specialize in finding the lowest fares (☞ Discounts & Deals, *below*), can be especially helpful when booking a plane ticket. When you're quoted a price, **ask your agent if the price is likely to get any lower.** Good agents know the seasonal fluctuations of airfares and can usually anticipate a sale or fare war. However, waiting can be risky: The fare could go *up* as seats become scarce, and you may wait so long that your preferred flight sells out. A wait-and-see strategy works best if your plans are flexible, but if you must arrive and depart on certain dates, don't delay.

CHECK WITH CONSOLIDATORS

Consolidators buy tickets for scheduled flights at reduced rates from the airlines then sell them at prices that beat the best fare available directly from the airlines, usually without advance restrictions. Sometimes you can even get your money back if you need to return the ticket. Carefully read the fine print detailing penalties for changes and cancellations, and **confirm your consolidator reservation with the airline.**

➤ CONSOLIDATORS: **United States Air Consolidators Association** (✉ 925 L St., Suite 220, Sacramento, CA 95814, ☎ 916/441–4166, FAX 916/441–3520).

CONSIDER A CHARTER

Charters usually have the lowest fares but are not dependable. Departures are infrequent and seldom on time, flights can be delayed for up to 48 hours or can be canceled for any reason up to 10 days before you're scheduled to leave. Itineraries and prices can change after you've booked your flight, so you must **be very careful to choose a legitimate charter carrier.** Don't commit to a charter operator that doesn't follow proper booking procedures. Be especially careful when buying a charter ticket. Read the fine print regarding refund policies. If you can't pay with a credit card, **make your check payable to a charter carrier's escrow account** (unless you're dealing with a travel agent, in which case his or her check should be made payable to the escrow account). The name of the bank should be in the charter contract.

Airlines routinely overbook planes, knowing that not everyone with a ticket will show up, but sometimes everyone does. When that happens, airlines ask for volunteers to give up their seats. In return these volunteers usually get a certificate for a free flight and are rebooked on the next flight out. If there are not enough volunteers the airline must choose who will be denied boarding. The first to get bumped are passengers who checked in late and those flying on discounted tickets, **so get to the gate and check in as early as possible,** especially during peak periods.

Always **bring a photo ID to the airport.** You may be asked to show it before you are allowed to check in.

ENJOY THE FLIGHT

For more legroom, **request an emergency-aisle seat**; don't however, sit in the row in front of the emergency aisle or in front of a bulkhead, where seats may not recline.

If you don't like airline food, **ask for special meals when booking.** These can be vegetarian, low-cholesterol, or kosher, for example.

To avoid jet lag try to maintain a normal routine while traveling. At night **get some sleep.** By day **eat light meals, drink water (not alcohol), and move about the cabin** to stretch your legs.

Some carriers have prohibited smoking throughout their systems; others allow smoking only on certain routes or even certain departures from that route, so **contact your carrier regarding its smoking policy.**

COMPLAIN IF NECESSARY

If your baggage goes astray or your flight goes awry, complain right away. Most carriers require that you file a claim immediately.

➤ AIRLINE COMPLAINTS: U.S. Department of Transportation **Aviation Consumer Protection Division** (✉ C-75, Room 4107, Washington, DC 20590, ☎ 202/366–2220). **Federal Aviation Administration (FAA) Consumer Hotline** (☎ 800/322–7873).

WITHIN SWEDEN

Sweden is larger than it looks on a map, and many native travelers choose to fly between major cities, using trains and buses for local travel. If you are traveling from south to north, flying is a necessity. All major cities and towns are linked with regular flights by **Scandinavian Airlines System (SAS).**

For international travelers, one or two stopovers can often be purchased more cheaply along with an international ticket. With **SAS**, the least expensive tickets (Jackpot) are round-trip, must include a Saturday night, and can be bought only within Scandinavia from 7 to 14 days ahead. Ask about low rates for hotels and car rental in connection with Jackpot tickets. Weekend Jackpot tickets can be bought right up to flight time. SAS also gives couples traveling together a discount off some tickets and significant discounts on SAS hotels and car rentals. Low-priced round-trip weekend excursions from one Scandinavian capital to another (minimum three-day stay) can be bought one day in advance from SAS.

➤ WITHIN SWEDEN: **Scandinavian Airlines System SAS** (☎ 08/727000 or 08/974175).

AIRPORTS

The major gateway to Sweden is **Arlanda International Airport** in Stockholm. Göteborg's Landvetter airport is also served by major carriers. Flying time from New York to Stockholm is eight hours.

➤ AIRPORT INFORMATION: **Arlanda International Airport** (☎ 011–46–8/767–6100). **Landvetter** (☎ 031/941100).

B

BOAT TRAVEL

An excellent way of seeing Sweden is from the many ferry boats that ply the archipelagos and main lakes. In Stockholm, visitors should buy a special *Båtluffarkort* (Inter Skerries Card, SKr250) from Waxholmsbolaget (✉ Sodra Blasieholmsh wharf, ☎ 08/6795830). This gives unlimited travel on the archipelago ferry boats for a 16-day period.

Highly popular four-day cruises are available on the Göta Canal, which makes use of rivers, lakes, and, on its last lap, the Baltic Sea. This lovely waterway, which links Göteborg on the west coast with Stockholm on the east, has a total of 65 locks, and you travel on fine old steamers, some of which date almost from the canal's opening in 1832. The oldest and most desirable is the *Juno*, built in 1874. Prices start at SKr5,900 for a bed in a double cabin. For more information, contact the **Göta Canal Steamship Company** (✉ Box 272, S401 24 Göteborg, ☎ 031/806315, FAX 031/158311).

BUS TRAVEL

There is excellent bus service between all major towns and cities. Consult the Yellow Pages under *Bussresear-*

rangörer for the telephone numbers of the companies concerned.

Bus tours can be effective for smaller regions within Sweden, but there is an excellent train system that offers much greater coverage in less time than buses. Detailed information on bus routes is available through local tourist offices (☞ Visitor Information, *below*.)

➤ BUS COMPANY: **Swebus** (✉ Cityterminalen, Klarabergsviadukten 72, ☎ 020/640640) operates out of Stockholm.

C

CAMERAS, CAMCORDERS, & COMPUTERS

Always **keep your film, tape, or computer disks out of the sun.** Carry an extra supply of batteries, and **be prepared to turn on your camera, camcorder, or laptop** to prove to security personnel that the device is real. Always **ask for hand inspection of film,** which becomes clouded after successive exposure to airport x-ray machines, and **keep videotapes and computer disks away from metal detectors.**

➤ PHOTO HELP: **Kodak Information Center** (☎ 800/242–2424). *Kodak Guide to Shooting Great Travel Pictures,* available in bookstores or from Fodor's Travel Publications (☎ 800/533–6478; $16.50 plus $4 shipping).

CUSTOMS

Before departing, **register your foreign-made camera or laptop with U.S. Customs** (☞ Customs & Duties, *below*). If your equipment is U.S.-made, call the consulate of the country you'll be visiting to find out whether the device should be registered with local customs upon arrival.

CAR RENTAL

Rates in Stockholm begin at $110 a day and $210 a week for an economy car without air conditioning, and with a manual transmission and unlimited mileage. This does not include tax on car rentals, which is 25% in Sweden.

Major car-rental companies such as **Avis, Hertz, Europcar/InterRent, Bonus, Budget,** and **OK** have facilities in all major towns and cities as well as at airports. Some service stations offer car rentals, including **Shell, Statoil, Texaco,** and **Q8.** See the Yellow Pages under *Biluthyrning* for telephone numbers and addresses.

➤ OUTSIDE SWEDEN: **Avis** (☎ 800/331–1084, (☎ 800/879–2847 in Canada). **Budget** (☎ 800/527–0700, 0800/181181 in the U.K.). **Dollar** (☎ 800/800–4000; 0990/565656 in the U.K., where it is known as Eurodollar). **Hertz** (☎ 800/654–3001, 800/263–0600 in Canada, 0345/555888 in the U.K.). **National Inter-Rent** (☎ 800/227–3876; 01345/222525 in the U.K., where it is known as Europcar InterRent).

CUT COSTS

To get the best deal, **book through a travel agent who is willing to shop around.**

Also **ask your travel agent about a company's customer-service record.** How has it responded to late plane arrivals and vehicle mishaps? Are there often lines at the rental counter, and, if you're traveling during a holiday period, does a confirmed reservation guarantee you a car?

Be sure to **look into wholesalers,** companies that do not own fleets but rent in bulk from those that do and often offer better rates than traditional car-rental operations. Prices are best during off-peak periods. Rentals booked through wholesalers must be paid for before you leave the United States.

➤ RENTAL WHOLESALERS: **Auto Europe** (☎ 207/842–2000 or 800/223–5555, FAX 800–235–6321). **Europe by Car** (☎ 212/581–3040 or 800/223–1516, FAX 212/246–1458). The **Kemwel Group** (☎ 914/835–5555 or 800/678–0678, FAX 914/835–5126).

NEED INSURANCE?

When driving a rented car you are generally responsible for any damage to or loss of the vehicle. Before you rent, **see what coverage you already have** under the terms of your personal auto-insurance policy and credit cards.

Collision policies that car-rental companies sell for European rentals typically do not cover stolen vehicles. Before you buy additional coverage for theft, find out if your credit card or personal auto insurance will cover the loss.

BEWARE SURCHARGES

Before you pick up a car in one city and leave it in another, **ask about drop-off charges or one-way service fees,** which can be substantial. Note, too, that some rental agencies charge extra if you return the car before the time specified on your contract. To avoid a hefty refueling fee, **fill the tank just before you turn in the car,** but be aware that gas stations near the rental outlet may overcharge.

MEET THE REQUIREMENTS

Ask about age requirements: Several countries require drivers to be over 20 years old, but some car-rental companies require that drivers be at least 25. In Sweden your own driver's license is acceptable for a limited time; check with the country's tourist board before you go. An International Driver's Permit is a good idea; it's available from the American or Canadian automobile association, or, in the United Kingdom, from the Automobile Association or Royal Automobile Club.

CHILDREN & TRAVEL

CHILDREN IN SWEDEN

In Sweden children are to be seen *and* heard and are genuinely welcome in most public places.

Be sure to plan ahead and **involve your youngsters** as you outline your trip. When packing, include things to keep them busy en route. On sightseeing days try to schedule activities of special interest to your children. If you are renting a car don't forget to **arrange for a car seat** when you reserve. Most hotels in Sweden allow children under a certain age to stay in their parents' room at no extra charge, but others charge them as extra adults; be sure to **ask about the cutoff age for children's discounts.** Many youth hostels offer special facilities (including multiple-bed rooms and separate kitchens) for families with children. Family hostels also provide an excellent opportunity for children to meet youngsters from other countries. Contact the AYH (☞ Students, *below*).

DISCOUNTS

Children are entitled to discount tickets (often as much as 50% off) on buses, trains, and ferries throughout Scandinavia, as well as reductions on special City Cards. Children under 12 pay half-price and children under 2 pay 10% on SAS and Linjeflyg round-trips. The only restriction on this discount is that the family travel together and return to the originating city in Scandinavia at least two days later. With the ScanRail Pass—good for rail journeys throughout Scandinavia—children under 4 (on lap) travel free; those 4–11 pay half-fare and those 12–25 pay 75% of the adult fare.

FLYING

As a general rule, infants under two not occupying a seat fly at greatly reduced fares and occasionally for free. If your children are two or older **ask about children's airfares.**

In general the adult baggage allowance applies to children paying half or more of the adult fare. When booking, **ask about carry-on allowances for those traveling with infants.** In general, for babies charged 10% of the adult fare you are allowed one carry-on bag and a collapsible stroller, which may have to be checked; you may be limited to less if the flight is full.

According to the FAA it's a good idea to use safety seats aloft for children weighing less than 40 pounds. Airlines, however, can set their own policies: U.S. carriers allow FAA-approved models but usually require that you buy a ticket, even if your child would otherwise ride free, since the seats must be strapped into regular seats. Airline rules vary regarding their use, so it's important to **check your airline's policy about using safety seats during takeoff and landing.** Safety seats cannot obstruct any of the other passengers in the row, so get an appropriate seat assignment as early as possible.

When making your reservation, **request children's meals or a free-standing bassinet** if you need them; the latter are available only to those seated at the bulkhead, where there's enough legroom. Remember, however, that bulkhead seats may not have their own overhead bins, and there's no storage space in front of you—a major inconvenience.

GROUP TRAVEL

If you're planning to take your kids on a tour, look for companies that specialize in family travel.

➤ FAMILY-FRIENDLY TOUR OPERATORS: **Families Welcome!** (✉ 92 N. Main St., Ashland, OR 97520, ☎ 541/482–6121 or 800/326–0724, ℻ 541/482–0660). **Rascals in Paradise** (✉ 650 5th St., Suite 505, San Francisco, CA 94107, ☎ 415/978–9800 or 800/872–7225, ℻ 415/442–0289).

Whenever possible, **pay with a major credit card** so you can cancel payment if there's a problem, provided that you can provide documentation. This is a good practice whether you're buying travel arrangements before your trip or shopping at your destination.

If you're doing business with a particular company for the first time, **contact your local Better Business Bureau and the attorney general's offices** in your state and the company's home state, as well. Have any complaints been filed?

Finally, if you're buying a package or tour, always **consider travel insurance** that includes default coverage (☞ Insurance, *below*).

➤ LOCAL BBBs: **Council of Better Business Bureaus** (✉ 4200 Wilson Blvd., Suite 800, Arlington, VA 22203, ☎ 703/276–0100, ℻ 703/525–8277).

When shopping, **keep receipts** for all of your purchases. Upon reentering the country, **be ready to show customs officials what you've bought.** If you feel a duty is incorrect, appeal the assessment. If you object to the way your clearance was handled, get the inspector's badge number. In either case, first ask to see a supervisor, then write to the port director at the address listed on your receipt. Send a copy of the receipt and other appropriate documentation. If you still don't get satisfaction you can take your case to customs headquarters in Washington.

ENTERING SWEDEN

Travelers 21 or older entering Sweden from non-EU countries may import duty-free: 1 liter of liquor or 2 liters of fortified wine; 2 liters of wine; 15 liters of beer; 200 cigarettes or 100 cigarillos or 50 cigars or 250 grams of tobacco; 50 grams of perfume; ¼ liter of aftershave; and other goods up to the value of SKr 1,700. Travelers from the United Kingdom or other EU countries may import duty-free: 1 liter of liquor or 3 liters of fortified wine; 5 liters of wine; 15 liters of beer; 300 cigarettes or 150 cigarillos or 75 cigars or 400 grams of tobacco; and other goods, including perfume and aftershave, of any value.

ENTERING THE U.S.

You may bring home $400 worth of foreign goods duty-free if you've been out of the country for at least 48 hours and haven't already used the $400 allowance or any part of it in the past 30 days.

Travelers 21 and older may bring back 1 liter of alcohol duty-free. In addition, regardless of your age, you are allowed 200 cigarettes and 100 non-Cuban cigars. (At press time, a federal rule restricting tobacco access to persons 18 years and older did not apply to importation.) Antiques, which the U.S. Customs Service defines as objects more than 100 years old, enter duty-free, as do original works of art done entirely by hand, including paintings, drawings, and sculptures.

You may also send packages home duty-free: up to $200 worth of goods for personal use, with a limit of one parcel per addressee per day (and no alcohol or tobacco products or perfume worth more than $5); label the package PERSONAL USE, and attach a list of its contents and their retail value. Do not label the package UNSOLICITED GIFT, or your duty-free exemption will drop to $100. Mailed items do not affect your duty-free allowance on your return.

➤ INFORMATION: **U.S. Customs Service** (Inquiries, ✉ Box 7407, Washington, DC 20044, ☎ 202/927–6724; complaints, Office of Regulations and Rulings, 1301 Constitution Ave. NW, Washington, DC 20229; registration of equipment, ✉ Resource Management, 1301 Constitution Ave. NW, Washington DC, 20229, ☎ 202/927–0540).

ENTERING CANADA

If you've been out of Canada for at least seven days you may bring in C$500 worth of goods duty-free. If you've been away for fewer than seven days but more than 48 hours, the duty-free allowance drops to C$200; if your trip lasts 24–48 hours, the allowance is C$50. You may not pool allowances with family members. Goods claimed under the C$500 exemption may follow you by mail; those claimed under the lesser exemptions must accompany you.

Alcohol and tobacco products may be included in the seven-day and 48-hour exemptions but not in the 24-hour exemption. If you meet the age requirements of the province or territory through which you reenter Canada you may bring in, duty-free, 1.14 liters (40 imperial ounces) of wine or liquor *or* 24 12-ounce cans or bottles of beer or ale. If you are 16 or older you may bring in, duty-free, 200 cigarettes and 50 cigars; these items must accompany you.

You may send an unlimited number of gifts worth up to C$60 each duty-free to Canada. Label the package UNSOLICITED GIFT—VALUE UNDER $60. Alcohol and tobacco are excluded.

➤ INFORMATION: **Revenue Canada** (✉ 2265 St. Laurent Blvd. S, Ottawa, Ontario K1G 4K3, ☎ 613/993–0534, 800/461–9999 in Canada).

ENTERING THE U.K.

From countries outside the EU, including Sweden, you may import, duty-free, 200 cigarettes or 50 cigars; 1 liter of spirits or 2 liters of fortified or sparkling wine or liqueurs; 2 liters of still table wine; 60 milliliters of perfume; 250 milliliters of toilet water; plus £136 worth of other goods, including gifts and souvenirs.

➤ INFORMATION: **HM Customs and Excise** (✉ Dorset House, Stamford St., London SE1 9NG, ☎ 0171/202–4227).

SMART TRAVEL TIPS

THE GOLD GUIDE / SMART TRAVEL TIPS

D

DINING

Although restaurants in Sweden's major cities offer the full range of dining experiences, eating out in any of the smaller towns will probably be limited to traditional local fare, or imported fast-food joints such as McDonald's and Pizza Hut. Local food can be very good, especially in the seafood and game categories, but bear in mind that northern climes beget exceptionally hearty, and heavy, meals. Sausage appears in a thousand forms, likewise potatoes. Some particular northern tastes can seem very different, such as the fondness for pickled and fermented fish—to be sampled carefully at first—and a universal obsession with sweet pastries, ice cream, and chocolate. Other novelties for the visitor might be the use of fruit in main dishes and soups, or sour milk on breakfast cereal, or preserved fish paste as a spread for crackers, or the prevalence of crackers and complete absence of sliced bread. The Swedish *smörgåsbord* is often the traveling diner's best bet, since it includes fresh fish and vegetables alongside meat and starches; it's also among the lower-priced menu choices.

Restaurant meals are a big-ticket item throughout Sweden, but there are ways to keep the cost of eating down. Take full advantage of the large, buffet breakfast usually included in the cost of a hotel room. At lunch, look for the "menu" that offers a set two- or three-course meal for a set price, or limit yourself to a hearty appetizer. At dinner, pay careful attention to the price of wine and drinks, since the high tax on alcohol raises these costs considerably. For more information on affordable eating, *see* Costs *in* Money, *below.*

DISABILITIES & ACCESSIBILITY

ACCESS IN SWEDEN

Facilities for travelers with disabilities in Sweden are generally good, and most of the major tourist offices offer special booklets and brochures on travel and accommodations.

LODGING

The **Best Western** chain (☎ 800/528–1234) offers properties with wheel-chair-accessible rooms in Stockholm. If wheelchair-accessible rooms are not available, ground-floor rooms are provided.

TIPS AND HINTS

When discussing accessibility with an operator or reservationist, **ask hard questions.** Are there any stairs, inside *or* out? Are there grab bars next to the toilet *and* in the shower/tub? How wide is the doorway to the room? To the bathroom? For the most extensive facilities meeting the latest legal specifications, **opt for newer accommodations,** which are more likely to have been designed with access in mind. Older buildings or ships may offer more limited facilities. Be sure to **discuss your needs before booking.**

➤ COMPLAINTS: **Disability Rights Section** (⊠ U.S. Department of Justice, Box 66738, Washington, DC 20035–6738, ☎ 202/514–0301 or 800/514–0301, FAX 202/307–1198, TTY 202/514–0383 or 800/514–0383) for general complaints. **Aviation Consumer Protection Division** (☞ Air Travel, *above*) for airline-related problems. **Civil Rights Office** (⊠ U.S. Department of Transportation, Departmental Office of Civil Rights, S-30, 400 7th St. SW, Room 10215, Washington, DC, 20590, ☎ 202/366–4648) for problems with surface transportation.

TRAVEL AGENCIES & TOUR OPERATORS

The Americans with Disabilities Act requires that travel firms serve the needs of all travelers. That said, you should note that some agencies and operators specialize in making travel arrangements for individuals and groups with disabilities.

➤ TRAVELERS WITH MOBILITY PROBLEMS: **Access Adventures** (⊠ 206 Chestnut Ridge Rd., Rochester, NY 14624, ☎ 716/889–9096), run by a former physical-rehabilitation counselor. **Accessible Journeys** (⊠ 35 W. Sellers Ave., Ridley Park, PA 19078, ☎ 610/521–0339 or 800/846–4537, FAX 610/521–6959), for escorted tours exclusively for travelers with mobility impairments. **Flying Wheels Travel** (⊠ 143 W. Bridge St., Box 382, Owatonna, MN 55060, ☎ 507/451–5005 or 800/535–6790, FAX 507/451–1685), a travel agency specializing in

European cruises and tours. **Hinsdale Travel Service** (⊠ 201 E. Ogden Ave., Suite 100, Hinsdale, IL 60521, ☎ 630/325–1335), a travel agency that benefits from the advice of wheelchair traveler Janice Perkins. **Wheelchair Journeys** (⊠ 16979 Redmond Way, Redmond, WA 98052, ☎ 425/885–2210 or 800/313–4751), for general travel arrangements.

DISCOUNTS & DEALS

Be a smart shopper and **compare all your options before making a choice.** A plane ticket bought with a promotional coupon may not be cheaper than the least expensive fare from a discount ticket agency. For high-price travel purchases, such as packages or tours, keep in mind that what you get is just as important as what you save. Just because something is cheap doesn't mean it's a bargain.

LOOK IN YOUR WALLET

When you use your credit card to make travel purchases you may get free travel-accident insurance, collision-damage insurance, and medical or legal assistance, depending on the card and the bank that issued it. American Express, MasterCard, and Visa provide one or more of these services, so **get a copy of your credit card's travel-benefits policy.** If you are a member of the American Automobile Association (AAA) or an oil-company-sponsored road-assistance plan, always **ask hotel or car-rental reservationists about auto-club discounts.** Some clubs offer additional discounts on tours, cruises, or admission to attractions. And don't forget that auto-club membership entitles you to free maps and trip-planning services.

DIAL FOR DOLLARS

To save money, **look into "1-800" discount reservations services,** which use their buying power to get a better price on hotels, airline tickets, even car rentals. When booking a room, always **call the hotel's local toll-free number** (if one is available) rather than the central reservations number—you'll often get a better price. Always ask about special packages or corporate rates.

When shopping for the best deal on hotels and car rentals **look for guaranteed exchange rates,** which protect you against a falling dollar. With your rate locked in you won't pay more even if the price goes up in the local currency.

➤ AIRLINE TICKETS: ☎ 800/FLY–4–LESS.

➤ HOTEL ROOMS: **Hotels Plus** (☎ 800/235–0909). **International Marketing & Travel Concepts (IMTC)** (☎ 800/790–4682). **Steigenberger Reservation Service** (☎ 800/223–5652). **Travel Interlink** (☎ 800/888–5898).

SAVE ON COMBOS

Packages and guided tours can both save you money, but don't confuse the two. When you buy a package your travel remains independent, just as though you had planned and booked the trip yourself. Fly/drive packages, which combine airfare and car rental, are often a good deal. If you **buy a rail/drive pass** you'll save on train tickets and car rentals. All Eurail- and Europass holders get a discount on Eurostar fares through the Channel Tunnel.

JOIN A CLUB?

Many companies sell discounts in the form of travel clubs and coupon books, but these cost money. You must use participating advertisers to get a deal, and only after you recoup the initial membership cost or book price do you begin to save. If you plan to use the club or coupons frequently you may save considerably. Before signing up, find out what discounts you get for free.

➤ DISCOUNT CLUBS: **Entertainment Travel Editions** (⊠ 2125 Butterfield Rd., Troy, MI 48084, ☎ 800/445–4137; $23–$48, depending on destination). **Great American Traveler** (⊠ Box 27965, Salt Lake City, UT 84127, ☎ 800/548–2812; $49.95 per year). **Moment's Notice Discount Travel Club** (⊠ 7301 New Utrecht Ave., Brooklyn, NY 11204, ☎ 718/234–6295; $25 per year, single or family). **Privilege Card International** (⊠ 237 E. Front St., Youngstown, OH 44503, ☎ 330/746–5211 or 800/236–9732; $74.95 per year). **Sears's Mature Outlook** (⊠ Box 9390, Des Moines, IA 50306, ☎ 800/336–6330; $14.95 per year). **Travelers Advantage** (⊠ CUC Travel Service, 3033 S.

Parker Rd., Suite 1000, Aurora, CO 80014, ☎ 800/548–1116 or 800/648–4037; $49 per year, single or family). **Worldwide Discount Travel Club** (✉ 1674 Meridian Ave., Miami Beach, FL 33139, ☎ 305/534–2082; $50 per year family, $40 single).

DRIVING

Sweden has an excellent highway network of more than 80,000 km (50,000 mi). The fastest routes are those with numbers prefixed with an E (for "European"), some of which are the equivalent of American highways or British motorways. All main and secondary roads are well surfaced, but some minor roads, particularly in the north, are gravel. In remote northern areas, road conditions can be unpredictable, and careful planning is required for safety's sake. It is wise to **use a four-wheel-drive vehicle** and to **travel with at least one other car** in these areas. If you plan on extensive road touring, **buy the *Vägatlas över Sverige,*** a detailed road atlas published by the Mötormännens Riksförbund, available at bookstores for around SKr270.

Drive on the right, and, no matter where you sit in a car, **seat belts are mandatory.** You must also **have at least low-beam headlights on** at all times. Signs indicate five basic speed limits, ranging from 30 kph (19 mph) in school or playground areas to 110 kph (68 mph) on long stretches of E roads.

Be aware that there are relatively low legal blood-alcohol limits and tough penalties for driving while intoxicated in Sweden. Penalties include suspension of the driver's license and fines or imprisonment and are enforced by random police roadblocks in urban areas on weekends. An accident involving a driver with an illegal blood-alcohol level usually voids all insurance agreements, so the driver becomes responsible for his own medical bills and damage to the cars.

Gasoline costs about $1.00 per liter of lead-free gas, roughly four times the typical U.S. price. Gas stations are self-service: pumps marked SEDEL are automatic and accept SKr20 and SKr100 bills; pumps marked KASSA are paid for at the cashier; the KONTO pumps are for customers with Swedish gas credit cards.

Parking meters and, increasingly, timed ticket machines, operate in larger towns and cities, usually between 8 AM and 6 PM. The fee varies from about SKr6 to SKr35 per hour. Parking garages in urban areas are mostly automated, often with machines that accept credit cards; LEDIGT on a garage sign means space is available.

The **Larmtjänst** organization, run by a confederation of Swedish insurance companies, provides a 24-hour breakdown service. Its phone numbers are listed in the Yellow Pages.

CAR FERRY

If you are traveling to Sweden by car, you can approach through Denmark, using ferry crossings to Malmö or Helsingborg (☞ Ferries, *below*). Ferry costs are steep. **Make reservations—** they're vital.

➤ AUTO CLUBS: In the U.S., **American Automobile Association** (☎ 800/564–6222). In the U.K., **Automobile Association** (AA, ☎ 0990/500–600), **Royal Automobile Club** (RAC, membership ☎ 0990/722–722; insurance 0345/121–345).

E

ELECTRICITY

To use your U.S.-purchased electric-powered equipment, **bring a converter and adapter.** The electrical current in Sweden is 220 volts, 50 cycles alternating current (AC); wall outlets take Continental-type plugs, with two round prongs.

If your appliances are dual-voltage, you'll need only an adapter. Don't use 110-volt outlets, marked FOR SHAVERS ONLY, for high-wattage appliances such as blow-dryers. Most laptops operate equally well on 110 and 220 volts and so require only an adapter.

EMERGENCIES

Anywhere in Sweden, dial ☎ 112 for emergency assistance.

F

FERRIES

Taking a ferry isn't only fun, it's often necessary. Many companies arrange package trips, some offering a rental car and hotel accommodations as part of the deal.

Ferry crossings often last overnight. The trip between Copenhagen and Oslo, for example, takes approximately 16 hours, most lines leaving at about 5 PM and arriving about 9 the next morning. The direct cruise between Stockholm and Helsinki takes 12 hours, usually leaving at about 6 PM and arriving the next morning at 9. The shortest ferry route runs between Helsingør, Denmark, and Helsingborg, Sweden; it takes only 25 minutes.

➤ FERRY LINES: The main ferry operators running within Scandinavian waters are **Color Line** (✉ Box 30, DK–9850 Hirsthals, Denmark, ☎ 45/99–56–19–66, FAX 45/98–94–50–92; ✉ Hjortneskaia, Box 1422 Vika, N–0115 Oslo, Norway, ☎ 47/22–94–44–00, FAX 47/22–83–07–71; ✉ c/o Bergen Line, Inc., 505 5th Ave., New York, NY 10017, ☎ 800/323–7436, FAX 212/983–1275; ✉ Tyne Commission Quay, North Shields NE29 6EA, Newcastle, England, ☎ 0191/296–1313, FAX 091/296–1540), and **Scand-Lines** (✉ Box 1, DK–3000 Helsingør, Denmark, ☎ 45/49–26–26–83, FAX 45/49–26–11–24; ✉ Knutpunkten 44, S–252 78 Helsingborg, Sweden, ☎ 46/42–186100, FAX 46/42–187410).

The chief operator between England and many points within Scandinavia is **DFDS/Scandinavian Seaways** (✉ Sankt Annae Plads 30, DK–1295 Copenhagen, Denmark, ☎ 45/33–42–30–00, FAX 45/33–42–30–69; ✉ DFDS Travel Centre, 15 Hanover St., London W1R 9HG, ☎ 0171/409–5050, FAX 0171/409–6035; ✉ Scandinavia House, Parkeston Quay, Harwich, Essex, CO12 4QG, England, ☎ 01255/243–456, FAX 01255/244–370; ✉ 6555 NW 9th Ave., Suite 207, Fort Lauderdale, FL 33309, ☎ 800/533–3755, FAX 954/491–7958; ✉ Box 8895, Scandiahamnen, S–402 72 Göteborg, Sweden, ☎ 46/8–650650), with ships connecting Harwich and Newcastle to Göteborg and Amsterdam.

Connections from Denmark to Norway and Sweden are available through DFDS and the **Stena Line** (✉ Trafikhamnen, DK–9900 Frederikshavn, Denmark, ☎ 45/96–20–02–00, FAX 45/96–20–02–81; ✉ Jernbanetorget 2, N–0154 Oslo 1, Norway, ☎ 47/23–17–90–00, FAX 47/22–41–44–40; ✉ Scandinavia AB, S–405 19 Göteborg, Sweden, ☎ 46/31–775–0000, FAX 46/31–858595).

The **Silja Line** (✉ Kungsgatan 2, S–111 43 Stockholm, Sweden, ☎ 46/8–22–21–40, FAX 46/8–667–8681; ✉ c/o Scandinavian Seaways, Parkeston Quay Scand. House, Harwich, England, ☎ 44/255–240–240, FAX 44/255–240–268) offers luxurious cruises to Finland, with departures from Stockholm to Åbo, Helsingfors, Helsinki and Turku, and a crossing from Umeå to Vaasa.

Travel by car often necessitates travel by ferry. Some well-known vehicle and passenger ferries run between Dragør, Denmark (just south of Copenhagen), and Limhamn, Sweden (just south of Malmö); between Helsingør, Denmark, and Helsingborg, Sweden; and between Copenhagen and Göteborg, Sweden. On the Dragør/Limhamn ferry (ScandLines), taking a car one-way costs SKr395 (about $60 or £39). An easy trip runs between Copenhagen and Göteborg on **Stena Line** (in Sweden, ☎ 031/75–00–00). The Helsingør/Helsingborg ferry (ScandLines also) takes only 25 minutes; taking a car along one-way costs SKr330 (about $50 or £33). Fares for round-trip are cheaper, and on weekends the Öresund Runt pass (for crossing between Dragoør and Limhamn one way and Helsingborg and Helsingoør the other way) costs only SKr495 (about $75 or £49).

G

GAY & LESBIAN TRAVEL

➤ GAY- AND LESBIAN-FRIENDLY TRAVEL AGENCIES: **Advance Damron** (✉ 1 Greenway Plaza, Suite 800, Houston, TX 77046, ☎ 713/850–1140 or 800/695–0880, FAX 713/888–1010). **Club Travel** (✉ 8739 Santa Monica Blvd., West Hollywood, CA 90069, ☎ 310/358–2200 or 800/429–8747, FAX 310/358–2222). **Islanders/Kennedy Travel** (✉ 183 W. 10th St., New York, NY 10014, ☎ 212/242–3222 or 800/

988–1181, FAX 212/929–8530). **Now Voyager** (✉ 4406 18th St., San Francisco, CA 94114, ☎ 415/626–1169 or 800/255–6951, FAX 415/626–8626). **Yellowbrick Road** (✉ 1500 W. Balmoral Ave., Chicago, IL 60640, ☎ 773/561–1800 or 800/642–2488, FAX 773/561–4497). **Skylink Women's Travel** (✉ 3577 Moorland Ave., Santa Rosa, CA 95407, ☎ 707/585–8355 or 800/225–5759, FAX 707/584–5637), serving lesbian travelers.

H

HEALTH

MEDICAL PLANS

No one plans to get sick while traveling, but it happens, so **consider signing up with a medical-assistance company.** Members get doctor referrals, emergency evacuation or repatriation, 24-hour telephone hot lines for medical consultation, cash for emergencies, and other personal and legal assistance. Coverage varies by plan, so **review the benefits carefully.**

➤ MEDICAL-ASSISTANCE COMPANIES: **International SOS Assistance** (✉ Box 11568, Philadelphia, PA 19116, ☎ 215/244–1500 or 800/523–8930; ✉ 1255 University St., Suite 420, Montréal, Québec H3B 3B6, ☎ 514/874–7674 or 800/363–0263; ✉ 7 Old Lodge Pl., St. Margarets, Twickenham TW1 1RQ, England, ☎ 0181/744–0033). **MEDEX Assistance Corporation** (✉ Box 5375, Timonium, MD 21094-5375, ☎ 410/453–6300 or 800/537–2029). **Traveler's Emergency Network** (✉ 3100 Tower Blvd., Suite 1000B, Durham, NC 27707, ☎ 919/490–6055 or 800/275–4836, FAX 919/493–8262). **TravMed** (✉ Box 5375, Timonium, MD 21094, ☎ 410/453–6380 or 800/732–5309). **Worldwide Assistance Services** (✉ 1133 15th St. NW, Suite 400, Washington, DC 20005, ☎ 202/331–1609 or 800/821–2828, FAX 202/828–5896).

I

INSURANCE

Travel insurance is the best way to **protect yourself against financial loss.** The most useful policies are trip-cancellation-and-interruption, default, medical, and comprehensive insurance.

Without insurance you will lose all or most of your money if you cancel your trip, regardless of the reason. It's essential that you **buy trip-cancellation-and-interruption insurance,** particularly if your airline ticket, cruise, or package tour is nonrefundable and cannot be changed. When considering how much coverage you need, look for a policy that will cover the cost of your trip plus the nondiscounted price of a one-way airline ticket, should you need to return home early. Also **consider default or bankruptcy insurance,** which protects you against a supplier's failure to deliver.

Medicare generally does not cover health-care costs outside the United States, nor do many privately issued policies. If your own policy does not cover you outside the United States, **consider buying supplemental medical coverage.** Remember that travel health insurance is different from a medical-assistance plan (☞ Health, *above*).

Citizens of the United Kingdom can buy an annual travel-insurance policy valid for most vacations during the year in which it's purchased. If you are pregnant or have a preexisting medical condition, make sure you're covered.

If you have purchased an expensive vacation, particularly one that involves travel abroad, comprehensive insurance is a must. **Look for comprehensive policies that include trip-delay insurance,** which will protect you in the event that weather problems cause you to miss your flight, tour, or cruise. A few insurers sell waivers for preexisting medical conditions. Companies that offer both features include Access America, Carefree Travel, Travel Insured International, and Travel Guard (☞ *below*).

Always **buy travel insurance directly from the insurance company;** if you buy it from a travel agency or tour operator that goes out of business you probably will not be covered for the agency or operator's default, a major risk. Before you make any purchase, **review your existing health and home-owner's policies** to find out whether they cover expenses incurred while traveling.

➤ TRAVEL INSURERS: In the U.S., **Access America** (✉ 6600 W. Broad St., Richmond, VA 23230, ☎ 804/285–3300 or 800/284–8300), **Carefree Travel Insurance** (✉ Box 9366, 100 Garden City Plaza, Garden City, NY 11530, ☎ 516/294–0220 or 800/323–3149), **Near Travel Services** (✉ Box 1339, Calumet City, IL 60409, ☎ 708/868–6700 or 800/654–6700), **Travel Guard International** (✉ 1145 Clark St., Stevens Point, WI 54481, ☎ 715/345–0505 or 800/826–1300), **Travel Insured International** (✉ Box 280568, East Hartford, CT 06128–0568, ☎ 860/528–7663 or 800/243–3174), **Travelex Insurance Services** (✉ 11717 Burt St., Suite 202, Omaha, NE 68154-1500, ☎ 402/445–8637 or 800/228–9792, FAX 800/867–9531), **Wallach & Company** (✉ 107 W. Federal St., Box 480, Middleburg, VA 20118, ☎ 540/687–3166 or 800/237–6615). In Canada, **Mutual of Omaha** (✉ Travel Division, 500 University Ave., Toronto, Ontario M5G 1V8, ☎ 416/598–4083, 800/268–8825 in Canada). In the U.K., **Association of British Insurers** (✉ 51 Gresham St., London EC2V 7HQ, ☎ 0171/600–3333).

L

LANGUAGE

Despite the fact that Swedish is in the Germanic family of languages, it is a myth that someone who speaks German can understand Swedish. Fortunately, English is widely spoken in Sweden. German is the most common third language. Outside major cities, English becomes rarer, and it's a good idea to **take along a dictionary or phrase book.** Even here, however, anyone under the age of 50 is likely to have studied English in school.

Swedish, Danish, and Norwegian are similar, and fluent speakers can generally understand each other. A foreigner will most often be struck by the lilting rhythm of spoken Swedish, which takes a bit of getting used to for Danes and Norwegians, who often choose to speak English with Swedes.

After "z," the Swedish alphabet has three extra letters, "å," "æ" or "ä," and "ø" or "ö,". The character "ö" is pronounced a bit like a very short "er", similar to the French "eu"; "æ" or "ä," which sounds like the "a" in "ape" but with a glottal stop, or the "a" in "cat," depending on the region, and the "å" (also written "aa"), which sounds like the "o" in "ghost." The important thing about these characters isn't that you pronounce them correctly—but that you know to look for them in the phone book at the very end. Mr. Søren Åstrup, for example, will be found after "Z." Æ or Ä and Ø or Ö follow. Another oddity in the phone book is that v and w are interchangeable; Wittström, for example, comes before Vittviks, not after.

LODGING

In the larger cities, lodging ranges from first-class business hotels run by SAS, Sheraton, and Scandic to good-quality tourist-class hotels, such as RESO, Best Western, Scandic Budget, and Sweden Hotels, to a wide variety of single-entrepreneur hotels. In the countryside, look for independently run inns and motels, called guest houses. Before you leave home, **ask your travel agent about discounts** (☞ Discounts, *below*), including summer hotel checks for Best Western, Scandic, and Inter Nor hotels, and enormous year-round rebates at SAS hotels for travelers over 65. All EuroClass (business class) passengers can get discounts of at least 10% at SAS hotels when they book through SAS.

Apart from the more modest inns and the cheapest budget establishments, private baths and showers are standard. Whatever their size, almost all Swedish hotels provide scrupulously clean accommodation and courteous service. Prices in hotels are normally on a per-room basis and include all taxes and service charges and usually breakfast (deluxe establishments do not include breakfast).

Scandinavian breakfasts resemble what many people would call lunch, usually including breads, cheeses, marmalade, hams, lunch meats, eggs, juice, cereal, milk, and coffee. Generally, the farther north you go, the larger the breakfasts become.

Two things about Swedish hotels usually surprise North Americans: the relatively limited dimensions of Scandinavian beds and the generous size of Scandinavian breakfasts. Scandinavian double beds are often about 60 inches wide or slightly less, close in size to the U.S. queen size. If you want one, **make special reservations for a king-size bed** (72 inches wide): They are difficult to find.

Older hotels may have some rooms described as "double," which in fact have one double bed plus one foldout sofa big enough for two people. This arrangement is occasionally called a combi-room but is being phased out. **Ask ahead** for a private bathroom if this is important to you, as many older hotels, particularly the country inns and independently run smaller hotels in the cities, do not have private bathrooms.

APARTMENT AND VILLA RENTALS

If you want a home base that's roomy enough for a family and comes with cooking facilities, **consider a furnished rental.** These can save you money, however some rentals are luxury properties, economical only when your party is large. Home-exchange directories list rentals (often second homes owned by prospective house swappers), and some services search for a house or apartment for you (even a castle if that's your fancy) and handle the paperwork. Some send an illustrated catalog; others send photographs only of specific properties, sometimes at a charge. Up-front registration fees may apply.

➤ RENTAL AGENTS: **Europa-Let/Tropical Inn-Let** (✉ 92 N. Main St., Ashland, OR 97520, ☎ 541/482–5806 or 800/462–4486, FAX 541/482–0660). **Property Rentals International** (✉ 1008 Mansfield Crossing Rd., Richmond, VA 23236, ☎ 804/378–6054 or 800/220–3332, FAX 804/379–2073).

CAMPING

There are 760 registered campsites nationwide, many close to uncrowded bathing places and with fishing, boating, or canoeing; they may also offer bicycle rentals. Prices range from SKr70 to SKr130 per 24-hour period. Many campsites also offer accommodations in log cabins at various prices, depending on the facilities offered, and some have special facilities for guests with dis-

abilities. Most are open between June and September, but about 200 remain open in winter for skiing and skating enthusiasts.

➤ CAMPSITES: **Sveriges Campingvärdarnas Riksförbund** (Swedish Campsite Owners' Association or SCR, ✉ Box 255, S451 17 Uddevalla, ☎ 0522/39345, FAX 0522/33849), publishes, in English, an abbreviated list of sites; contact the office for a free copy.

CHALET RENTAL

With 250 chalet villages with high standards, Sweden enjoys popularity with its chalet accommodations, often arranged on the spot at tourist offices.

➤ CONTACTS: **Swedish Touring Association** (STF, ☎ 08/4632200, FAX 08/6781938). **Scandinavian Seaways** (☎ 0171/4096060 and 031/650600) in Göteborg arranges package deals that combine a ferry trip from Britain across the North Sea and a stay in a chalet village.

DISCOUNTS

Sweden offers Inn Checks, or prepaid hotel vouchers, for accommodations ranging from first-class hotels to country cottages. These vouchers, which must be purchased from travel agents or from the Scandinavian Tourist Board (☞ Visitor Information, *below*) before departure, are sold individually and in packets for as many nights as needed and offer savings of up to 50%. For further information about Scandinavian hotel vouchers, contact the Scandinavian Tourist Board.

HOME EXCHANGES

If you would like to exchange your home for someone else's, **join a home-exchange organization,** which will send you its updated listings of available exchanges for a year and will include your own listing in at least one of them. Making the arrangements is up to you.

➤ EXCHANGE CLUBS: **HomeLink International** (✉ Box 650, Key West, FL 33041, ☎ 305/294–7766 or 800/638–3841, FAX 305/294–1148) charges $83 per year.

HOTEL RESERVATIONS

The official annual guide, *Hotels in Sweden,* published by and available free from the Swedish Travel and Tourism Council (☞ Visitor Information, *below*), gives comprehensive information about hotel facilities and prices.

Make reservations whenever possible. Even countryside inns, which usually have space, are sometimes packed with vacationing Europeans. Sweden virtually shuts down during the entire month of July, so summer-time hotel reservations are especially important, especially if staying outside the city areas during July and early August.

➤ RESERVATION SERVICES: **Countryside Hotels** (✉ Box 69, 830 13 Åre, ☎ 0647/51860, FAX 0647/51920) is comprised of 35 select resort hotels, some of them restored manor houses or centuries-old inns. **Hotellcentralen** (✉ Central Station, 111 20, ☎ 08/7892425, FAX 08/7918666) is an independent agency that makes advance telephone reservations for any Swedish hotel at no cost. **Scandic** (☎ 08/6105050). **RESO** (☎ 08/4114040). **Best Western** (☎ 08/330600 or 020/792752). The **Sweden Hotels** group (☎ 08/7898900)has about 100 independently owned hotels and its own classification scheme—*A, B,* or *C*—based on facilities. **Radisson SAS** (☎ 020/797592).

M

MAIL

Postcards and letters up to 20 grams can be mailed for SKr7 to destinations within Europe, SKr8 to the United States and the rest of the world.

MONEY

The unit of currency is the krona (plural kronor), which is divided into 100 öre and is written as SKr or SEK. The 10-öre coin was phased out in 1991, leaving only the 50-öre, SKr1, and SKr5 coins. These have been joined by an SKr10 coin. Bank notes are at present SKr20, 50, 100, 500, and 1,000. At press time, the exchange rate was SKr8.08 to the dollar, SKr13.27 to the pound, and SKr5.52 to the Canadian dollar.

In this book currency is abbreviated SKr. In Sweden you may see prices indicated with Kr only, and you may see exchange rates in banks quoted for SEK.

ATMS

Before leaving home, **make sure that your credit cards have been programmed for ATM use in Sweden.** Note that Discover is accepted mostly in the United States. Local bank cards often do not work overseas or may access only your checking account; **ask your bank about a MasterCard/Cirrus or Visa debit card,** which works like a bank card but can be used at any ATM displaying a MasterCard/Cirrus or Visa logo. These cards, too, may tap only your checking account; check with your bank about their policy.

➤ ATM LOCATIONS: **Cirrus** (☎ 800/424–7787). A list of **Plus** locations is available at your local bank.

BANK AND CREDIT CARDS

The 1,200 or so blue **Bankomat** cash dispensers nationwide have been adapted to take some foreign cards, including MasterCard, Visa, and bank cards linked to the Cirrus network. For more information, contact Bankomat Centralen (☎ 08/7257240) in Stockholm or your local bank.

COSTS

Costs are high in Sweden. Throughout the region, be aware that sales taxes can be very high, but foreigners can get some refunds by shopping at tax-free stores (☞ Taxes, *below*).

Some sample prices of everyday items are: cup of coffee, SKr15–SKr20; a beer, SKr30–SKr45; mineral water, SKr10–SKr20; cheese roll, SKr20–SKr40; pepper steak à la carte, SKr120–SKr160; cheeseburger, SKr40; pizza, starting at SKr30.

You can **reduce the cost of food by planning.** Breakfast is often included in your hotel bill; if not, you may wish to buy fruit, sweet rolls, and a beverage for a picnic breakfast. **Opt for a restaurant lunch instead of dinner,** since the latter tends to be significantly more expensive. Instead of beer or wine, **drink tap water**—liquor can cost four times the price of the same brand in a store—but do specify tap water, as the term "water" can refer to soft drinks and bottled water, which are also expensive.

THE GOLD GUIDE / SMART TRAVEL TIPS

Liquor and strong beer (over 3% alcohol) can be purchased only in state-owned shops, at very high prices, during weekday business hours, usually 9:30 to 6. A 70- or 75-centiliter bottle of whiskey, for example, can easily cost SKr250 (about $35). (When you visit relatives in Scandinavia, a bottle of liquor or fine wine bought duty-free on the trip over is often a much-appreciated gift.)

CURRENCY EXCHANGE

Traveler's checks and foreign currency can be exchanged at banks all over Sweden and at post offices displaying the NB EXCHANGE sign.

For the most favorable rates, **change money at banks.** Although fees charged for ATM transactions may be higher abroad than at home, Cirrus and Plus exchange rates are excellent, because they are based on wholesale rates offered only by major banks. You won't do as well at exchange booths in airports or rail and bus stations, in hotels, in restaurants, or in stores, although you may find their hours more convenient. To avoid lines at airport exchange booths, **get a small amount of local currency before you leave home.** Since rates fluctuate daily, you should check them at the time of your departure.

➤ EXCHANGE SERVICES: **International Currency Express** (☎ 888/842–0880 on the East Coast or 888/278–6628 on the West Coast for telephone orders). **Thomas Cook Currency Services** (☎ 800/287–7362 for telephone orders and retail locations).

TIPPING

In addition to the 12% value-added tax, most hotels usually include a service charge of 15%; it is not necessary to tip unless you have received extra services. Similarly, a service charge of 13% is usually included in restaurant bills. It is a custom, however, to leave small change when buying drinks. Taxi drivers and hairdressers expect a tip of about 10%.

TRAVELER'S CHECKS

Whether or not to buy traveler's checks depends on where you are headed. **Take cash if your trip includes rural areas** and small towns, traveler's checks to cities. If your checks are lost or stolen, they can usually be replaced within 24 hours. To ensure a speedy refund, buy your checks yourself (don't ask someone else to make the purchase). When making a claim for stolen or lost checks, the person who bought the checks should make the call.

OPENING AND CLOSING TIMES

BANKS

Banks are open weekdays 9:30 AM to 3 PM, but some stay open until 5:30 on most days. The bank at Arlanda Airport is open every day with extended hours, and the Forex and Valuta Specialisten currency-exchange offices also have extended hours.

MUSEUMS

The opening times for museums vary widely, but most are open from 10 AM to 4 PM weekdays and over the weekend but are closed on Monday. Consult the guide in *På Stan,* the entertainment supplement published in *Dagens Nyheter's* Friday edition, or *Stockholm This Week.*

SHOPS

Shops are generally open weekdays from 9 AM, 9:30 AM, or 10 AM until 6 PM and Saturday from 9 AM to 1 or 4 PM. Most of the large department stores stay open later in the evenings, and some open on Sunday. Several supermarkets open on Sunday, and there are a number of late-night food shops such as the 7-Eleven chain.

OUTDOOR ACTIVITIES AND SPORTS

BIKING

Rental costs average around SKr90 per day. Tourist offices and **Svenska Turistförening** (Swedish Touring Association of STF, ✉ Box 25, S101 20 Stockholm, ☎ 08/4632200, FAX 08/6781938) have information about cycling package holidays that include bike rentals, overnight accommodations, and meals. The bicycling organization, **Cykelfrämjandet** (National Cycle Association, ✉ Torsg. 31, Box 6027, S102 31 Stockholm, ☎ 08/321680 Mon.–Thurs. 9–noon, FAX 08/310503), publishes a free English-language guide to cycling trips.

BOATING AND SAILING

STF, in cooperation with Telia (Sweden's PTT, or Postal, Telephone, and Telegraph authority), publishes an annual guide in Swedish to all the country's marinas. It is available from **Telia Infomedia** (☎ 08/6341700) or in your nearest Telebutik. **Svenska Kanotförbundet** (Swedish Canoeing Association, ✉ Skeppsbron 11, 611 35 Nyköping, ☎ 0155/69508) publishes a similar booklet.

GOLFING

Sweden has 365 golf clubs; you can even play by the light of the midnight sun at Boden in the far north. **Svenska Golfförbundet** (Swedish Golfing Association, ✉ Box 84, S182 11 Danderyd, ☎ 08/6221500, FAX 08/7558439) publishes an annual guide in Swedish; it costs around SKr100, including postage.

SKIING

There are plenty of downhill and cross-country facilities in Sweden. The best-known resorts are in the country's western mountains: Åre in the north, with 29 lifts; Idre Fjäll, to the south of Åre, offering accommodations for 10,000; and Sälen in the folklore region of Dalarna. You can ski through May at Riksgränsen in the far north.

TENNIS

Contact **Svenska Tennisförbundet** (Swedish Tennis Association, ✉ Lidingöv. 75, Box 27915, S115 94 Stockholm, ☎ 08/6679770, FAX 08/6646606).

P

PACKING FOR SWEDEN

Bring a folding umbrella and a lightweight raincoat, as it is common for the sky to be clear at 9 AM, rainy at 11 AM, and clear again in time for lunch. **Pack casual clothes,** as Swedes tend to dress more casually than their Continental brethren. If you have trouble sleeping when it is light or are sensitive to strong sun, **bring an eye mask and dark sunglasses;** the sun rises as early as 4 AM in some areas, and the far-northern latitude causes it to slant at angles unseen elsewhere on the globe. **Bring bug repellent** if you plan to venture away from the capital cities; large mosquitoes can be a real nuisance in the far-northern reaches of Sweden.

Bring an extra pair of eyeglasses or contact lenses in your carry-on luggage, and if you have a health problem, **pack enough medication** to last the entire trip or have your doctor write you a prescription using the drug's generic name, because brand names vary from country to country. It's important that you **don't put prescription drugs or valuables in luggage to be checked**: it might go astray. To avoid problems with customs officials, carry medications in the original packaging. Also, don't forget the addresses of offices that handle refunds of lost traveler's checks.

LUGGAGE

In general, you are entitled to check two bags on flights within the United States and on international flights leaving the United States. A third piece may be brought on board, but it must fit easily under the seat in front of you or in the overhead compartment.

If you are flying between two foreign destinations, note that baggage allowances may be determined not by piece but by weight—generally 88 pounds (40 kilograms) in first class, 66 pounds (30 kilograms) in business class, and 44 pounds (20 kilograms) in economy. If your flight between two cities abroad *connects* with your transatlantic or transpacific flight, the piece method still applies.

Airline liability for baggage is limited to $1,250 per person on flights within the United States. On international flights it amounts to $9.07 per pound or $20 per kilogram for checked baggage (roughly $640 per 70-pound bag) and $400 per passenger for unchecked baggage. Insurance for losses exceeding these amounts can be bought from the airline at check-in for about $10 per $1,000 of coverage; note that this coverage excludes a rather extensive list of items, which is shown on your airline ticket.

Before departure, **itemize your bags' contents** and their worth, and label the bags with your name, address, and phone number. (If you use your home address, cover it so that potential thieves can't see it readily.) Inside each bag, **pack a copy of your**

itinerary. At check-in, **make sure that each bag is correctly tagged** with the destination airport's three-letter code. If your bags arrive damaged or fail to arrive at all, file a written report with the airline before leaving the airport.

PASSPORTS & VISAS

Once your travel plans are confirmed, **check the expiration date of your passport.** It's also a good idea to **make photocopies of the data page;** leave one copy with someone at home and keep another with you, separated from your passport. If you lose your passport, promptly call the nearest embassy or consulate and the local police; having a copy of the data page can speed replacement.

U.S. CITIZENS

All U.S. citizens, even infants, need only a valid passport to enter Sweden for stays of up to three months.

➤ INFORMATION: **Office of Passport Services** (☎ 202/647–0518).

CANADIANS

You need only a valid passport to enter Sweden for stays of up to three months.

➤ INFORMATION: **Passport Office** (☎ 819/994–3500 or 800/567–6868).

U.K. CITIZENS

Citizens of the United Kingdom need only a valid passport to enter Sweden for stays of up to three months.

➤ INFORMATION: **London Passport Office** (☎ 0990/21010) for fees and documentation requirements and to request an emergency passport.

S

SENIOR-CITIZEN TRAVEL

To qualify for age-related discounts, **mention your senior-citizen status up front** when booking hotel reservations (not when checking out) and before you're seated in restaurants (not when paying the bill). Note that discounts may be limited to certain menus, days, or hours. When renting a car, **ask about promotional car-rental discounts,** which can be cheaper than senior-citizen rates.

➤ EDUCATIONAL TRAVEL PROGRAMS: **Elderhostel** (✉ 75 Federal St., 3rd floor, Boston, MA 02110, ☎ 617/

426–8056). **Interhostel** (✉ University of New Hampshire, 6 Garrison Ave., Durham, NH 03824, ☎ 603/862–1147 or 800/733–9753, FAX 603/862–1113).

TRAIN TRAVEL

Travelers over 60 can buy a **SeniorRail Card** for about $27. It gives 30% discounts on train travel in 21 European countries for a whole year from purchase.

SHOPPING

Prices in Sweden are never low, but quality is high, and specialties are sometimes less expensive here than elsewhere. Swedish crystal is just one of the items to look for. Keep an eye out for sales, called *rea* in Swedish.

STUDENTS

To save money, **look into deals available through student-oriented travel agencies.** To qualify you'll need a bona fide student ID card. Members of international student groups are also eligible.

➤ STUDENT IDs AND SERVICES: **Council on International Educational Exchange** (✉ CIEE, 205 E. 42nd St., 14th floor, New York, NY 10017, ☎ 212/822–2600 or 888/268–6245, FAX 212/822–2699), for mail orders only, in the United States. **Travel Cuts** (✉ 187 College St., Toronto, Ontario M5T 1P7, ☎ 416/979–2406 or 800/667–2887) in Canada.

➤ HOSTELING: **Hostelling International—American Youth Hostels** (✉ 733 15th St. NW, Suite 840, Washington, DC 20005, ☎ 202/783–6161, FAX 202/783–6171). **Hostelling International—Canada** (✉ 400-205 Catherine St., Ottawa, Ontario K2P 1C3, ☎ 613/237–7884, FAX 613/237–7868). **Youth Hostel Association of England and Wales** (✉ Trevelyan House, 8 St. Stephen's Hill, St. Albans, Hertfordshire AL1 2DY, ☎ 01727/855215 or 01727/845047, FAX 01727/844126). Membership in the U.S., $25; in Canada, C$26.75; in the U.K., £9.30).

➤ STUDENT TOURS: **AESU Travel** (✉ 2 Hamill Rd., Suite 248, Baltimore, MD 21210-1807, ☎ 410/323–4416 or 800/638–7640, FAX 410/323–4498).

T

VALUE-ADDED TAX (V.A.T.)

One way to beat high prices is to **take advantage of tax-free shopping.** Value-added tax (called *moms* all over Scandinavia) is 25% and is automatically included in prices. Throughout Sweden, you can make major purchases free of tax if you have a foreign passport. Non-EU residents can obtain a 15% refund on goods of SKr200 or more. To receive your refund at any of the 15,000 stores that participate in the tax-free program, you'll be asked to fill out a form and show your passport. The form can then be turned in at any airport or ferry customs desk. Keep all your receipts and tags; occasionally, customs authorities ask to see your purchases, so pack them where they will be accessible.

Sweden's country code is 46.

DIRECTORY ASSISTANCE AND OPERATOR INFORMATION

For international calls, the operator assistance number is ☎ 0018; directory assistance is ☎ 07977. Within Sweden, dial ☎ 90130 for operator assistance and ☎ 07975 for directory assistance.

INTERNATIONAL CALLS

The foreign dialing code is 009, followed by the country code, then your number (☞ Local Access Codes, *below*).

LOCAL CALLS

Post offices do not have telephone facilities, but there are plenty of pay phones, and long-distance calls can be made from special telegraph offices called *Telebutik,* marked TELE.

A local call costs a minimum of SKr2. For calls outside the locality, dial the area code (see telephone directory). Public phones are of three types: one takes SKr1 and SKr5 coins (newer public phones also accept SKr10 coins); another takes only credit cards; and the last takes only the prepaid *Telefonkort.*

A *Telefonkort* (telephone card), available at Telebutik, Pressbyrån (large blue-and-yellow newsstands), or hospitals, costs SKr35, SKr60, or SKr100. If you're making numerous domestic calls, the card saves money. Many of the pay phones in downtown Stockholm and Göteborg take only these cards, so it's a good idea to carry one.

CALLING HOME

Before you go, **find out the local access codes** for your destinations. AT&T, MCI, and Sprint long-distance services make calling home relatively convenient, but you may find the local access number blocked in many hotel rooms. First ask the hotel operator to connect you. If the hotel operator balks, ask for an international operator, or dial the international operator yourself. One way to improve your odds of getting connected to your long-distance carrier is to travel with more than one company's calling card (a hotel may block Sprint, for example, but not MCI). If all else fails, call your phone company collect in the United States or call from a pay phone in the hotel lobby.

➤ TO OBTAIN ACCESS CODES: AT&T USADirect (☎ 800/874–4000). MCI Call USA (☎ 800/444–4444). Sprint Express (☎ 800/793–1153).

➤ LOCAL ACCESS CODES: AT&T USADirect (☎ 020/795611). MCI Call USA (☎ 020/795922). Sprint Express (☎ 020/799011).

Buying a prepackaged tour or independent vacation can make your trip to Sweden less expensive and more hassle-free. Because everything is prearranged you'll spend less time planning.

Operators that handle several hundred thousand travelers per year can use their purchasing power to give you a good price. Their high volume may also indicate financial stability. But some small companies provide more personalized service; because they tend to specialize, they may also be more knowledgeable about a given area.

A GOOD DEAL?

The more your package or tour includes, the better you can predict the ultimate cost of your vacation. Make sure you know exactly what is covered, and **beware of hidden costs.** Are taxes, tips, and service charges included? Transfers and baggage handling? Entertainment and excursions? These can add up.

If the package or tour you are considering is priced lower than in your wildest dreams, **be skeptical.** Also, **make sure your travel agent knows the accommodations** and other services. Ask about the hotel's location, room size, beds, and whether it has a pool, room service, or programs for children, if you care about these. Has your agent been there in person or sent others you can contact?

BUYER BEWARE

Each year consumers are stranded or lose their money when tour operators—even very large ones with excellent reputations—go out of business. So **check out the operator.** Find out how long the company has been in business, and ask several agents about its reputation. **Don't book unless the firm has a consumer-protection program.**

Members of the National Tour Association and United States Tour Operators Association are required to set aside funds to cover your payments and travel arrangements in case the company defaults. Nonmembers may carry insurance instead. Look for the details, and for the name of an underwriter with a solid reputation, in the operator's brochure. Note: When it comes to tour operators, **don't trust escrow accounts.** Although the Department of Transportation watches over charter-flight operators, no regulatory body prevents tour operators from raiding the till. You may want to protect yourself by buying travel insurance that includes a tour-operator default provision. For more information, *see* Consumer Protection, *above.*

It's also a good idea to choose a company that participates in the American Society of Travel Agent's Tour Operator Program (TOP). This gives you a forum if there are any disputes between you and your tour operator; ASTA will act as mediator.

➤ TOUR-OPERATOR RECOMMENDATIONS: **American Society of Travel Agents** (☞ Travel Agencies, *below*). **National Tour Association** (✉ NTA, 546 E. Main St., Lexington, KY 40508, ☎ 606/226–4444 or 800/755–8687). **United States Tour Operators Association** (✉ USTOA, 342 Madison Ave., Suite 1522, New York, NY 10173, ☎ 212/599–6599, FAX 212/599–6744).

USING AN AGENT

Travel agents are excellent resources. In fact, large operators accept bookings made only through travel agents. But it's a good idea to **collect brochures from several agencies,** because some agents' suggestions may be influenced by relationships with tour and package firms that reward them for volume sales. If you have a special interest, **find an agent with expertise in that area;** ASTA (☞ Travel Agencies, *below*) has a database of specialists worldwide. Do some homework on your own, too: Local tourism boards can provide information about lesser-known and small-niche operators, some of which may sell only direct.

SINGLE TRAVELERS

Prices for packages and tours are usually quoted per person, based on two sharing a room. If traveling solo, you may be required to pay the full double-occupancy rate. Some operators eliminate this surcharge if you agree to be matched with a roommate of the same sex, even if one is not found by departure time.

GROUP TOURS

Among companies that sell tours to Sweden, the following are nationally known, have a proven reputation, and offer plenty of options. The classifications used below represent different price categories, and you'll probably encounter these terms when talking to a travel agent or tour operator. The key difference is usually in accommodations, which run from budget to better, and better-yet to best.

➤ SUPER-DELUXE: **Abercrombie & Kent** (✉ 1520 Kensington Rd., Oak Brook, IL 60521-2141, ☎ 630/954–2944 or 800/323–7308, FAX 630/954–3324). **Travcoa** (✉ Box 2630, 2350 S.E. Bristol St., Newport Beach, CA 92660, ☎ 714/476–2800 or 800/992–2003, FAX 714/476–2538).

➤ DELUXE: **Globus** (✉ 5301 S. Federal Circle, Littleton, CO 80123-2980, ☎ 303/797–2800 or 800/221–0090, FAX 303/347–2080). **Maupintour** (✉ 1515 St. Andrews Dr., Lawrence, KS 66047, ☎ 913/843–1211 or 800/255–4266, FAX 913/843–8351). **Tauck Tours** (✉ Box 5027, 276 Post Rd. W, Westport, CT 06881-5027, ☎ 203/226–6911 or 800/468–2825, FAX 203/221–6828).

➤ FIRST-CLASS: **Bennett Tours** (✉ 270 Madison Ave., New York, NY 10016-0658, ☎ 212/532–5060 or 800/221–2420, FAX 212/779–8944). **Brendan Tours** (✉ 15137 Califa St., Van Nuys, CA 91411, ☎ 818/785–9696 or 800/421–8446, FAX 818/902–9876). **Brekke Tours** (✉ 802 N. 43rd St., Ste. D, Grand Forks, ND 58203, ☎ 701/772–8999 or 800/437–5302, FAX 701/780–9352). **Caravan Tours** (✉ 401 N. Michigan Ave., Chicago, IL 60611, ☎ 312/321–9800 or 800/227–2826, FAX 312/321–9845). **Collette Tours** (✉ 162 Middle St., Pawtucket, RI 02860, ☎ 401/728–3805 or 800/832–4656, FAX 401/728–1380). **Finnair** (☎ 800/950–5000). **KITT Holidays** (✉ 2 Appletree Sq., #150, 8011 34th Ave. S., Minneapolis, MN 55425, ☎ 612/854–8005 or 800/262–8728, FAX 612/854–6948). **Scantours** (✉ 1535 6th St., #205, Santa Monica, CA 90401-2533, ☎ 310/451–0911 or 800/223–7226, FAX 310/395–2013). **Scan Travel Center** (✉ 66 Edgewood Ave., Larchmont, NY 10538, ☎ 803/671–6758 or 800/759–7226). **Trafalgar Tours** (✉ 11 E. 26th St., New York, NY 10010, ☎ 212/689–8977 or 800/854–0103, FAX 800/457–6644).

➤ BUDGET: **Cosmos** (☞ Globus, *above*). **Trafalgar** (☞ *above*).

PACKAGES

Like group tours, independent vacation packages are available from major tour operators and airlines. The companies listed below offer vacation packages in a broad price range.

➤ AIR/HOTEL/SIGHTSEEING: **DER Tours** (✉ 9501 W. Devon St., Rosemont, IL 60018, ☎ 800/937–1235; FAX 800/282–7474, 800/860–9944 for brochures). **Icelandair** (☎ 800/757–3876).

THEME TRIPS

➤ ADVENTURE: **Borton Overseas** (✉ 1621 E. 79th St., Bloomington, MN 55425, ☎ 612/883–0704 or 800/843–0602, FAX 612/883–0221). **Scandinavian Special Interest Network** (✉ Box 313, Sparta, NJ 07871, ☎ 201/729–8961, FAX 201/729–6565).

➤ BICYCLING: **Euro-Bike Tours** (✉ Box 990, De Kalb, IL 60115, ☎ 800/321–6060, FAX 815/758–8851).

➤ CRUISING: **Bergen Line** (✉ 405 Park Ave., New York, NY 10022, ☎ 212/319–1300 or 800/323–7436, FAX 212/319–1390). **EuroCruises** (✉ 303 W. 13th St., New York, NY 10014, ☎ 212/691–2099 or 800/688–3876). **Swan Hellenic/Classical Cruises & Tours** (✉ 132 E. 70th St., New York, NY 10021, ☎ 800/252–7745, FAX 212/774–1545).

➤ CUSTOMIZED PACKAGES: **Scandinavian Special Interest Network** (☞ Adventure, *above*).

➤ FISHING: **Scandinavian Special Interest Network** (☞ Adventure, *above*).

➤ GENEALOGY: **Brekke Tours** (✉ 802 N. 43rd St., Ste. D, Grand Forks, ND 58203, ☎ 701/772–8999 or 800/437–5302, FAX 701/780–9352).

➤ LEARNING: **Earthwatch** (✉ Box 9104, 680 Mount Auburn St., Watertown, MA 02272, ☎ 617/926–8200 or 800/776–0188, FAX 617/926–8532) for research expeditions.

➤ MUSIC: **Dailey-Thorp Travel** (✉ 330 W. 58th St., #610, New York, NY 10019-1817, ☎ 212/307–1555 or 800/998–4677, FAX 212/974–1420).

TRAIN TRAVEL

Statens Järnvägar, or SJ, the state railway company, has a highly efficient network of comfortable, electric trains. On nearly all long-distance routes there are buffet cars and, on overnight trips, sleeping cars and couchettes in both first and second class. Seat reservations are advisable, and on some trains—indicated with *R, IN,* or *IC* on the timetable—they are compulsory. An extra fee of SKr15 is charged to reserve a seat on a trip of less than 150 km (93 mi); on longer trips there is no extra charge.

Reservations can be made right up to departure time. SJ also organizes reduced-cost package trips in conjunction with local tourist offices. The **high-speed X2000 train** has been introduced on several routes; the Stockholm–Göteborg run takes just under three hours. Travelers younger than 19 years travel at half-fare. Up to two children younger than 12 years may travel free if accompanied by an adult.

Statens Järnvägar (SJ) (⊠ Central Station, Vasag. 1, ☎ 08/762–2000 or 020/75–7575).

To save money, **look into rail passes,** but be aware that if you don't plan to cover many miles, you may come out ahead by buying individual tickets.

➤ FROM THE U.K.: The **British Rail European Travel Center** (⊠ Victoria Station, London, ☎ 0171/8342345) can be helpful in arranging connections to Sweden's SJ (Statens Järnvägar).

DISCOUNT PASSES

Sweden is one of 17 countries in which you can **use EurailPasses,** which provide unlimited first-class rail travel, in all of the participating countries, for the duration of the pass. If you plan to rack up the miles, get a standard pass. These are available for 15 days ($522), 21 days ($678), one month ($838), two months ($1,188), and three months ($1,468). InterRail passes are also valid in Sweden.

For SKr150 you can buy a *Reslustkort,* which gets you 50% reductions on *röda avgångar* ("red," or off-peak, departures).

The **ScanRail Pass** comes in various denominations: five days of travel within 15 days ($222 first class, $176 second class); 10 days within a month ($354 first class, $284 second class); or one month ($516 first class, $414 second class).

In addition to standard EurailPasses, **ask about special rail-pass plans.** Among these are the Eurail Youthpass (for those under age 26), the Eurail Saverpass (which gives a discount for two or more people traveling together), a Eurail Flexipass (which allows a certain number of travel days within a set period), the

Euraildrive Pass, and the Europass Drive (which combines travel by train and rental car).

Whichever pass you choose, remember that you must **purchase your pass before you leave** for Europe.

Many travelers assume that rail passes guarantee them seats on the trains they wish to ride. Not so. You need to **book seats ahead even if you are using a rail pass;** seat reservations are required on some European trains, particularly high-speed trains, and are a good idea on trains that may be crowded—particularly in summer on popular routes. You will also need a reservation if you purchase sleeping accommodations.

➤ RAIL PASSES: Swedish rail passes are sold by travel agents as well as **Rail Europe** (⊠ 226–230 Westchester Ave., White Plains, NY 10604, ☎ 914/682–5172 or 800/438–7245; ⊠ 2087 Dundas East, Suite 105, Mississauga, Ontario L4X 1M2, ☎ 416/ 602–4195).

Eurail and EuroPasses are available through travel agents and **Rail Europe** (⊠ 226-230 Westchester Ave., White Plains, NY 10604, ☎ 914/682–5172 or 800/438–7245; ⊠ 2087 Dundas East, Suite 105, Mississauga, Ontario L4X 1M2, ☎ 416/602–4195), **DER Tours** (⊠ Box 1606, Des Plaines, IL 60017, ☎ 800/782–2424, FAX 800/ 282–7474), or **CIT Tours Corp.** (⊠ 342 Madison Ave., Suite 207, New York, NY 10173, ☎ 212/697– 2100 or 800/248–8687, or 800/248– 7245 in western U.S.).

A good travel agent puts your needs first. Look for an agency that has been in business at least five years, emphasizes customer service, and has someone on staff who specializes in your destination. In addition, **make sure the agency belongs to the American Society of Travel Agents** (ASTA). If your travel agency is also acting as your tour operator, *see* Buyer Beware in Tour Operators, *above).

➤ LOCAL AGENT REFERRALS: American Society of Travel Agents (ASTA), ☎ 800/965–2782 24-hr hot line, FAX 703/684–8319). **Alliance of Canadian Travel Associations** (⊠ Suite 201,

1729 Bank St., Ottawa, Ontario K1V 7Z5, ☎ 613/521–0474, FAX 613/521–0805). **Association of British Travel Agents** (⌂ 55–57 Newman St., London W1P 4AH, ☎ 0171/637–2444, FAX 0171/637–0713).

Travel catalogs specialize in useful items, such as compact alarm clocks and travel irons, that can **save space when packing.** They also offer dual-voltage appliances, currency converters, and foreign-language phrase books.

➤ MAIL-ORDER CATALOGS: **Magellan's** (☎ 800/962–4943, FAX 805/568–5406). **Orvis Travel** (☎ 800/541–3541, FAX 540/343–7053). **Travel-Smith** (☎ 800/950–1600, FAX 800/950–1656).

U

The U.S. government can be an excellent source of inexpensive travel information. When planning your trip, **find out what government materials are available.**

➤ ADVISORIES: **U.S. Department of State** (⌂ Overseas Citizens Services Office, Room 4811 N.S., Washington, DC 20520); enclose a self-addresses, stamped envelope. Interactive hot line (☎ 202/647–5225, FAX 202/647–3000). Computer bulletin board (☎ 301/946–4400).

➤ PAMPHLETS: **Consumer Information Center** (⌂ Consumer Information Catalogue, Pueblo, CO 81009, ☎ 719/948–3334) for a free catalog that includes travel titles.

Before you go, call or write to the tourist board for general information. From the U.K., contact the individual countries' tourist boards.

➤ SCANDINAVIAN TOURIST BOARD: U.S. and Canada: (⌂ Box 4649, Grand Central Station, New York, NY 10163–4649, ☎ 212/885–9700, FAX 212/885–9710).

➤ SWEDISH TRAVEL AND TOURISM COUNCIL: **U.K.:** (⌂ 73 Welbeck St., London W1M 8AN, ☎ 0171/935–9784, FAX 0171/935–5853). **Stockholm** (⌂ Box 3030, Kungsg. 36, 103 61 Stockholm, ☎ 08/7255500, FAX 08/7255531). **Stockholm Information Service at Sweden House** (Sverigehuset, ⌂ Hamng. 27, Box 7542, S103 93 Stockholm, ☎ 08/7892490).

W

The tourist season runs from mid-May through mid-September; however, many attractions close in late August, when the schools reopen at the end of the Swedish vacation season. In general, the weather is not overly warm, and a brisk breeze and brief rainstorms are possible anytime. Nights can be chilly, even in summer. The weather can be glorious in the spring and fall, and many visitors prefer sightseeing when there are fewer people around.

Visit in summer if you want to experience the delightfully long summer days. In June, the sun rises in Copenhagen at 4 AM and sets at 11 PM and daylight lasts even longer farther north, making it possible to extend your sightseeing into the balmy evenings. Many attractions extend their hours during the summer, and many shut down altogether when summer ends. Sweden has typically unpredictable north European summer weather, but, as a general rule, it is likely to be warm but not hot from May until September. In Stockholm, the weeks just before and after Mid-summer offer almost 24-hour light, whereas in the far north, above the Arctic Circle, the sun doesn't set between the end of May and the middle of July. Fall, spring, and even winter are pleasant, despite the area's reputation for gloom. The days become shorter quickly, but the sun casts a golden light one does not see farther south. On dark days, fires and candlelight will warm you indoors.

Away from the protection of the Gulf Stream, northern Sweden experiences very cold, clear weather that attracts skiers; even Stockholm's harbor, well south in Sweden but facing the Baltic Sea, freezes over completely.

CLIMATE

STOCKHOLM

Jan.	30F	−1C	May	57F	14C	Sept.	59F	15C
	23	−5		43	6		48	9
Feb.	30F	−1C	June	66F	19C	Oct.	48F	9C
	23	−5		52	11		41	5
Mar.	37F	3C	July	72F	22C	Nov.	41F	5C
	25	−4		57	14		34	1
Apr.	46F	8C	Aug.	68F	20C	Dec.	36F	2C
	34	1		55	13		28	−2

➤ FORECASTS: **Weather Channel Connection** (☎ 900/932–8437), 95¢ per minute from a Touch-Tone phone.

1 Destination: Sweden

SWEDISH SPECTACULAR

SWEDEN REQUIRES THE VISITOR to travel far, in terms of both distance and attitude. Approximately the size of California, Sweden reaches as far north as the Arctic fringes of Europe, where glacier-topped mountains and thousands of acres of pine, spruce, and birch forests are broken here and there by wild rivers, countless pristine lakes, and desolate moorland. In the more populated south, roads meander through mile after mile of softly undulating countryside, skirting lakes and passing small villages with their ubiquitous sharp-pointed church spires. Here, the lush forests that dominate Sweden's northern landscape have largely fallen to the plow.

Once the dominant power of the region, Sweden has traditionally looked mostly inward, seeking to find its own, Nordic solutions. During the cold war, it tried with considerable success to steer its famous "Middle Way" between the two superpowers, both economically and politically. Its citizens were in effect subjected to a giant social experiment aimed at creating a perfectly just society, one that adopted the best aspects of both socialism and capitalism.

In the late 1980s, as it slipped into the worst economic recession since the 1930s, Sweden made adjustments that lessened the role of its all-embracing welfare state in the lives of its citizens. Although fragile, the conservative coalition, which defeated the long-incumbent Social Democrats in the fall of 1991, attempted to make further cutbacks in welfare spending as the country faced one of the largest budget deficits in Europe. In a kind of nostalgic backlash, the populace voted the Social Democrats back into power in 1994, hoping to recapture the party's policy of cradle-to-grave protection. The world economy hasn't exactly cooperated, and the country's budget deficit is only now crawling back to parity. An influx of immigrants is reshaping what was once a homogeneous society. As a result, the mostly blond, blue-eyed Swedes may now be more open to the outside world than at any other time in their history. Indeed, another major change was Sweden's decision to join the European Union (EU) as of January 1995, a move that represents a radical break with its traditional independent stance on international issues. So far, the domestic benefits of membership are not tangible, but the country's exporting industries have made considerable gains.

The country possesses stunning natural assets. In the forests, moose, deer, bears, and lynx roam, coexisting with the whine of power saws and the rumble of automatic logging machines as mankind exploits a natural resource that remains the country's economic backbone. Environmental awareness, however, is high. Fish abound in sparkling lakes and tumbling rivers, sea eagles and ospreys soar over myriad pine-clad islands in the archipelagoes off the east and west coasts.

The country is Europe's fourth largest, 482,586 square km (173,731 square mi) in area, and its population of 8.7 million is thinly spread. If, like Greta Garbo—one of its most famous exports—you enjoy being alone, you've come to the right place. A law called *Allemansrätt* guarantees public access to the countryside; NO TRESPASSING signs are seldom seen.

Sweden stretches 1,563 km (977 mi) from the barren Arctic north to the fertile plains of the south. Contrasts abound, but they are neatly tied together by a superbly efficient infrastructure, embracing air, road, and rail. You can catch salmon in the far north and, thanks to the excellent domestic air network, have it cooked by the chef of your luxury hotel in Stockholm later the same day.

The seasons contrast savagely: Sweden is usually warm and exceedingly light in the summer, then cold and dark in the winter. The sea may freeze, and in the north, iron railway lines may snap.

Sweden is also an arresting mixture of ancient and modern. The countryside is dotted with runic stones recalling its Viking past: trade beginning in the 8th century eastward to Kiev and as far south as Constantinople and the Mediterranean, expanding to the British Isles in the 9th through 11th centuries, and settling in Normandy in the 10th century. Small timbered farmhouses and maypoles around which villagers still dance at Midsummer in their traditional costumes evoke both the pagan early history and the more recent agrarian culture.

Many of the country's cities are sci-fi modern, their shop windows filled with the latest in consumer goods and fashions, but Swedes are reluctant urbanites: their hearts and souls are in the forests and the archipelagoes, and to there they faithfully retreat in the summer and on weekends to take their holidays, pick berries, or just listen to the silence. The skills of the wood-carver, the weaver, the leather worker, and the glassblower are all highly prized. Similarly, Swedish humor is earthy and slapstick. Despite the praise lavished abroad on introspective dramatic artists such as August Strindberg and Ingmar Bergman, it is the simple trouser-dropping farce that will fill Stockholm's theaters, the scatological joke that will get the most laughs.

Again, despite the international musical success of the Swedish rock groups Ace of Base, Roxette, and Abba, the domestic penchant is more often for the good, old-fashioned dance band. Gray-haired men in pastel sweaters playing saxophones are more common on TV than heavy-metal rockers. Strangely, in ultramodern concert halls and discos, it is possible to step back in time to the 1950s, if not the 1940s.

Despite the much-publicized sexual liberation of Swedes, the joys of hearth and home are most prized in what remains in many ways an extremely conservative society. Conformity, not liberty, is the real key to the Swedish character. However, the good of the collective is slowly being replaced by that of the individual as socialism begins to lose its past appeal.

At the same time, Swedes remain devoted royalists and patriots, avidly following the fortunes of King Carl XVI Gustaf, Queen Silvia, and their children in the media, and raising the blue-and-yellow national flag each morning on the flagpoles of their country cottages. Few nations, in fact, make as much of an effort to preserve and defend their natural heritage. It is sometimes difficult in cities such as Stockholm, Göteborg, or Malmö to realize that you are in an urban area. Right in the center of Stockholm, thanks to a cleanup program in the 1970s, you can fish for salmon or go for a swim. In Göteborg's busy harbor, you can sit aboard a ship bound for the archipelago and watch fish jump out of the water; in Malmö hares hop around in the downtown parks. It is this pristine quality of life that can make a visit to Sweden a step out of time, a relaxing break from the modern world.

— By Chris Mosey

NEW AND NOTEWORTHY

Scandinavia's largest country, Sweden has always been politically independent and commercially prolific, but despite strong exports, domestically Swedes are still fighting the effects of the worst economic recession to hit the country since the 1930s. The downturn began in the late '80s and shook the very foundations of Sweden's social structure, changing it in a way that not even the country's membership in the EU, which it joined in January 1995, could measurably influence.

But this is good news for you, as the weak kronor means that Sweden has become a relatively inexpensive place to vacation, although hotel and restaurant prices are still relatively higher than those in the United States.

Stockholm is the 1998 Cultural Capital of Europe, and in the nick of time the Moderna Museet (Museum of Modern Art) has moved back to its newly refurbished home on Skeppsholmen. The yearlong celebrations and the strength of the dollar will make travel to Sweden in 1998 even more appealing.

WHAT'S WHERE

In Sweden, streamlined, ultramodern cities give way to lush forests and timbered farmhouses, and modern western European democracy coexists with strong affection for a monarchy. With 277,970 square km (107,324 square mi) for only

8.6 million residents, almost all have room to live as they choose.

Stockholm, one of Europe's most beautiful capitals, is built on 14 small islands. Bustling, skyscraper-lined boulevards are a short walk from twisting medieval streets in this modern yet pastoral city. South of the city, in Småland province, are isolated villages whose names are bywords when it comes to fine crystal glassware: Kosta, Orrefors, Boda, and Strømbergshyttan. Skåne, the country's southernmost province, is an area of fertile plains, sand beaches, scores of castles and manor houses, thriving farms, medieval churches, and summer resorts.

Sweden's second-largest city, Göteborg, is on the west coast. A Viking port in the 11th century, today the city is home to the Scandinavium indoor arena; Nordstan, one of Europe's largest indoor shopping malls; and Liseberg, Scandinavia's largest amusement park. A cruise on the Göta Canal provides a picturesque coast-to-coast journey through the Swedish countryside.

Dalarna, the central region of Sweden, is considered the most typically Swedish of all the country's 24 provinces, a place of forests, mountains, and red-painted wooden farmhouses and cottages by the shores of pristine, sun-dappled lakes. The north of Sweden, Norrland, is a place of wide-open spaces. Golden eagles soar above snowcapped crags; huge salmon fight their way up wild, tumbling rivers; rare orchids bloom in Arctic heathland; wild rhododendrons splash the land with color.

PLEASURES AND PASTIMES

Beaches

Beaches in Sweden range from wide, sandy strands to steep, rocky shores, from oceanfront to lakefront, from resorts to remote nature preserves. Beaches are wide and sandy on the western side of the country, steep and rocky on the eastern side. The area most favored for the standard sunbathing and wave-frolicking vacation is known as the Swedish Riviera, on the coast south of Göteborg.

Camping

As soon as the winter frost abates, the Swedes migrate en masse to the country, with camping and sports gear in tow. Of the 760 registered campsites nationwide, many offer fishing, boating, or canoeing, and about 200 remain open in winter for skiing and skating. Many campsites also offer accommodations in log cabins at various prices, and some have special facilities for guests with disabilities.

Dining

The nation's standard home-cooked meal is basically peasant fare—sausages, potatoes, and other hearty foods to ward off the winter cold. However, it has also produced the *smörgåsbord*, a generous and artfully arranged buffet featuring both hot and cold dishes. Fish—fresh, smoked, or pickled—is a Swedish specialty; herring and salmon both come in myriad traditional and new preparations.

Husmanskost (home-cooking) recipes are often served in restaurants as a *dagens rätt* (daily special) at lunch. Examples are *pyttipanna* (literally, "bits in the pan"—beef and potato hash topped with a fried egg), *Janssons frestelse* ("Jansson's Temptation"—gratin of potatoes with anchovies), or pea soup with pancakes, a traditional meal on Thursday.

Look for *kräftor* (crayfish), boiled with dill, salt, and sugar, then cooled overnight. Swedes eat them with hot buttered toast, caraway seeds, and schnapps or beer. Autumn heralds an exotic assortment of mushrooms and wild berries. Trout and salmon are common, as are various cuts of elk and reindeer. To the foreign palate, the best of Norrland's culinary specialties is undoubtedly *löjrom,* pinkish caviar from a species of Baltic herring, eaten with chopped onions and sour cream, and the various desserts made from the cloudberries that thrive here.

CATEGORY	COST*
$$$$	over SKr500
$$$	SKr250–SKr500
$$	SKr120–SKr250
$	under SKr120

Prices are per person for a two-course meal, including service charge and tax but not wine.

Fishing

It is not unusual to see a fisherman landing a thrashing salmon from the quayside in central Stockholm. Outside the city limits, the country is laced with streams and lakes full of fish, and there's excellent deep-sea fishing off the Baltic coast.

Lodging

Service in a Swedish hotel, no matter the price category, is always unfailingly courteous and efficient. You'll find that accommodations on the expensive side offer great charm and beauty, but the advantages of location held by less luxurious establishments shouldn't be overlooked. The woodland setting of a camper's *stuga* may be just as desirable and memorable as the gilded antiques of a downtown hotel.

In summer many discounts, special passes, and summer packages are available. Your travel agent or the Swedish Travel and Tourism Council (in New York) will have full details. The Scandic Hotel Summer Check plan enables you to pay for accommodations in advance with checks costing SKr595 each for one night in a double room; with a supplementary PlusCheck, which costs SKr110, you can stay in one of their city-center hotels. Sweden Hotel's Nordic Hotel Pass costs SKr90 and gives discounts of 15% to 50% from June 20 to August 17 and on weekends year-round.

Vandrarhem (youth hostels), also scrupulously clean and well run, are more expensive than elsewhere in Europe. The Swedish Touring Association (STF) has 394 hostels and cabins nationwide, most with four- to six-bed family rooms, around 100 with running hot and cold water. They are open to anyone regardless of age. Prices are about SKr100 per night for members of STF or organizations affiliated with Hostelling International. Nonmembers are charged an additional SKr35 per night. STF publishes an annual hostel handbook.

CATEGORY	COST*
$$$$	over SKr1,400
$$$	SKr1,100–SKr1,400
$$	SKr850–SKr1,100
$	under SKr850

Prices are for a standard double room, including breakfast and tax.

Sailing

Deep at heart, modern Swedes are still seafaring Vikings. Sweden's cultural dependence on boats runs so deep that a popular gift at Christmas is candles containing creosote, providing the comforting scent of dock and hull for when sailors can't be on their boats—which is most of the year. In summer, thousands of craft jostle among the islands of the archipelago and clog the lakes and rivers. Statistics claim there are more than 250,000 boats in the Stockholm archipelago alone. Boating opportunities for visitors are plentiful, from hourly rentals to chartered cruises in anything from kayaks to motor launches to huge luxury ferry liners.

Tennis

When Björn Borg began to win Wimbledon with almost monotonous regularity, Sweden became a force in world tennis. As such, the country is filled with indoor and outdoor courts, and major competitions, namely the Stockholm Open, take place regularly. One of the most unusual is the annual Donald Duck Cup, in Båstad, for children ages 11 to 15: ever since the young Björn won a Donald Duck trophy, the tournament has attracted thousands of youngsters who hope to imitate his success.

FODOR'S CHOICE

Dining

★ **Ulriksdals Wärsdhus, Stockholm.** The lunchtime smörgåsbord is renowned at this restaurant in an 1868 country inn. $$$$

★ **The Place, Göteborg.** Sample delicious and exotic dishes, from smoked breast of pigeon to beef tartar with caviar. $$$

★ **Wedholms Fisk, Stockholm.** Traditional Swedish fare here, especially the fresh fish, is simple but outstanding. $$$

★ **Örtagården, Stockholm.** This delightful vegetarian, no-smoking restaurant is above the Östermalmstorg food market. $

Lodging

★ **Berns, Stockholm.** This 132-year-old hotel employs discreet lighting, modern Italian furniture, and swank marble, granite, and wood inlays to create a wonderful art deco atmosphere. *$$$$*

⭐ **Marina Plaza, Helsingborg.** The use of space, style, and elegance—especially in the lofty lobby atrium—lends a decidedly modern appeal to this lodging. *$$$*

Castles and Churches

⭐ **Drottningholms Slott, Stockholm.** One of the most delightful European palaces embraces all that was best in the art of living practiced by mid-18th-century royalty.

⭐ **Kalmar Slott, Småland.** The "Key to the Realm" during the Vasa era, this Renaissance palace commands the site of an 800-year-old fortress on the Baltic shore.

⭐ **Kungliga Slottet, Stockholm.** In this magnificent granite edifice, you can tour the State Apartments, the Royal Armory, and the Treasury, where the crown jewels are kept.

Museums

⭐ **Skansen, Stockholm.** Farmhouses, windmills, barns, and churches are just some of the buildings brought from around the country for preservation at this museum.

⭐ **Vasa Museet, Stockholm.** Visit the *Vasa*, a warship that sank on its maiden voyage in 1628, was raised nearly intact in 1961, and now resides in its own museum.

⭐ **Zorn Museet, Mora.** Many fine paintings by Anders Zorn (1860–1920), Sweden's leading Impressionist painter, are displayed in this museum next to the beautiful house he built in his hometown.

Special Moments

⭐ Dogsledding in Norrland

⭐ Watching a Lucia procession at Christmastime

⭐ Sailing in the Stockholm archipelago

FESTIVALS AND SEASONAL EVENTS

WINTER

JAN. 13➤ **Knut** signals the end of Christmas festivities and "plundering" of the Christmas tree: trinkets are removed from the tree, edible ornaments gobbled up, and the tree itself thrown out.

FEB. (FIRST THURS., FRI., AND SAT.)➤ A **market** held in Jokkmokk features both traditional Lapp artifacts and plenty of reindeer. On **Shrove Tuesday** special buns called *semlor*—lightly flavored with cardamom, filled with almond paste and whipped cream—are traditionally placed in a dish of warm milk, topped with cinnamon, and eaten.

MAR. (FIRST SUN.)➤ The **Vasaloppet Ski Race** treks 88 km (55 mi) from Sälen to Mora in Dalarna, and attracts entrants from all over the world.

SPRING

APR➤ On Maundy Thursday, small girls dress up as witches and hand out "Easter letters" for small change. *Påskris*, twigs tipped with brightly dyed feathers, decorate homes.

On April 30, for the **Feast of Valborg,** bonfires are lit to celebrate the end of winter. The liveliest celebrations involve the students of the university cities of Uppsala, 60 km (37 mi) north of Stockholm, and Lund, 16 mi (10 mi) north of Malmö.

MAY 1➤ **Labor Day** marches and rallies are held nationwide.

JUNE 6➤ **National Day** is celebrated, with parades, speeches, and band concerts nationwide.

SUMMER

JUNE➤ **Midsummer's Eve** and **Day** celebrations are held on the Friday evening and Saturday that fall between June 20 and 26. Swedes decorate their homes with flower garlands, raise maypoles, and dance around them to folk music.

AUG.➤ **Stockholm Water Festival** celebrates the city's clean water environment with water-sports performances, a fireworks competition, and many other events all over town. Crayfish are considered a delicacy in Sweden, and the second Wednesday of August marks the **Crayfish premiere,** when friends gather to eat them at outdoor parties.

AUTUMN

NOV. 11➤ **St. Martin's Day** is celebrated primarily in the southern province of Skåne. Roast goose is served, accompanied by *svartsoppa,* a bisque made of goose blood and spices.

DEC.➤ For each of the four weeks of **Advent,** leading up to Christmas, a candle is lit in a four-pronged candelabra.

DEC. 10➤ **Nobel Day** sees the presentation of the Nobel prizes by King Carl XVI Gustaf at a glittering banquet held in the Stockholm City Hall.

DEC. 13➤ On **Santa Lucia Day** young girls are selected to be "Lucias"; they wear candles—today usually electric substitutes—in their hair and sing hymns with their handmaidens and "star boys" at ceremonies around the country.

DEC. 24➤ **Christmas Eve** is the principal day of Christmas celebration. Traditional Christmas dishes include ham, rice porridge, and *lutfisk* (ling that is dried and then boiled).

DEC. 31➤ **New Year's Eve** is the Swedes' occasion to set off an astounding array of fireworks. Every household has its own supply, and otherwise quiet neighborhood streets are full of midnight merrymakers.

2 Stockholm

POSITIONED WHERE the waters of Lake Mälaren rush into the Baltic, Stockholm is one of Europe's most beautiful capitals. Nearly 1.6 million people now live in the greater Stockholm area, yet it remains a quiet, almost pastoral city. Built on 14 small islands joined by bridges crossing open bays and narrow channels, Stockholm is a handsome, civilized city filled with parks, squares, and airy boulevards, yet it is also a bustling, modern metropolis. Glass-and-steel skyscrapers abound, but you are never more than a five-minute walk from twisting medieval streets and waterside walkways.

The first written mention of Stockholm dates from 1252, when a powerful regent named Birger Jarl built a fortified castle and township here. King Gustav Vasa took it over in 1523, and King Gustavus Adolphus made it the heart of an empire a century later.

During the Thirty Years' War (1618–48), Sweden gained importance as a Baltic trading state, and Stockholm grew commensurately. But by the beginning of the 18th century, Swedish influence had begun to wane and Stockholm's development had slowed. It did not revive until the Industrial Revolution, when the hub of the city moved north from Gamla Stan.

Nowadays most Stockholmers live in high-rise suburbs that branch out to the pine forests and lakesides around the capital. They are linked by a highly efficient infrastructure of roads, railways, and one of the safest subway systems in the world. Air pollution is minimal, and the city streets are relatively clean and safe.

EXPLORING STOCKHOLM

Although Stockholm is built on a group of islands adjoining the mainland, the waterways between them are so narrow, and the bridges so smoothly integrated, that the city really does feel more or less continuous. The island of Gamla Stan and its smaller neighbors, Riddarholmen and Helgeandsholmen, lie pretty much at town center. South of Gamla Stan, Södermalm spreads over a wide area, where the many art galleries and bars attract a slightly bohemian crowd. North of Gamla Stan is Norrmalm, the financial and business heart of the city. West of Norrmalm is the island of Kungsholmen, site of Stadshuset, the City Hall, and most of the city government offices. East of Norrmalm is Östermalm, an old residential neighborhood where many of the embassies and consulates are found. Finally, between Östermalm and Södermalm lies the island of Djurgården, once a royal game preserve, now the site of lovely parks and museums such as Skansen, the open-air cultural heritage park.

Modern Stockholm

The area bounded by Stadshuset, Hötorget, Stureplan, and Dramaten is essentially Stockholm's downtown, where the city comes closest to feeling like a bustling metropolis. Shopping, nightlife, business, traffic, dining, festivals—all are at their most intense in this part of town.

A Good Walk

Start at the redbrick **Stadshuset** ①, a powerful symbol of Stockholm. Cross the bridge to Klara Mälarstrand and follow the waterfront to Drottninggatan, a pedestrian street that will take you north to the hub of the city, **Sergels Torg** ②. The **Kulturhuset** ③ is in the imposing glass

Stockholm

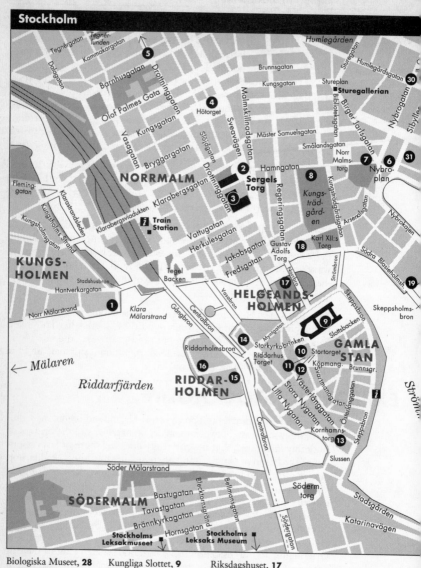

ÖSTERMALM

Kommendörsgatan
Karlaplan
Karlavägen
Millesgården
N. DJURGÅRDEN

Linnégatan
Narvavägen
Banérgatan
Oxenstiernsgatan
Gardesgatan
Skarpögatan

Artillerigatan
Skeppargatan
Grevgatan
Styrmangatan
Storgatan
Linnégatan
Strandvägen

29

Riddargatan

Oscars
Kyrka

Strandvägen
Djurgårdsbron

Djurgårdsbrunnsviken

23

24

Rosendalsvägen

22

DJURGÅRDEN

Sirishovsvägen

20 21

28

Hazeliusbacken

26

27

SKEPPSHOLMEN

Svensksundsvägen

Alkärret
Djurgårdsvägen

25

Falkenb G.

Djurgårds
Slätten
Sollidsbacken
Singelbacken

Allmänna Gränd

KASTELL-
HOLMEN

Baltic →

Saltsjön

BECKHOLMEN

N

KEY

0   500 yards

i Tourist Information

0   500 meters

— Rail Lines

building on the southern side of Sergels Torg. Continuing north on Drottninggatan, you'll come to the market-filled **Hötorget** ④. The intersection of Kungsgatan and Sveavägen, at the corner of Konserthuset, is one of the busiest pedestrian crossroads in town.

Head north up Sveavägen for a brief detour to see the spot where Prime Minister Olof Palme was assassinated in 1986. A plaque has been laid on the right-hand side of the street, just before the intersection with Olof Palmes Gata; his grave is in Adolf Fredrik's Kyrkogård, a few blocks farther on. Continue north along Sveavägen, and turn left up Tegnérgatan to find **Strindbergsmuseet Blå Tornet** ⑤, where playwright August Strindberg lived from 1908 to 1912. Return to Hötorget by way of Drottninggatan.

Next, walk east along Kungsgatan, one of Stockholm's main shopping streets, to Stureplan, where you'll find Sturegallerian, an elegant mall (☞ Shopping, *below*). Head southeast along Birger Jarlsgatan—named for the nobleman generally credited with founding Stockholm around 1252—where there are still more interesting shops and restaurants. When you reach Nybroplan, take a look at the grand **Kungliga Dramatiska Teatern** ⑥.

Heading west up Hamngatan, stop in at **Hallwylska Museet** ⑦ for a tour of the private collection of Countess von Hallwyl's treasures. Continue along Hamngatan to **Kungsträdgården** ⑧, a park since 1562. You'll find many outdoor cafés and restaurants here, and usually public concerts and events in the summer. At the northwest corner of the park you will find Sverigehuset, or Sweden House, the tourist center (☞ Visitor Information *in* Stockholm A to Z, *below*); on the opposite side of Hamngatan is the NK department store (☞ Shopping, *below*).

TIMING

Allow about 4½ hours for the walk, plus an hour each for guided tours of Stadshuset and Hallwylska Museet (September–June, Sunday only). Note the Strindbergsmuseet Blå Tornet is closed Monday.

Sights to See

⑦ **Hallwylska Museet** (Hallwyl Museum). This private turn-of-the-century palace with imposing wood-panel rooms houses a collection of furniture, paintings, and musical instruments in a bewildering mélange of styles assembled by Countess von Hallwyl, who left it to the state on her death. ☒ *Hamng. 4,* ☎ *08/6664499.* ☒ *SKr50.* ☉ *Guided tours only. Tours in English July and Aug., daily at 1; Sept.–June, Sun. at 1.*

④ **Hötorget** (Hay Market). Once the city's hay market, this is now a popular gathering place with an excellent outdoor fruit and vegetable market. Also lining the square are the Konserthuset, the PUB department store, and a multiscreen cinema Filmstaden Sergel (☞ Nightlife and the Arts, *below*). ☒ *Just west of Sveaväg.*

NEED A
BREAK?

Stop at **Kungshallen** (☒ Hötorget opposite Filmstaden Sergel, ☎ 08/ 218005) and choose from an array of international goodies. Or, get a window table at the **café** inside Filmstaden Sergel.

③ **Kulturhuset** (Culture House). Here you'll find an array of exhibitions for children and adults, plus a library, theater, cyber-café, exhibition center, and restaurant. ☒ *Sergels Torg 3,* ☎ *08/7000100. Call for details.*

⑥ **Kungliga Dramatiska Teatern** (Royal Dramatic Theater). Locally known as Dramaten, this theater is housed in a grand but appealing building with gilded statuary that looks out over the city harbor. Performances are in Swedish. ⊠ *Nybroplan,* ☎ 08/6670680.

👆 **❽ Kungsträdgården** (King's Garden). This is one of Stockholm's smallest yet most central parks. Once the royal kitchen garden, it now hosts a large number of festivals and happenings each season. There is a playground, an ice-skating rink in winter, and numerous cafés and restaurants. ⊠ *Between Hamng. and the Operan.*

❷ Sergels Torg. This area in Stockholm center was named after Johan Tobias Sergel (1740–1814), one of Sweden's greatest sculptors. The busy junction is dominated by modern, functional buildings and a sunken pedestrian square with subterranean connections to the rest of the neighborhood.

★ **❶ Stadshuset** (City Hall). The architect Ragnar Östberg, one of the founders of the National Romantic movement, completed Stockholm's City Hall in 1923. Headquarters of the city council, the building is functional but ornate: its immense **Blå Hallen** (Blue Hall) is the venue for the Nobel Prize dinner, Stockholm's principal social event. A trip to the top of the 348-ft tower, most of which can be achieved by elevator, is rewarded by a breathtaking panorama of the city and Riddarfjärden. ⊠ *Hantverkarg. 1,* ☎ 08/50829059. ⊡ *SKr30, tower SKr15.* ☉ *Guided tours only, daily 10–4:30. Tours in English, June–Aug., daily 10, 11, noon, 2; May and Sept., daily 10, noon, and 2; Oct.–Apr., daily 10 and noon.*

NEED A
BREAK?

After climbing the Stadshuset tower, relax on the fine grass terraces, which lead down to the bay and overlook Lake Mälaren. Or, have lunch in **Stadshuskällaren** (City Hall Cellar, ☎ 08/6505454), where the annual Nobel Prize banquet is held. You can also head a few blocks down Hantverkargatan to find several good small restaurants.

❺ Strindbergsmuseet Blå Tornet (Strindberg Museum, Blue Tower). Hidden away over a grocery store, this museum is dedicated to Sweden's most important author and dramatist, August Strindberg (1849–1912). This was actually Strindberg's home from 1908 until his death, and the interior has been expertly reconstructed with authentic furnishings and other objects, including one of his pens. It also has a library, printing press, and picture archives, and it is the site of literary, musical, and theatrical events. ⊠ *Drottningg. 85,* ☎ 08/4115354. ⊡ *SKr30.* ☉ *Tues. 11–7, Wed.–Fri. 11–4, weekends noon–4.*

Gamla Stan and Skeppsholmen

Gamla Stan (Old Town) sits on a cluster of small islands between two of Stockholm's main islands and is the site of the medieval city. Skeppsholmen is the island just east. Narrow, twisting cobbled streets here are lined with superbly preserved old buildings.

A Good Walk

Start at the waterfront edge of Kungsträdgården and cross Strömsbron to the **Kungliga Slottet** ⑨, where you can see the changing of the guard at noon every day. Walk up the sloping cobblestone drive called Slottsbacken and bear right past the Obelisk to find the main entrance to the palace. Stockholm's 15th-century Gothic cathedral, **Storkyrkan** ⑩, stands at the top of Slottsbacken, but its entrance is at the other end, on Trångsund.

Following Källargränd from the Obelisk or Trångsund from Storkyrkan, you will reach the small **Stortorget** ⑪, marvelously atmospheric amid magnificent old merchants' houses. The **Stockholms Fondbörs** ⑫ fronts the square.

Walk past Svartmangatan's many ancient buildings, including the Tyska Kyrkan, or German Church, with its magnificent oxidized copper spire and airy interior. Continue along Svartmangatan, take a right on Tyska Stallplan to Prästgatan, and just to your left you'll find Mårten Trotzigs Gränd; this picturesque, lamplit alley stairway leads downhill to **Järntorget** ⑬. From here you can take Västerlånggatan back north across Gamla Stan, checking out the pricey fashion boutiques, galleries, and souvenir shops along the way.

Cut down Storkyrkobrinken to the 17th-century Dutch Baroque **Riddarhuset** ⑭. A short walk takes you over Riddarholmsbron to Riddarholmen—Island of Knights—on which stands **Riddarholms Kyrkan** ⑮. Also on Riddarholmen is the white 17th-century palace that houses the **Svea Hovrätt** ⑯. Returning across Riddarholmsbron, take Myntgatan back toward Kungliga Slottet and turn left at Mynttorget to cross the bridge and pass through the refurbished stone **Riksdagshuset** ⑰ on Helgeandsholmen, Holy Ghost Island. Another short bridge puts you on Drottninggatan; take a right onto Fredsgatan and walk to Gustav Adolfs Torg.

The **Operan** ⑱ occupies the waterfront between Gustav Adolfs Torg and Kungsträdgården. A little farther along on Strömgatan, a host of tour boats dock in front of the stately Grand Hotel. Pass the Grand and visit the **National Museet** ⑲. Cross the footbridge to the idyllic island of Skeppsholmen, where you'll find the **Östasiatiska Museet** ⑳, with a fine collection of Buddhist art. On Skeppsholmen you will also find the **Moderna Museet** ㉑. The adjoining island, Kastellholmen, is a pleasant place for a stroll, especially on a summer evening, with views of the Baltic harbor and Djurgården's lighted parks.

TIMING

Allow three hours for the walk, and double that if you want to tour the various parts of the palace. The National Museet and Östasiatiska Museet will take up to an hour each to view. Note that Kungliga Slottet is closed Monday off-season, and the Stockholms Leksakmuseet, Moderna Museet, National Museet, and Östasiatiska Museet are always closed Monday. The Riddarhuset is open weekdays only; off-season, hit the Riddarholms Kyrkan on a Wednesday or weekend.

Sights to See

⑬ **Järntorget** (Iron Square). Named after its original use as an iron and copper marketplace, this square was also the venue for public executions. ⊠ *Intersection of Västerlångg. and Österlångg.*

OFF THE   **STOCKHOLMS LEKSAKMUSEET** – In Södermalm, Stockholm's Toy Museum
BEATEN PATH has a collection of toys and dolls from all over the world, as well as a
             children's theater with clowns, magicians, storytellers, and puppet
             shows. The museum is near the Mariatorget subway station, two stops
             south of Gamla Stan. ⊠ *Mariatorget 1, Södermalm,* ☎ *08/6416100.*
             ⊠ *SKr30.* ☉ *Tues.–Fri. 10–4, weekends noon–4.*

★ ❾ **Kungliga Slottet** (Royal Palace). Watch the changing of the guard in the curved terrace entrance of this magnificent granite edifice designed by Nicodemus Tessin and completed in 1760. View the palace's fine furnishings and Gobelin tapestries on a tour of the **Representationsvän** (State Apartments), or survey the crown jewels, which are no longer used in this self-consciously egalitarian country, in the **Skattkammaren** (Treasury). The **Livrustkammaren** (Royal Armory) has an outstanding collection of weaponry, coaches, and royal regalia. Entrances to the Treasury and Armory are on the Slottsbacken side of the palace. ⊠ *Gamla Stan,* ☎ *State Apartments 08/4026130, Treasury 08/4026130, Royal Armory 08/6664475.* ✑ *State Apartments SKr45, Treasury SKr40, Royal Armory SKr55.* ☉ *State Apartments and Treasury, June–Aug., daily 10–4; Sept.–May, Tues.–Sun. noon–3. Armory, May–Aug., daily 11–4; Sept.–May, Tues.–Sun. 11–4.*

㉑ **Moderna Museet** (Museum of Modern Art). Reopened in its original venue on Skeppsholmen, the museum's excellent collection includes works by Picasso, Kandinsky, Dali, Brancusi, and other international artists. You can also view examples of significant Swedish painters and sculptors and an extensive section on photography. ⊠ *Skeppsholmen,* ☎ *08/6664250,* ✑ *SKr50.* ☉ *Tues.–Thurs. noon–7, Fri.–Sun. noon–5.*

⑲ **National Museet** (National Museum). Important old masters—Rembrandt included—and works of many Swedish artists line the walls here. ⊠ *Södra Blasieholmshamnen,* ☎ *08/6664250.* ✑ *SKr50.* ☉ *Wed. and Fri.–Sun. 11–5, Tues. and Thurs. 11–8 (closes some Tues. at 5, mid-May–mid-Oct.).*

⑱ **Operan** (Opera House). Stockholm's Baroque Opera House is almost more famous for its restaurants and bars than for its opera and ballet productions. It has been one of Stockholm's artistic and literary watering holes since the first Operakällaren restaurant (☞ Dining, *below*) opened on the site in 1787. ⊠ *Gustav Adolfs Torg,* ☎ *08/248240.*

⑳ **Östasiatiska Museet** (Museum of Far Eastern Antiquities). Those with an affinity to Asian disciplines will enjoy this fascinating collection of Chinese and Japanese Buddhist sculptures and artifacts. ⊠ *Skeppsholmen,* ☎ *08/6664250.* ✑ *SKr50.* ☉ *Tues. noon–8, Wed.–Sun. noon–5.*

⑮ **Riddarholms Kyrkan** (Riddarholm Church). Dating from 1270, the Grey Friars monastery is the second-oldest structure in Stockholm and the burial place for Swedish kings for more than four centuries. The most famous figures interred within are King Gustavus Adolphus, hero of the Thirty Years' War, and the warrior King Karl XII, renowned for his daring invasion of Russia, who died in Norway in 1718. The latest of the 17 Swedish kings to be put to rest here was Gustav V, in 1950. The various rulers' sarcophagi, usually embellished with their monograms, are visible in the small chapels given over to the various dynasties. The redbrick structure, distinguished by its delicate iron fretwork spire, is rarely used for services. ⊠ *Riddarholmen,* ☎ *08/4026000.* ✑ *SKr10.* ☉ *June–Aug., daily noon–4; May and Sept., Wed. and weekends noon–3.*

⑭ **Riddarhuset** (House of Nobles). Before the abolition of the aristocracy early in the 20th century, the House of Nobles was the gathering place for the First Estate of the realm. Hanging from its walls are 2,325 escutcheons, representing all the former noble families of Sweden. Thanks to the building's excellent acoustic properties, Riddarhuset is often used for concerts. ⊠ *Riddarhustorget,* ☎ *08/7233999.* ✑ *SKr40.* ☉ *Weekdays 11:30–12:30.*

⑰ **Riksdagshuset** (Parliament Building). When in session, the Swedish Parliament meets in this 1905 building. ⊠ *Riksg. 3A,* ☎ *08/7864000.* ✑ *Free.* ☉ *Tours in English late June–late Aug., weekdays 2:30 and 2; late Aug.–late June, weekends 1:30. Call ahead for bookings.*

⑫ **Stockholms Fondbörs** (Stockholm Stock Exchange). The Swedish Academy meets at the Stock Exchange every year to decide the winner of the Nobel Prize for Literature. The Stock Exchange itself is computerized and rather quiet. There are no tours in English, but there is a film about the Stock Exchange in Swedish. ✉ *Källargränd 2,* ☎ *08/ 6138892.* ⊙ *Group tours by appointment only.*

⑩ Storkyrkan (Great Church). Swedish kings were crowned in the 15th-century Great Church as late as 1907. Today, its main attractions are a dramatic wooden statue of Saint George slaying the dragon, carved by Bernt Notke of Lübeck in 1489, and the *Parhelion,* a painting of Stockholm dating from 1520, the oldest in existence. ✉ *Trångsund 1,* ☎ *08/7233000.*

⑪ Stortorget (Great Square). Here in 1520, the Danish king Christian II ordered a massacre of Swedish noblemen, paving the way for a national revolt against foreign rule and the founding of Sweden as a sovereign state under King Gustav Vasa, who ruled from 1523 to 1560. One legend holds that if it rains heavily enough on the anniversary of the massacre, the old stones still run red.

NEED A
BREAK?
> Among the cafés, pubs, and restaurants just south along Västerlång-gatan, stop at the **Grå Munken** (Gray Monk, ✉ Västerlång. 18, at Stora Gråmunkegränd) for a coffee and pastry.

⑯ Svea Hovrätt (Swedish High Court). The Swedish High Court commands a prime site on the island of Riddarholmen, on a quiet and restful quayside. Sit on the water's edge and watch the boats on Riddarfjärden (Bay of Knights) and, beyond it, Lake Mälaren. From here you can see the lake, the magnificent arches of Västerbron (West Bridge) in the distance, the southern heights, and above all the imposing profile of the City Hall, which appears almost to be floating on the water. At the quay you may see one of the Göta Canal ships. ✉ *Riddarholmen.* ⊙ *Not open to the public.*

Djurgården and Skansen

Djurgården is Stockholm's pleasure island: on it you will find the outdoor museum Skansen, the Gröna Lund amusement park, and the *Vasa,* a 17th-century warship raised from the harbor bed in 1961, as well as other delights.

A Good Walk

You can approach Djurgården from the water aboard the small ferries that leave from Slussen at the southern end of Gamla Stan or from Nybrokajen, or New Bridge Quay, in front of the Kungliga Dramatiska Teatern. Alternatively, starting at the theater, stroll down the Strandvägen quayside—taking in the magnificent old sailing ships and the fine views over the harbor—and cross Djurgårdsbron, or Djurgården Bridge, to the island. As you turn immediately to the right, your first port of call should be the **Vasa Museet** ㉒, with a dramatic display of the splendid 17th-century warship. Especially if you have kids in tow, visit the fairy-tale house, **Junibacken** ㉓, just off Djurgårdsbron. Return to the main street, Djurgårdsvägen, to find the entrance to the **Nordiska Museet** ㉔, worth a visit for an insight into Swedish folklore.

Continue on Djurgårdsvägen to the amusement park **Gröna Lund Tivoli** ㉕, where Stockholmers of all ages come to play. Beyond the park, cross Djurgårdsvägen to **Skansen** ㉖.

From Skansen, continue following Djurgårdsvägen to Prins Eugens Väg, and follow the signs to the beautiful turn-of-the-century **Waldemarsudde** ㉗. On the way back to Djurgårdsbron, follow the small street called Hazeliusbacken to the charmingly archaic **Biologiska Museet** ㉘ before heading back into town.

TIMING

Allow half a day for this tour, unless you're planning to turn it into a full-day event with lengthy visits to Skansen, Junibacken, and Gröna Land Tivoli. The Vasa Museet warrants two hours, and the Nordiska and Biologiska museums need an hour each. Waldemarsudde requires another half hour. Gröna Lund Tivoli is closed from mid-September to late April. Note the Nordiska Museet closes Monday, and the Biologiska Museet and Waldemarsudde are closed Monday off-season.

Sights to See

㉘ Biologiska Museet (Biological Museum). The Biological Museum, in the shadow of Skansen, exhibits real stuffed animals in various simulated environments. ✉ *Hazeliusporten*, ☎ *08/4428215*. ✺ *SKr20*. ☾ *Apr.–Sept., daily 10–3; Oct.–Mar., Tues.–Sun. 10–3.*

NEED A BREAK?

On Hazeliusbacken, the **Cirkus Theater** (✉ Djurgårdsslätten, ☎ 08/6608081) has a lovely terrace café. Or, for terrace dining, head to **Hasselbacken Hotel** (✉ Hazeliusbacken 20, ☎ 08/6705000).

㉕ Gröna Lund Tivoli. On a smaller scale than Copenhagen's Tivoli and Göteborg's Liseberg, the amusement park Gröna Lund Tivoli is a clean, well-organized pleasure garden with a wide range of rides, attractions, and restaurants. ✉ *Allmänna Gränd 9*, ☎ *08/6707600*. ✺ *SKr40 not including coupons or passes for rides.* ☾ *May.–Aug., daily. Call ahead for prices and hours.*

★ ㉓ Junibacken. In this fairy-tale house, you travel in small carriages through the storybook world of children's book writer Astrid Lindgren, creator of the irrepressible character Pippi Longstocking. Each of Lindgren's tales is explained as various scenes are revealed. It's perfect for children ages five and up. ✉ *Galärvarsv.*, ☎ *08/6600600*. ☾ *Daily 10–6.*

㉔ Nordiska Museet (Nordic Museum). In this splendid late-Victorian structure you'll find peasant costumes from every region of the country and exhibits on the Sami (pronounced *sah*-mee)—Lapps, formerly seminomadic reindeer herders who inhabit the far north. Families with children should visit the delightful "village-life" play area on the ground floor. ✉ *Djurgårdsv. 616*, ☎ *08/6664600*. ✺ *SKr50*. ☾ *Tues.–Sun. 11–5.*

★ ㉖ Skansen. The world's first open-air museum, Skansen was founded in 1891 by philologist and ethnographer Artur Hazelius, who is buried here. He preserved examples of traditional Swedish architecture, including farmhouses, windmills, barns, a working glassblower's hut, and churches, brought from all parts of the country. Not only is Skansen a delightful trip out of time in the center of a modern city, it also provides an easily assimilated insight into the life and culture of Sweden's various regions. In addition, the park has a zoo, carnival area, aquarium, theater, and cafés. ✉ *Djurgårdsslätten 4951*, ☎ *08/4428000*. ✺ *May.–Aug., SKr45; Sept.–Apr., weekdays SKr30, weekends SKr40. Aquarium SKr45.* ☾ *May.–Aug., daily 9–5; Sept.–Apr., daily 9–4.*

NEED A BREAK?

For a snack with a view at Skansen, try the **Solliden Restaurant** (☎ 08/6601055) near the front of the park, overlooking the city. The cozy **Bredablick Tower Café** (☎ 08/6634778) is at the back of Skansen, next to the children's circus.

★ ㉒ Vasa Museet. The warship *Vasa* sank on its maiden voyage in 1628, was forgotten for three centuries, located in 1956, and raised from the seabed in 1961. Its hull was found to be largely intact, because the Baltic's brackish waters do not support the worms that can eat through ships' timbers. Now largely restored to her former, if brief, glory, the man-of-war resides in a handsome new museum. ⊠ *Galärvarvet, Djurgården,* ☎ *08/6664800.* ☜ *SKr50.* ☉ *Thurs.–Tues. 10–5, Wed. 10–8. Jun.–Jul., English tours every hr; Aug.–May, weekdays 12:30 and 2:30, weekends 10:30, 12:30, 2:30, and 4:30.*

㉗ **Waldemarsudde.** This estate, Djurgården's gem, was bequeathed to the Swedish people by Prince Eugen on his death in 1947. It maintains an important collection of Nordic paintings from 1880 to 1940, in addition to the prince's own works. ⊠ *Prins Eugens väg 6,* ☎ *08/6621833.* ☜ *SKr50.* ☉ *June–Aug., Wed. and Fri.–Sun. 11–5, Tues. and Thurs. 7 AM–9 PM; Sept.–May, Tues.–Sun. 11–4.*

Östermalm and Kaknästornet

Marked by waterfront rows of Renaissance-era buildings with palatial rooftops and ornamentation, Östermalm is a quieter, more residential section of central Stockholm, its elegant streets lined with museums and fine shopping. On Strandvägen, or Beach Way, the boulevard that follows the harbor's edge from the busy downtown area to the staid diplomatic quarter, you can choose one of the three routes. The waterside walk, with its splendid views of the city harbor, bustles with tour boats and sailboats. The inside walk skirts upscale shops and exclusive restaurants. On the tree-shaded paths down the middle you just might meet the occasional horseback rider, properly attired in helmet, jacket, and high polished boots.

A Good Walk

Walk east from the Kungliga Dramatiska Teatern in Nybroplan along Strandvägen. At Djurgårdsbron, stop to admire the ornate little bridge, then turn left up Narvavägen to the **Historiska Museet** ㉙. Cross Narvavägen at Oscars Kyrka, then head up the street to Karlaplan, a pleasant, circular park with a fountain. Go across or around the park to find Karlavägen, a long boulevard lined with small shops and galleries. At Sibyllegatan, turn left and proceed southwest to **Östermalmstorg** ㉚, where you'll find the Saluhall, an excellent indoor food market. Continue down Sibyllegatan to the **Musik Museet** ㉛, installed in the city's oldest industrial building. Then go back to Nybroplan, where you can catch Bus 69 going east to **Kaknästornet** ㉜ for a spectacular view of Stockholm from the tallest tower in Scandinavia.

TIMING

This tour requires a little more than a half day. You'll want to spend around an hour in each of the museums. The bus ride from Nybroplan to Kaknästornet takes about 15 minutes, and the tower merits another half hour. Note the Historiska Museet and Musik Museet are closed Monday, and the Millesgården is closed Monday off-season.

Sights to See

㉙ **Historiska Museet** (Museum of National Antiquities). Viking treasures and the Gold Room are the main draw here, but well-presented changing exhibitions also cover various periods of Swedish history, and an excellent shop sells books and gifts. ⊠ *Narvav. 1317,* ☎ *08/7839400.* ☜ *SKr55.* ☉ *Tues.–Sun. 11–5, Thurs. until 8.*

NEED A BREAK? For a great coffee and a quick snack, the bistro **Cassi** (⊠ Narvav. 30, just off Karlaplan) is just to the right.

OFF THE BEATEN PATH **MILLESGÅRDEN –** This gallery and sculpture garden north of the city is dedicated to the former owner of the property, the American-Swedish sculptor Carl Milles (1875–1955). On display are Milles's own works as well as his private collection. The setting is exquisite: sculptures top columns on terraces in a magical garden high above the harbor and the city. Millesgården can be easily reached via subway to Ropsten, where you catch the Lidingö train and get off at Herserud, the second stop. The trip takes about 30 minutes. ⊠ *Carl Milles väg 2, Lidingö,* ☎ *08/7315060.* ⌦ *SKr50.* ☉ *May–Sept., daily 10–5; Oct.–Apr., Tues.–Sun. noon–4.*

㉜ **Kaknästornet** (Kaknäs TV Tower). The 511-ft-high Kaknäs radio and television tower, completed in 1967, is the tallest building in Scandinavia. Surrounded by an impressive array of satellite dishes, it is also used as a linkup station for a number of Swedish satellite TV channels and radio stations. Eat a meal in a restaurant 426 ft above the ground and enjoy panoramic views of the city and the archipelago. ⊠ *Mörkakroken, off Djurgårdsbrunsv.,* ☎ *08/6678030.* ⌦ *SKr20.* ☉ *May.–Aug., daily 9 AM–10 PM; Sept.–May, daily 10–9.*

☙ ㉛ **Musik Museet.** The Music Museum presents a history of music and instruments in its displays. Children are invited to touch and play some of the instruments, and a motion-sensitive "Sound Room" allows visitors to produce musical effects simply by gesturing and moving around. ⊠ *Sibylleg. 2,* ☎ *08/6664530.* ⌦ *SKr30.* ☉ *Tues.–Sun. 11–4.*

㉚ **Östermalmstorg.** The market square and its neighboring streets represent old, established Stockholm. **Saluhall** is more like a collection of boutiques than an indoor food market; the fish displays can be especially intriguing. At the other end of the square, **Hedvig Eleonora Kyrka**, a church with characteristically Swedish faux-marble painting throughout its wooden interior, is the site of frequent lunchtime concerts in spring and summer. ⊠ *Nybrog.*

NEED A BREAK?	The little restaurants inside the **Saluhall** (⊠ Östermalmstorg) offer everything from take-out coffee to sit-down meals.

DINING

The Stockholm restaurant scene has evolved of late, with more upscale restaurants offering good value and inexpensive restaurants appearing on the scene. And local chefs are trying their hand at innovation, some making waves in the culinary world: in 1997, Sweden won the Chef of the Year Contest held in Lyon, France. Among Swedish dishes, the best bets are fish, particularly salmon, and the smörgåsbord buffet, which usually offers variety at a good price. Reservations are usually necessary on weekends.

Downtown Stockholm and Beyond

$$$$ ✕ **Operakällaren.** Open since 1787, the haughty grand dame of Stockholm is more a Swedish institution than a great gastronomic experience. Thick Oriental carpeting, shiny polished brass, handsome carved-wood chairs and tables, and a decidedly stuffy atmosphere fill the room. The crystal chandeliers are said to be Sweden's finest, and the high windows on the south side give magnificent views of the Royal Palace. The restaurant is famed for its seasonal smörgåsbord, offered from early June through Christmas. Coveted selections include pickled herring, *rollmops* (rolled herring), reindeer and elk in season, and ice cream with cloudberry sauce. In summer, the veranda opens as the Operabryggan Café, facing Kungsträdgården and the waterfront. ⊠ *Operahuset, Jakobs Torg 2,* ☎ *08/67658010. Reservations essential. Jacket and tie. AE, DC, MC, V. Main dining room closed in July.*

20

Dining
Calle P, **28**
Cassi, **37**
De Fyras Krog, **48**
Den Gyldene
Freden, **46**
Diana, **44**
Edsbacka Krog, **9**
Eriks, **45**
Eriks Bakficka, **38**
Fredsgatan 12, **22**
Garlic and Shots, **53**

Gåsen, **16**
Grands Franska
Matsalen, **31**
Greitz, **12**
Hannas Krog, **55**
Il Conte, **35**
Källaren Aurora, **39**
Måtten Trotzig, **47**
Nils Emil, **57**
Operakällaren, **30**
Örtagården, **25**

Paul & Norbert, **33**
Rolfs Kök, **5**
Saigon Bar, **11**
Spisen, **54**
Stallmästare-
gården, **7**
Tranan, **1**
Ulriksdals
Wärdshus, **3**
Wedholms Fisk, **29**

Lodging
af Chapman, **60**
Alexandra, **56**
Amaranten, **18**
Anno 1647, **51**
Arcadia, **2**
Bema, **6**
Berns, **27**
Birger Jarl, **15**
Bosön, **36**
Central Hotel, **13**
City, **14**

KEY

i Tourist Information

—— Rail Lines

N

0   550 yards

0   500 meters

$$$$ ✕ **Ulriksdals Wärdshus.** The lunchtime smörgåsbord is unbeatable at
★   this beautifully situated country inn, built in 1868. The inn is in the
park of an 18th-century palace, with a traditional interior overlooking orchards and a peaceful lake. This restaurant is arguably one of
the most expensive in Stockholm, but the impeccable service and outstanding cuisine make it worthwhile. ⊠ *Ulriksdals Slottspark, Solna,*
☎ *08/850815. Reservations essential. Jacket required. AE, DC, MC,*
V. No dinner Sun.

$$$ ✕ **Edsbacka Krog.** In 1626, Edsbacka, just outside town, became
Stockholm's first licensed inn. Its exposed rough-hewn beams, plaster
walls, and open fireplaces still give it the feel of a country inn for the
gentry. The Continental-Swedish cuisine is reliably superb. The owner,
Christer Lindström, is an award-winning chef; his tarragon chicken with
winter vegetables is worth the occasional long wait. ⊠ *Sollentunav.*
220, Sollentuna, ☎ *08/963300. AE, DC, MC, V. Closed Sun. No*
lunch Sat., no dinner Mon.

$$$ ✕ **Fredsgatan 12.** The government crowd files in at lunch, the rest of
★   us come at night. An array of cleverly named fish and meat dishes are
well prepared. While enjoying one of the peculiar drinks at the bar,
you can get nice view of the kitchen—always a good sign of an un-
abashed chef. ⊠ *Fredsg. 12,* ☎ *08/248052. AE, DC, MC, V.*

$$$ ✕ **Gåsen.** This is a classic Östermalm restaurant: very classy, cozy, and
costly. The Swedish-French menu is excellent, including such dishes as
smoked breast of goose with apple chutney, grilled turbot with fresh
beet root and spinach, and Arctic raspberry ice cream with blue cu-
raçao sauce. The service is usually impeccable. ⊠ *Karlav. 28,* ☎ *08/*
6110269. Jacket and tie. AE, DC, MC, V. Closed weekends May–Aug.,
Sun. Sept.–Apr., and July.

$$$ ✕ **Greitz.** Home-style Swedish cuisine is served in this classy and com-
fortable restaurant. Try the *sotare* (grilled Baltic herring with parsley
and butter) or perch and salmon roe with sautéed white beets. The decor
is revamped café style, with the once-stained wood paneling around
the room painted burgundy red. ⊠ *Vasag. 50,* ☎ *08/234820. AE, DC,*
MC, V. Closed Sun. and July.

$$$ ✕ **Stallmästaregården.** A historic old inn with an attractive courtyard
and garden, Stallmästaregården is in the Haga Park, just north of
Norrtull, about 15 minutes by car or bus from the city center. Fine sum-
mer meals are served in the courtyard overlooking the waters of
Brunnsviken. Specialties include *anka roti,* charcoal-grilled duck kebab.
⊠ *Norrtull, near Haga,* ☎ *08/6101300. AE, DC, MC, V. Closed Sun.*

$$$ ✕ **Wedholms Fisk.** Noted for its fresh seafood dishes, Wedholms Fisk
★   is appropriately set by a bay in Stockholm center, on Berzelii Park. High
ceilings, large windows, and tasteful modern paintings from the owner's
personal collection create a spacious, sophisticated atmosphere. The
traditional Swedish cuisine, which consists almost exclusively of
seafood, is simple but outstanding. Try the poached sole in lobster-and-
champagne sauce or the Pilgrim mussels Provençale. ⊠ *Nybrokajen*
17, ☎ *08/6117874. AE, DC, MC, V. Closed Sun. and July.*

$$ ✕ **Calle P.** Palm leaves function as plates at this trendy restaurant, which
★   has an unusual menu of Asian-accented dishes such as spicy wild pig
and herb-poached trout on a bed of exotic greens. On the edge of a
small park, it provides the younger crowd with plenty of people-watch-
ing and hip background music. ⊠ *Berzelli Park,* ☎ *08/6782120. AE,*
DC, MC, V. Closed Sun.

$$ ✕ **Rolfs Kök.** Small and modern, Rolfs combines an informal atmosphere with excellent Swedish-French cuisine, serving three meals a day
at reasonable prices. The lamb is usually a good bet, as are the stir-
fried Asian dishes. ⊠ *Tegnérg. 41,* ☎ *08/101696. AE, DC, MC, V. No*
lunch weekends.

$$ ✕ **Saigon Bar.** With time-warp speed you are whisked from Stockholm to an American G.I. bar in Saigon, '70s trappings and all. Unusual dishes include Indonesian-style fish served on sweet and spicy potato hash and lamb cutlets with eggplant and bamboo-shoot gratin. The wok special is always a good bet. ✉ *Tegnérg. 19–21, from Rdmandsg. T-banan, east along Tegnérg.* ☎ *08/203887. AE, DC, MC, V. No lunch.*

$$ ✕ **Tranan.** A young yuppie crowd frequents Tranan for its bar, which often has live music, and for its unpretentious restaurant. The stark walls and checkered floor are from Tranan's days as a workingman's beer parlor. The chef prepares traditional Swedish cuisine. ✉ *Karlbergsv. 14,* ☎ *08/300765. AE, DC, MC, V.*

Gamla Stan and Skeppsholmen

$$$$ ✕ **Eriks.** One of the namesake restaurants of the famous chef (in Sweden, at least) Erik Lallerstedt, this restaurant serves traditional Swedish fare of the higher school, with a concentration on meat and fish dishes. Everything is well prepared, delicious, and expensive. For calm, choose the upstairs floor; the ground floor always bustles. You'll be dining among Sweden's rich and famous. ✉ *Österlångg. 17,* ☎ *08/238500. AE, DC, MC, V.*

$$$$ ✕ **Grands Franska Matsalen.** From this classic French restaurant in the Grand Hotel, you can enjoy an inspiring view of Gamla Stan and the Royal Palace across the inner harbor waters. The menu changes five times a year, but the emphasis is always on Swedish ingredients, used to create such dishes as medallions of deer with shiitake mushrooms in wild-berry cream sauce. The lofty measure of opulence here is commensurate with the bill. ✉ *Grand Hotel, Södra Blasieholmshamnen 8,* ☎ *08/ 6115214. Reservations essential. Jacket required. AE, DC, MC, V.*

$$$ ✕ **De Fyras Krog.** The name "Inn of the Four Estates" refers to the four social classes originally represented in the Swedish Riksdag—Nobility, Clergy, Burghers, and Peasants. The decor carries out the theme, with rococo furnishings, church pews, an upper gallery, and a stone-flagged cellar dining room to represent the four lifestyles. De Fyras Krog offers a menu of Swedish regional specialties and an intimate atmosphere. ✉ *Jårntorgsg. 5,* ☎ *08/241414. AE, DC, MC, V. Closed Sun.*

$$$ ✕ **Den Gyldene Freden.** Sweden's most famous old tavern has been open for business in 1722. Every Thursday, the Swedish Academy meets here in a private room on the second floor. The haunt of bards and barristers, artists and ad people, Freden could probably serve sawdust and still be popular, but the food and staff are worthy of the restaurant's hallowed reputation. The cuisine has a Swedish orientation, but Continental influences are spicing up the menu. Season permitting, try the oven-baked fillets of turbot served with chanterelles and crêpes; the gray hen fried with spruce twigs and dried fruit is another good selection. ✉ *Österlångg. 51,* ☎ *08/109046. AE, DC, MC, V. Closed Sun. No lunch.*

$$$ ✕ **Källaren Aurora.** Extremely elegant, if a little staid, this Gamla Stan cellar restaurant is set in a beautiful 17th-century house. Its largely foreign clientele enjoys top-quality Swedish and international cuisines served in intimate small rooms. Try charcoal-grilled spiced salmon, veal Parmesan, or orange-basted halibut fillet. ✉ *Munkbron 11,* ☎ *08/ 219359. AE, DC, MC, V. No lunch.*

$$ ✕ **Cassi.** This downtown restaurant, with an espresso bar dominating the front room, specializes in French bistro cuisine at reasonable prices. ✉ *Narvav. 30,* ☎ *08/6617461. DC, MC, V. Closed Sat.*

$$ ✕ **Diana.** This atmospheric Gamla Stan cellar dates from the Middle Ages. The menu draws on the best indigenous ingredients from the Swedish forest and shoreline. In summer customers may be predominantly foreign or businesspeople from the provinces. ⊠ *Brunnsgränd 2,* ☎ *08/107310. AE, DC, MC, V. Closed Sun.*

$$ ✕ **Måtten Trotzig.** The nouveau functional dining space is both a dining room and bar. A short menu demonstrates the chef's imagination, blending multicultural accents into interesting twists. The staff is young, the service professional. ⊠ *Västerlångg. 79,* ☎ *08/240231. AE, DC, MC, V.*

Östermalm

$$$$ ✕ **Paul & Norbert.** This quaint, romantic restaurant is rustic but re-
★ fined. It's on the city's most elegant avenue, overlooking one of its most picturesque bays. French-style preparations include indigenous wild game dishes such as reindeer, elk, partridge, and grouse; fish dishes are also a draw. ⊠ *Strandv. 9,* ☎ *08/6638183. Reservations essential. AE, DC, MC, V. Closed weekends.*

$$$ ✕ **Il Conte.** This warm Italian-style restaurant is close to Stockholm's most elegant avenue, Strandvägen. Il Conte offers delicious Italian dishes and wines served by an attentive staff. Tasteful decor creates an alluring, refined atmosphere. ⊠ *Grevg. 9,* ☎ *08/6612628. Reservations essential. AE, DC, MC, V. No lunch.*

$$ ✕ **Eriks Bakficka.** A favorite among locals, Eriks Bakficka is a block from the elegant waterside street Strandvägen, a few steps down from street level. The restaurant serves a wide variety of Swedish dishes, and there's a lower-priced menu in the pub section. The same owner operates Eriks in Gamla Stan (☞ *above*). ⊠ *Frederikshovsg. 4,* ☎ *08/6601599. AE, DC, MC, V. Closed weekends in July.*

$ ✕ **Örtagården.** This is a truly delightful vegetarian, no-smoking restau-
★ rant above the Östermalmstorg food market. It offers an attractive buffet of soups, salads, hot dishes, and homemade bread—not to mention the SKr5 bottomless cup of coffee—in a turn-of-the-century atmosphere. ⊠ *Nybrog. 31,* ☎ *08/6621728. AE, MC, V.*

Södermalm

$$$ ✕ **Garlic and Shots.** The menu here can be summed up in one word: garlic—the accent of every dish, save one at lunchtime. Crowds flock for the stuff and for the good prices. Garlic-flavored desserts and 22 kinds of vodka are served. Reservations are advised. ⊠ *Folkungag. 85,* ☎ *08/6408446. AE, DC, MC, V.*

$$$ ✕ **Spisen.** A new menu has given this noteworthy restaurant a welcome lift. Try the poached herring, dipped in garlic oil. Prized lunches and home-baked bread add to the alluring atmosphere. Look for the bar— it's hidden—which offers live jazz each Thursday. ⊠ *Renstiernas Gata 30,* ☎ *08/7022229. AE, DC, MC, V.*

$$ ✕ **Hannas Krog.** What started out as an interesting neighborhood spot has become one of Södermalm's trendiest restaurants. Guests are serenaded at 10 minutes before the hour by a mooing cow that emerges from the cuckoo clock just inside the door. Dishes are tasty and good— ranging from Caribbean shrimp specialties to Provençale lamb dishes— if a bit pricey. The restaurant handles crowds in a relaxed atmosphere with consistent service. ⊠ *Skåneg. 80,* ☎ *08/6438225. Reservations essential. AE, DC, MC, V. No lunch weekends and July.*

$$ ✕ **Nils Emil.** This bustling restaurant in Södermalm is known for a royal
★ following, delicious Swedish cuisine, and generous helpings at reasonable prices; try the *kåldomar* (ground beef wrapped in cabbage) or the Baltic herring. The paintings of personable owner-chef Nils Emil's island birthplace in the Stockholm archipelago are by a well-known Swedish artist, Gustav Rudberg. ⊠ *Folkungag. 122,* ☎ *08/6407209.*

Reservations essential. Jacket and tie. AE, DC, MC, V. Closed July. No lunch Sat.

LODGING

In spite of the prohibitively expensive reputation of Stockholm's hotels, great deals can be found during the summer, when prices are substantially lower and numerous discounts are available. More than 50 hotels offer the "Stockholm Package," providing accommodation for one night, breakfast, and the *Stockholmskortet,* or Stockholm Card, which gives free admission to museums and travel on public transport. All rooms in the hotels reviewed are equipped with shower or bath unless otherwise noted. Details are available from travel agents, tourist bureaus, or **Stockholm Information Service** (⌧ Box 7542, S103 93 Stockholm, ☎ 08/7892400, ℻ 08/7892450). Also try **Hotellcentralen** (⌧ Centralstation, S111 20 Stockholm, ☎ 08/7892425, ℻ 08/7918666), where you'll be charged a fee if you call; service is free if you go in person.

Note that you should book lodging far in advance if you plan to travel during the August Stockholm Water Festival.

Downtown Stockholm and Beyond

$$$$ ⚿ **Berns.** Successfully distinguishing itself from the rest of the crowd,
★ the 132-year-old Berns opted for an art deco look with the latest renovation. Indirect lighting, modern Italian furniture, and expensive marble, granite, and wood inlays now dominate the decor of the public areas and guest rooms. You can breakfast in the Red Room, immortalized by August Strindberg's novel of the same name: this was one of his haunts. Rates include the use of a nearby fitness center with a pool. ⌧ *Näckströmsg. 8, S111 47,* ☎ *08/7237200,* ℻ *08/6140700. 65 rooms, 3 suites. Restaurant, bar, no-smoking rooms, meeting room. AE, DC, MC, V.*

$$$$ ⚿ **Continental.** In city center across from the train station, the Continental is a reliable hotel that's especially popular with American guests. Rooms are equipped with a minibar, trouser press, and satellite television. An extravagant Scandinavian buffet is served in the Gustavian breakfast rooms. ⌧ *Klara Vattugränd 4, S101 22,* ☎ *08/244020,* ℻ *08/4113695. 268 rooms. Restaurant, bar, no-smoking rooms, sauna, meeting rooms. AE, DC, MC, V.*

$$$$ ⚿ **Royal Viking (Radisson SAS).** In 1984, what was slated as a convenient storage site only yards from Central Station became the Royal Viking hotel—its best quality, appropriately enough, is convenience, both in location and service. Guest rooms lack nothing except space. They have attractive natural textiles and artwork, sturdy writing desks, separate seating areas, and plush robes in the large bathrooms. Triple-glazed windows and plenty of insulation keep traffic noise to a minimum. The large atrium lobby is spacious, and the split-level lounge is elegant. There is a business-class SAS check-in counter in the lobby. ⌧ *Vasag. 1, S101 24,* ☎ *08/141000 or 800/4488355,* ℻ *08/108180. 319 rooms. Restaurant, bar, minibars, no-smoking rooms, indoor pool, sauna, convention center. AE, MC, V.*

$$$$ ⚿ **Sergel Plaza.** This stainless-steel-paneled hotel has a welcoming lobby, with cane chairs in a pleasantly skylit seating area. Well-lit rooms are practical but lack the luxury feel the price tag might lead you to expect. The decor is almost disappointing, with run-of-the-mill furnishings and too much gray. It's central, right on the main pedestrian mall, but most windows face only office buildings. ⌧ *Brunkebergstorg 9, S103 27,* ☎ *08/226600,* ℻ *08/215070. 406 rooms. Restaurant, bar, no-smoking rooms, sauna, shops, convention center. AE, DC, MC, V.*

$$$$ 🏨 **SkyCity Hotel.** This Radisson SAS–run hotel is dead center in the Arlanda Airport's SkyCity complex. With fully air-conditioned rooms, the hotel is equipped and furnished in a variety of tasteful styles. If your room faces the runway, you can watch the planes quietly take off and land. ✉ *SkyCity, 190 45 Stockholm-Arlanda,* 🕿 *08/59077300,* FAX *08/59378198. 230 rooms. Restaurant, bar, no-smoking rooms, fitness center, conference facilities. AE, DC, MC, V.*

$$$ 🏨 **Amaranten.** A little out of the way on the island of Kungsholmen, this large, modern hotel is, however, just a few minutes' walk from Stockholm's central train station. Rooms are contemporary, with satellite television and complimentary movie channels. Fifty rooms have air-conditioning and soundproofing for an extra charge. Guests can enjoy a brasserie and a piano bar. ✉ *Kungsholmsg. 31, Box 8054, S104 20,* 🕿 *08/6541060,* FAX *08/6526248. 410 rooms. Restaurant, piano bar, no-smoking rooms, indoor pool, sauna, meeting rooms. AE, DC, MC, V.*

$$$ 🏨 **Birger Jarl.** A short bus ride from the city center, this contemporary, conservative, thickly carpeted venue attracts business travelers, catered conferences, and tourists requiring unfussy comforts. Breakfast is an extensive buffet just off the lobby, but room service is also available. Rooms are not large but are well furnished and have nice touches, such as heated towel racks in the bathrooms; all double rooms have bathtubs. Four family-style rooms have extra floor space and sofa beds. ✉ *Tuleg. 8, S104 32,* 🕿 *08/151020,* FAX *08/6737366. 225 rooms. Coffee shop, no-smoking rooms, sauna, meeting rooms. AE, DC, MC, V.*

$$$ 🏨 **Central Hotel.** Less than 300 yards from the Central Station, this practical hotel was constructed in 1989. Rooms are small and face a pleasant, quiet courtyard; bathrooms have a shower only. ✉ *Vasag. 38, S101 20,* 🕿 *08/220840,* FAX *08/247573. 93 rooms. No-smoking rooms, meeting rooms. AE, DC, MC, V.*

$$$ 🏨 **City.** A large, modern-style hotel built in the 1940s and completely renovated in 1984, the City is near the city center and Hötorget market. It is owned by the Salvation Army, so alcohol is not served. Breakfast is served in the atrium restaurant Winter Garden. ✉ *Slöjdg. 7, S111 81,* 🕿 *08/7237200,* FAX *08/7237209. 293 rooms with bath. Restaurant, no-smoking rooms, sauna, meeting rooms. AE, DC, MC, V.*

$$$ 🏨 **Clas på Hörnet.** This may be the most exclusive—and smallest—hotel
★ in town, with only 10 rooms in an 18th-century inn converted into a small hotel in 1982. The rooms, comfortably furnished with period antiques, go quickly. The restaurant is worth visiting even if you don't spend the night: its old-fashioned dining room is tucked away on the ground floor of a restored 1739 inn and its Swedish and Continental menu includes outstanding *strömming* (Baltic herring) and cloudberry mousse cake. Restaurant reservations are essential, as are a jacket and tie. ✉ *Surbrunnsg. 20, S113 48,* 🕿 *08/165130, restaurant 08/165136,* FAX *08/6125315. 10 rooms. AE, DC, MC, V. Closed July.*

$$$ 🏨 **Lydmar.** Just opposite Hummlegården in the center of Stockholm lies this modern hotel, a 10-minute walk from the downtown hub of Sergels Torg. The lobby lounge is alive on weekends with the latest jazz sounds. ✉ *Stureg. 10, 114 36,* 🕿 *08/223160,* FAX *08/6608067. 61 rooms, 5 junior suites. AE, DC, MC, V.*

$$$ 🏨 **Tegnérlunden.** A quiet city park fronts this modern hotel, a 10-minute walk from the downtown hub of Sergels Torg, with the shops of Sveavägen along the way. Although the rooms are small and sparely furnished, they are clean and well maintained. The lobby is bright with marble, brass, and greenery, as is the sunny rooftop breakfast room. ✉ *Tegnérlunden 8, S113 59,* 🕿 *08/349780,* FAX *08/327818. 103 rooms. Breakfast room, no-smoking rooms, sauna, meeting room. AE, DC, MC, V.*

$$ ⊞ **Arcadia.** On a hilltop near a large waterfront nature preserve, this converted dormitory is still within 15 minutes of downtown by bus or subway, or 30 minutes on foot along pleasant shopping streets. Rooms are furnished in a spare, neutral style, with plenty of natural light. The adjoining restaurant serves meals on the terrace in summer. Take Bus 43 to Körsbärsvägen. ⊠ *Körsbärsv. 1, 114 89,* ☎ *08/160195,* FAX *08/ 166224. 82 rooms. Restaurant. AE, DC, MC, V.*

$$ ⊞ **Stockholm Plaza Hotel.** On one of Stockholm's foremost streets for shopping and entertainment, this hotel is ideal for the traveler who wants a central location. The building dates from the turn of the century and is furnished in an old world, elegant manner with reasonably sized rooms. ⊠ *Birger Jarlsg. 29, 103 95,* ☎ *08/145120,* FAX *08/1034923. 151 rooms. AE, DC, MC, V.*

$ ⊞ **Bema.** This small hotel is reasonably central, on the ground floor of an apartment block near Tegnérlunden. Room decor is Swedish modern, with beechwood furniture. One four-bed family room is available. Breakfast is served in your room. ⊠ *Upplandsg. 13, S111 23,* ☎ *08/ 232675,* FAX *08/205338. 12 rooms. AE, DC, MC, V.*

Gamla Stan and Skeppsholmen

$$$$ ⊞ **Grand.** The city's showpiece hotel is an 1874 landmark on the quayside at Blasieholmen, just across the water from the Royal Palace. Visiting political dignitaries, Nobel Prize winners, and movie stars come to enjoy the gracious Old World atmosphere, which extends to the comfortable, well-furnished rooms. One of the hotel's nicest features is a glassed-in veranda overlooking the harbor, where an excellent smörgåsbord buffet is served. Guests have access to the Sturebadet Health Spa nearby. ⊠ *Södra Blasieholmshamnen 8, Box 16424, S103 27,* ☎ *08/6793500,* FAX *08/6118686. 319 rooms, 20 suites. 2 restaurants, bar, no-smoking rooms, sauna, shops, meeting rooms. AE, DC, MC, V.*

$$$$ ⊞ **Lady Hamilton.** As charming and desirable as its namesake, the Lady
★ Hamilton opened in 1980 as a modern hotel inside a 15th-century building. Swedish antiques accent the light, natural-toned decor in all the guest rooms and common areas. Romney's "Bacchae" portrait of Lady Hamilton hangs in the foyer, where a large, smiling figurehead from an old ship supports the ceiling. The breakfast room, furnished with captain's chairs, looks out onto the lively cobblestone street, and the subterranean sauna rooms, in whitewashed stone, provide a secluded fireplace and a chance to take a dip in the building's original, medieval well. The honeymoon suite is impeccable. ⊠ *Storkyrkobrinken 5, S111 28,* ☎ *08/234680,* FAX *08/4111148. 34 rooms. Bar, breakfast room, no-smoking rooms, sauna, meeting room. AE, DC, MC, V.*

$$$$ ⊞ **Lord Nelson.** The owners of the Lady Hamilton and the Victory run this small hotel with a nautical atmosphere right in the middle of Gamla Stan. Space is at a premium—the rooms are little more than cabins—but service is excellent. Noise from traffic in the pedestrian street outside can be a problem during the summer. ⊠ *Västerlångg. 22, S111 29,* ☎ *08/232390,* FAX *08/101089. 31 rooms. Café, no-smoking rooms, sauna, meeting room. AE, DC, MC, V.*

$$$$ ⊞ **Reisen.** This 17th-century hotel on the waterfront in Gamla Stan has been open since 1819. It has a fine restaurant, grill, tea and coffee service in the library, and what is reputed to be the best piano bar in town. The swimming pool is built under the medieval arches of the foundations. ⊠ *Skeppsbron 1214, S111 30,* ☎ *08/223260,* FAX *08/ 201559. 114 rooms. 2 restaurants, bar, no-smoking floor, indoor pool, sauna, meeting rooms. AE, DC, MC, V.*

$$$$ ⊞ **Strand (Radisson SAS).** This Old World yellow-brick hotel, built in 1912 for the Stockholm Olympics, has been completely and tastefully modernized. It's on the water right across from the Royal Dramatic Theater. No two of its rooms are the same, but all are furnished with antiques and have such rustic touches as flowers painted on woodwork and furniture. The Piazza restaurant has an outdoor feel to it: Italian cuisine is the specialty, and the wine list is superb. A SAS check-in counter for business-class travelers adjoins the main reception area. ⊠ *Nybro-kajen 9, Box 163 96, S103 27,* ☎ *08/6787800,* ℻ *08/6112436. 148 rooms. Restaurant, no-smoking rooms, sauna, meeting rooms. AE, DC, MC, V.*

$$$$ ⊞ **Victory.** Slightly larger than its brother and sister hotels, the Lord Nelson and Lady Hamilton (☞ *above*), this extremely atmospheric Gamla Stan building dates from 1640. Decor is nautical, with items from the HMS *Victory* and Swedish antiques. Each room is named after a 19th-century sea captain. The noted Lejontornet restaurant keeps an extensive wine cellar. ⊠ *Lilla Nyg. 5, S111 28,* ☎ *08/143090,* ℻ *08/ 202177. 48 rooms. Restaurant, bar, bistro, no-smoking floor, 2 saunas, meeting rooms. AE, DC, MC, V.*

$$$ ⊞ **Gamla Stan.** This quiet, cozy hotel is tucked away in one of the Gamla Stan's 17th-century houses. Each of its 51 rooms is uniquely decorated. ⊠ *Lilla Nyg. 25,* ☎ *08/244450,* ℻ *08/216483. 51 rooms. No-smoking floor, meeting rooms. AE, DC, MC, V.*

$$ ⊞ **Mälardrottningen.** One of the more unusual establishments in Stockholm, Mälardrottningen, a Sweden Hotels property, was once Barbara Hutton's yacht. Since 1982, it has been a quaint and pleasant hotel, with a crew as service-conscious as any in Stockholm. Tied up on the freshwater side of Gamla Stan, it is minutes from everything. The small suites are suitably decorated in a navy-blue and maroon nautical theme. Some of the below-deck cabins are a bit stuffy, but in summer you can take your meals out on deck. Its chief assets are novelty and absence of traffic noise. ⊠ *Riddarholmen 4, S111 28,* ☎ *08/ 243600 or 800/4488355,* ℻ *08/243676. 59 cabins. Restaurant, bar, grill, no-smoking rooms, sauna, meeting rooms. AE, DC, MC, V.*

Östermalm

$$$$ ⊞ **Diplomat.** Within easy walking distance of Djurgården, this elegant hotel is less flashy than most in its price range. The building is a turn-of-the-century town house that housed foreign embassies in the 1930s and was converted into a hotel in 1966. Rooms have thick carpeting and high ceilings; those in the front, facing the water, have magnificent views over Stockholm Harbor. Check out the tearoom restaurant and second-floor bar. ⊠ *Strandv. 7C, S104 40,* ☎ *08/6635800,* ℻ *08/ 7836634. 133 rooms. Restaurant, bar, no-smoking rooms, sauna, meeting room. AE, DC, MC, V.*

$$$ ⊞ **Mornington.** A quiet, modern Best Western hotel that prides itself on a friendly atmosphere, the Mornington is within easy walking distance of Stureplan and downtown shopping areas and particularly handy to Östermalmstorg, with its food hall. Rooms tend to be small; decor is standard Best Western. ⊠ *Nybrog. 53, S102 44,* ☎ *08/6631240,* ℻ *08/6622179. 140 rooms. Restaurant, bar, no-smoking rooms, sauna, steam rooms, meeting rooms. AE, DC, MC, V.*

$$ ⊞ **Örnsköld.** Just behind the Royal Dramatic Theater in the heart of
★ the city, this hidden gem has the atmosphere of an old private club, with a brass-and-leather lobby and Victorian-style furniture in the moderately spacious, high-ceilinged rooms. Rooms over the courtyard are quieter, but those facing the street—not a busy one—are sunnier. The hotel

is frequented by actors appearing at the Royal Theater. ✉ *Nybrog. 6,*
114 34, ☎ *08/6670285,* FAX *08/6676991. 30 rooms. AE, MC, V.*

Södermalm

$$$$ 🏨 **Scandic Crown.** Working with what appears to be a dubious location (perched on a tunnel above a six-lane highway), the Scandic
Crown has pulled a rabbit out of a hat. The hotel was built in 1988
on special cushions; you know the highway is there, but it intrudes only
minimally, mainly in view. The intriguing labyrinth of levels, separate
buildings, and corridors is filled with such unique details as a rounded
stairway lighted from between the steps. The guest rooms are exquisitely
designed and modern, with plenty of stainless steel and polished wood
inlay to accent the maroon color scheme. Noteworthy is the Couronne
d'Or, a French eatery, and a cellar with wines dating from 1650 where
wine tasting is available. The hotel is at Slussen, easily accessible from
downtown. ✉ *Guldgränd 8, S104 65,* ☎ *08/7022500,* FAX *08/6428358.*
264 rooms. 2 restaurants, piano bar, no-smoking rooms, indoor pool,
beauty salon, sauna, meeting rooms. AE, DC, MC, V.

$$$ 🏨 **Anno 1647.** Named for the date the building was erected, this
★ small, pleasant, friendly hotel is in Södermalm, three stops on the sub-
way from the city center. Rooms vary in shape, but all have original,
well-worn pine floors, with 17th-century-style appointments. There's
no elevator in this four-story building. ✉ *Mariagränd 3, S116 41,* ☎
08/6440480, FAX *08/6433700. 42 rooms, 30 with bath. Snack bar. AE,*
DC, MC, V.

$$ 🏨 **Alexandra.** Although it is in the Södermalm area, to the south of
Gamla Stan, this small, modern hotel is only five minutes by subway
from the city center. A new floor was added in 1990. ✉ *Magnus*
Ladulåsg. 42, S118 27, ☎ *08/840320,* FAX *08/7205353. 75 rooms, 6*
two-room suites. Breakfast rooms, no-smoking rooms, sauna. AE,
DC, MC, V.

$ 🏨 **Gustav af Klint.** A "hotel ship" moored at Stadsgården quay, near
Slussen subway station, the *Gustav af Klint* is divided into two sections—a hotel and a hostel. The hostel section has 18 four-bunk cabins and 10 two-bunk cabins; a 14-bunk dormitory is also available from
May through mid-September. The hotel section has four single-bunk
and three two-bunk cabins with bedsheets and breakfast included. The
hostel rates are SKr120 per person in a four-bunk room, and SKr140
per person in a two-bunk room; these do not include bedsheets or breakfast. All guests share common bathrooms and showers. There is a cafeteria and a restaurant, and you can dine on deck in summer. ✉
Stadsgårdskajen 153, S116 45, ☎ *08/6404077,* FAX *08/6406416. 7*
hotel cabins, 28 hostel cabins, 28 dormitory beds. AE, MC, V.

Youth Hostels

Don't be put off by the "youth" bit: there's actually no age limit. The
standards of cleanliness, comfort, and facilities offered are usually extremely high. Hostels listed are on Skeppsholmen and Södermalm.

🏨 **af Chapman.** This circa-1888 sailing ship, permanently moored in
Stockholm Harbor just across from the Royal Palace, is a landmark
in its own right. Book early—the place is so popular in summer that
finding a bed may prove difficult. Breakfast (SKr45) is not included in
the room rate; there are no kitchen facilities. ✉ *Västra Brobänken,*
Skeppsholmen S111 49, ☎ *08/6795015,* FAX *08/6119875. 136 beds,*
2- to 6-bed cabins. Café June–Aug. DC, MC, V. Closed Dec. 25–Mar.
🏨 **Bosön.** Out of the way on the island of Lidingö, this hostel is part
of the Bosön Sports Institute, a national training center pleasantly close

to the water. You can rent canoes on the grounds and go out for a paddle. Breakfast is included in the room rate. There are laundry facilities and a kitchen for guest use. ✉ *Bosön, S181 47 Lidingö,* ☎ *08/6056600,* FAX *08/7671644. 70 beds. Cafeteria, sauna, coin laundry. MC, V.*

🏠 **Långholmen.** This former prison, built in 1724, was converted into a combined hotel and hostel in 1989. The hotel rooms are made available as additional hostel rooms in the summer. Rooms are small and windows are nearly nonexistent—you *are* in a prison—but that hasn't stopped travelers from flocking here. Each room has two to five beds, and all but 10 have bathrooms with shower. The hostel is on the island of Långholmen, which has popular bathing beaches and a Prison Museum. The Inn, next door, serves Swedish home cooking, the Jail Pub offers light snacks, and a garden restaurant operates in the summer. ✉ *Långholmen, Box 9116, S102 72,* ☎ *08/6680510. 254 beds June–Sept., 26 beds Sept.–May. Cafeteria, restaurant, sauna, beach, coin laundry. AE, DC, MC, V.*

🏠 **Skeppsholmen.** A former craftsman's workshop in a pleasant and quiet part of the island was converted into a hostel for the overflow from the *af Chapman,* an anchor's throw away. Breakfast (SKr45) is not included in the room rate. ✉ *Skeppsholmen, S111 49,* ☎ *08/ 6795017,* FAX *08/6117155. 155 beds, 2- to 6-bed rooms. DC, MC, V.*

Camping

You can camp in the Stockholm area for SKr80–SKr130 per night. Try any of the following sites: **Bromma** (✉ Ängby Camping, S161 55 Bromma, ☎ 08/370420, FAX 08/378226), **Skärholmen** (✉ Bredäng Camping, S127 31 Skärholmen, ☎ 08/977071, FAX 08/7087262), **Sollentuna** (✉ Rösjöbadens Camping, S191 56 Sollentuna, ☎ 08/962184, FAX 08/929295).

NIGHTLIFE AND THE ARTS

The hubs of Stockholm's nightlife are the streets Birger Jarlsgatan, Stureplan, and the city end of Kungsträdgården. On weekends, discos and bars are often packed with tourists and locals, and you might have to wait in line. Many establishments will post and enforce a minimum age requirement, which could be anywhere from 18 to 30, depending on the clientele they wish to serve.

The tourist guide *Stockholm This Week* is available free of charge at most hotels and tourist centers. The Friday editions of the daily newspapers *Dagens Nyheter* and *Svenska Dagbladet* carry current listings of events, films, restaurants, and museums in Swedish.

The **Stockholm Water Festival** (tel. 08/4595500) is *the* big event in Stockholm. People from all over the world come for the concerts, races, fireworks competition, and general partying between August 8–16.

Stockholm is the 1998 **Cultural Capital of Europe,** hosting events of all kinds—involving the arts, culture, nature—throughout the year. The program features an international dance and ballet series, an art manifestation in Kungsträdgården, guest circus performances, a jubilee exhibit of Orrefors glass at the National Museum, music festival at Ulriksdal's Castle, photographic festival, and theater festival with a whole host of European theaters taking part.

SCANDINAVIA BY TRAIN

The best way to experience the sights Scandinavia has to offer is by train.

With a *Scanrail Pass* choose unlimited rail travel throughout Denmark, Finland, Norway and Sweden for as many days as you need. Individual country rail passes are also available.

And with a *Scanrail 'n Drive,* you can take advantage of the benefits of both rail *and* car to get even more out of your Scandinavian vacation.

For information or reservations call your travel agent or Rail Europe:

1-800-4-EURAIL(US)

1-800-361-RAIL(CAN)

Your one source for European travel!

Pick up
the phone.

Pick up
the miles.

Calling Card

415 555 1234 2244
J.D. SMITH

WORLDPHONE

Use your MCI Card® to make an international call from virtually anywhere in the world and earn frequent flyer miles on one of seven major airlines.

Enroll in an MCI Airline Partner Program today. In the U.S., call **1-800-FLY-FREE**. Overseas, call MCI collect at **1-916-567-5151**.

1. To use your MCI Card, just dial the WorldPhone access number of the country you're calling from.
   (For a complete listing of codes, visit www.mci.com.)
2. Dial or give the operator your MCI Card number.
3. Dial or give the number you're calling.

# Austria (CC) ♦	022-903-012	# Netherlands (CC) ♦		0800-022-91-22
# Belarus (CC)		# Norway (CC) ♦		800-19912
From Brest, Vitebsk, Grodno, Minsk	8-800-103	# Poland (CC) ÷		00-800-111-21-22
From Gomel and Mogilev regions	8-10-800-103	# Portugal (CC) ÷		05-017-1234
# Belgium (CC) ♦	0800-10012	Romania (CC) ÷		01-800-1800
# Bulgaria	00800-0001	# Russia (CC) ÷ ♦		
# Croatia (CC) ★	99-385-0112	To call using ROSTELCOM ■		747-3322
# Czech Republic (CC) ♦	00-42-000112	For a Russian-speaking operator		747-3320
# Denmark (CC) ♦	8001-0022	To call using SOVINTEL ■		960-2222
# Finland (CC) ♦	08001-102-80	# San Marino (CC) ♦		172-1022
# France (CC) ♦	0-800-99-0019	# Slovak Republic (CC)		00-421-00112
# Germany (CC)	0130-0012	# Slovenia		080-8808
# Greece (CC) ♦	00-800-1211	# Spain (CC)		900-99-0014
# Hungary (CC) ♦	00▼800-01411	# Sweden (CC) ♦		020-795-922
# Iceland (CC) ♦	800-9002	# Switzerland (CC) ♦		0800-89-0222
# Ireland (CC)	1-800-55-1001	# Turkey (CC) ♦		00-8001-1177
# Italy (CC) ♦	172-1022	# Ukraine (CC) ÷		8▼10-013
# Kazakhstan (CC)	8-800-131-4321	# United Kingdom (CC)		
# Liechtenstein (CC) ♦	0800-89-0222	To call using BT ■		0800-89-0222
# Luxembourg	0800-0112	To call using MERCURY ■		0500-89-0222
# Monaco (CC) ♦	800-90-019	# Vatican City (CC)		172-1022

Is this a great time, or what? :-)

Nightlife

Bars

If you prefer exploring areas not entirely swamped by crowds, you will find a bar-hopping visit to Södermalm rewarding. Start at **Mosebacke Etablissement** (⊠ Mosebacke Torg 3, ☎ 08/6419020), a combined indoor theater and outdoor café with a spectacular view of the city. Wander along Götagatan with its lively bars and head for **Snaps/Rangus Tangus** (⊠ Medborgarplatsen, ☎ 08/6402868), an eatery and cellar bar with live music in a 300-year-old building. A trendy 20-something crowd props up the long bar at **WC** (⊠ Skåneg. 51, ☎ 08/7022963), with ladies' drink specials.

Limerick (⊠ Tegnérg. 10, ☎ 08/6734398) is a favorite Hibernian watering hole. Irish beer enthusiasts rally at **Dubliner** (⊠ Smålandsg. 8, ☎ 08/6797707). **The Tudor Arms** (⊠ Grevg. 31, ☎ 08/6602712) is just as popular as when it opened in the '70s. **Bagpiper's Inn** (⊠ Rörstrandsg. 21, ☎ 08/311855) is another favorite.

Casinos

Many hotels and bars have a roulette table and sometimes blackjack, operating according to Swedish rules. These are aimed at cutting the amount you can lose. The **Monte Carlo** (☎ 08/4110025), at the corner of Kungsgatan and Sveavägen, offers roulette and blackjack 11:30 AM–5 AM daily; there is food service and a bar, and a disco on weekends. Clientele tends to be on the rough side.

Discos and Cabaret

Stockholm's biggest nightclub, **Börsen** (⊠ Jakobsg. 6, ☎ 08/7878500), offers high-quality international cabaret shows. Another popular spot is the **Cabaret Club** (⊠ Barnhusg. 12, ☎ 08/4110608), where reservations are advised.

Café Opera (⊠ Operahuset, ☎ 08/4110026), at the waterfront end of Kungsträgården, is a popular meeting place for young and old alike. It has the longest bar in town, plus dining and roulette, and dancing after midnight; the kitchen offers a night menu until 2:30 AM. **Daily's Bar** (⊠ Kungsträdgården, ☎ 08/215655), a glitzy disco at the other end of Kungsträdgården, near Sweden House, has a restaurant and is open until 3 AM. **King Creole** (⊠ Kungsg. 18, ☎ 08/244700) offers big-band dance music alternating with rock. **Berns' Salonger** (⊠ Berzelii Park, ☎ 08/6140550), an elegant restaurant and bar in a renovated period building with a large balcony facing the Royal Dramatic Theater, turns into a lively disco at night. **Sture Compagniet** (⊠ Stureg. 4, ☎ 08/6117800) is a complex of bars, food service, and dance areas on three levels inside the Sture Gallerian shopping mall. **Penny Lane** (⊠ Birger Jarlsg. 29, ☎ 08/201411) is a soft-disco nightclub specifically for a 30- and 40-something crowd. **Mälarsalen** (⊠ Torkel Knutssonsg. 2, ☎ 08/6581300) caters to the nondrinking jitterbug and fox-trot crowd in Södermalm.

Gay Bars

Pronounced "Hus-et," the upscale **Hus 1** (⊠ Sveav. 57, ☎ 08/315533) dance club—with a restaurant, café, bookshop, and disco—has mirrored walls, weekend drag shows, and a SKr60 cover charge (SKr40 before 10). A hot spot for gays to hang out is the entrance to the **Kina Teater** (⊠ Berzelli Park). **Patricia** (⊠ Stadsgården, Berth 25, ☎ 08/7430570) is a floating disco and bar right next to Slussen.

Jazz Clubs

The best and most popular venue is **Fasching** (⊠ Kungsg. 63, ☎ 08/216267), where international and local bands play year-round. **Stam-**

pen (⊠ Stora Nyg. 5, ☎ 08/205793) is an overpriced, but atmospheric, club in Gamla Stan with traditional jazz nightly. Get there early
for a seat. New on the jazz scene is the lobby bar at the **Lydmar Hotel**
(⊠ Stureg. 10, ☎ 08/223160), where live jazz can be enjoyed on weekends and some weekdays.

Piano Bars

Piano bars are part of the Stockholm scene. The **Anglais Bar** at the Hotel
Anglais (⊠ Humlegårdsg. 23, ☎ 08/6141600) is recommended on weekends. Also try the **Clipper Club** at the Hotel Reisen (⊠ Skeppsbron 1214,
☎ 08/223260).

Rock Clubs

Lido (⊠ Hornsg. 92, subway to Zinkensdamm; ☎ 08/6682333) is on
Södermalm. Call ahead for reservations. **Krogen Tre Backar** (⊠ Tegnérg. 1214, ☎ 08/6734400) can be found just off Sveavgen.

The Arts

Stockholm's theater and concert season runs from September through
May, so you won't find many big-name artists at the height of the tourist
season except during the Stockholm Water Festival in August. For a list
of events, pick up the free booklet *Stockholm This Week,* available from
hotels and tourist information offices. Contact the Stockholm Information
Service for information in 1998 Cultural Capital of Europe happenings.
For tickets to theaters and shows try **Biljettdirekt** at Sweden House (☞
Visitor Information *in* Stockholm A to Z, *below*) or any post office.

Classical Music

Free concerts are held in **Kungsträdgården** every summer—for details, contact the tourist office or check *Stockholm This Week.* International orchestras perform at **Konserthuset** (⊠ Hötorget 8, ☎ 08/
102110), the main concert hall. The **Music at the Palace** series (☎ 08/
102247) runs June through August. Off-season, there are weekly concerts by Sweden's Radio Symphony Orchestra at **Berwaldhallen**
(Berwald Concert Hall, ⊠ Strandv. 69, ☎ 08/7841800).

Film

Stockholm has an abundance of cinemas, all listed in the Yellow Pages
under *Biografer.* Current billings are listed in evening papers, normally
with Swedish titles; call ahead if you're unsure. Foreign movies are sub-
titled. Most, if not all, cinemas take reservations over the phone. Popular showings can sell out ahead of time. Most cinemas are part of the
SF chain (☎ 08/840500), including the 14-screen **Filmstaden Sergel** (⊠
Hötorget, ☎ 08/7896001). The **Grand** (⊠ Sveav. 45, ☎ 08/4112400)
is said to be the best-quality cinema in town. **Biopalatset** and **Filmstaden
Söder** (⊠ Medborgarplatsen, ☎ 08/6443100 and 7896060) are on the
south side and have many films to choose from.

Opera

It is said that Queen Lovisa Ulrika began introducing opera to her sub-
jects in 1755. Since then, Sweden has become an opera center of standing producing such names as Jenny Lind, Jussi Björling, and Birgit
Nilsson. **Operan** (The Royal Opera House, ⊠ Jakobs Torg 2, ☎ 08/
248240), dating from 1898, is now the de facto home of Sweden's op-
eratic tradition. **Folkoperan** (⊠ Hornsg. 72, ☎ 08/6160750) is a modern company with its headquarters in Södermalm. Casting traditional
presentation and interpretation of the classics to the wind, its productions
are refreshingly new.

Theater

Kungliga Dramatiska Teatern (Royal Dramatic Theater, called Dramaten, ⊠ Nybroplan, ☎ 08/6670680) sometimes stages productions of international interest, in Swedish, of course. Productions by the **English Theatre Company** and the **American Drama Group Europe** are occasionally staged at various venues in Stockholm. See newspapers or contact Stockholm Information Service for details.

OUTDOOR ACTIVITIES AND SPORTS

Participant Sports

Beaches

The best bathing places in central Stockholm are on the island of Långholmen and at Rålambshov at the end of Norr Mälarstrand. Both are grassy or rocky lakeside hideaways. Topless sunbathing is virtually de rigueur.

Biking

Stockholm is laced with bike paths, and bicycles can be taken on the commuter trains (except during peak traveling times) for excursions to the suburbs. Average rental cost is SKr80 a day or SKr400 a week. **Cykelfrämjandet** (⊠ Torsg. 31, Box 6027, S102 31, ☎ 08/321680), a local bicyclists' association, publishes an English-language guide to cycling trips. Bikes can be rented from **Cykel & Mopeduthyrning** (⊠ Strandv. at Kajplats 24, ☎ 08/6607959). Also try **Skepp & Hoj** (⊠ Galärvarvsv. 2, ☎ 08/6605757), pronounced "ship ahoy."

Fitness Centers

Health and fitness is a Swedish obsession. The **Sports Club Stockholm** (⊠ City Sports Club, Birger Jarlsg. 6C. ☎ 08/6798310; Atlanta Sports Club, ⊠ St. Eriksg. 34, ☎ 08/6506625) chain has four centers in all, with women's and mixed gym facilities for SKr90 a day. For a relatively inexpensive massage, try the **Axelsons Gymnastiska Institut** (⊠ Gästrikeg. 1012, ☎ 08/165360). **Friskis & Svettis** (⊠ St. Eriksg. 54, 100 28 Stockholm, ☎ 08/6544414) is a local chain of indoor and, in summer, outdoor gyms specializing in aerobics. There are branches all over the Stockholm area. Monday through Thursday at 6 PM, from the end of May into late August, it hosts free sessions in Rålambshovsparken.

Golf

There are numerous golf courses around Stockholm. Contact **Stockholms Golfförbund** (⊠ Solkraftsv. 25, 135 70 Stockholm, ☎ 08/7426940) for information. Try **Lidingö Golfklubb** (⊠ Kyttingev. 2, Lidingö, ☎ 08/7317900), about a 20-minute drive from the city center. **Ingarö Golfklubb** (⊠ Fogelvik, Ingarö, ☎ 08/57028244) is also about 20 minutes away.

Running

Numerous parks with footpaths dot the central city area, among them **Haga Park** (which also has canoe rentals), **Djurgården,** and the wooded **Liljans Skogen.** A very pleasant public path follows the waterfront across from Djurgården, going east from Djurgårdsbron past some of Stockholm's finest old mansions and the wide-open spaces of Ladugårdsgärdet.

Skiing

The **Excursion Shop** in the Sweden House (⊠ Kungsträdgården, Stockholm, ☎ 08/7892415) has information on skiing as well as other sport and leisure activities and will advise on necessary equipment.

Swimming

In town center, **Centralbadet** (⊠ Drottningg. 88, ☎ 08/242403) has an extra-large indoor pool, whirlpool, steambath, and sauna. **Sturebadet** (⊠ Sturegallerian, ☎ 08/54501500) offers aquatic aerobics and a sauna.

Tennis

Former champion Björn Borg once played at **Kungliga Tennishallen** (Royal Tennis Hall, ⊠ Lidingöv. 75, ☎ 08/4591500). **Tennisstadion** (⊠ Fiskartorpsv. 20, ☎ 08/215454) also maintains good courts.

Spectator Sports

The ultramodern **Globen** (⊠ Box 10055, S121 27, Globentorget 2, ☎ 08/7251000), at 281 ft the world's tallest spherical building, hosts sports like ice hockey and equestrian events. It has its own subway station. North of the city lies the open-air **Råsunda Stadion** (⊠ Box 1216, Solnav. 51, S171 23 Solna, ☎ 08/7350935), famous as the home of soccer in Stockholm.

SHOPPING

If you like to shop till you drop then charge on down to any one of the three main department stores in the central city area. For bargains, peruse the boutiques and galleries in Västerlånggatan, the main street of Gamla Stan, and the crafts and art shops that line the raised sidewalk at the start of Hornsgatan on Södermalm. Drottninggatan, Birger Jarlsgatan, and Hamngatan also offer some of the city's best shopping.

Department Stores and Malls

Sweden's leading department store is **NK** (⊠ Hamng. 1820, across the street from Kungsträdgården, ☎ 08/7628000); the initials, pronounced enn-*koh*, stand for *Nordiska Kompaniet*. Prices are high, as is the quality. Also try **Åhléns** (⊠ Klarabergsg. 50, ☎ 08/6766000). Before becoming a famous actress, Greta Garbo used to work at the **PUB** (⊠ Drottningg. 63 and Hötorget, ☎ 08/7916000), with 42 independent boutiques. Garbo fans should visit the small exhibit on level H2, with an array of photographs beginning with her employee ID card.

Gallerian (⊠ Stureg.) is in the city center. **Sturegallerian** (⊠ Stureplan), the other main shopping mall, is on Stureplan.

Specialty Stores

Auction houses

There are three principal local auction houses. Perhaps the finest is **Lilla Bukowski** (⊠ Strandv. 7, ☎ 08/6140800), in its elegant quarters on the waterfront. **Auktions Kompaniet** (⊠ Regeringsg. 47, ☎ 08/235700) is next to NK downtown. **Stockholms Auktionsverk** (⊠ Jakobsg. 10, ☎ 08/4536700) is under the Gallerian shopping center.

Books

Hemlins (⊠ Västerlångg. 6, Gamla Stan, ☎ 08/106180) carries foreign titles and antique books.

Crafts

Swedish handicrafts from all over the country are available at **Svensk Hemslöjd** (⊠ Sveav. 44, ☎ 08/232115). Though prices are high at **Svenskt Hantwerk** (⊠ Kungsg. 55, ☎ 08/214726), so is the quality. For elegant home furnishings and timeless fabrics, affluent Stockholmers tend to favor **Svenskt Tenn** (⊠ Strandv. 5A, ☎ 08/6701600), best known for its selection of designer Josef Franck's furniture and fabrics.

Glass

Nordiska Kristall (✉ Kungsg. 9, ☎ 08/104372), near Sturegallerian, has a small gallery of one-of-a-kind art glass pieces. **Svenskt Glas** (✉ Birger Jarlsg. 8, ☎ 08/6797909) is near the Royal Dramatic Theater. The **Crystal Art Center** (✉ Tegelbacken 4, ☎ 08/217169), near Central Station, has a great selection of smaller glass items. **NK** (☞ *above*) carries a wide, representative line of Swedish glasswork in its Swedish Shop downstairs.

Men's Clothing

For suits and evening suits for both sale and rental, **Hans Allde** (✉ Birger Jarlsg. 58, ☎ 08/207191) provides good, old-fashioned service. For shirts, try **La Chemise** (✉ Smålandsg. 11, ☎ 08/6111494).

Women's Clothing

There are many boutiques on **Biblioteksgatan** and **Västerlånggatan** in Gamla Stan. A shop that specializes in lingerie but carries fashionable clothes as well is **Twilfit** (✉ Nybrog. 11, ☎ 08/6623817; ✉ Gallerian, ☎ 08/216996; and ✉ Gamla Brog. 3638, ☎ 08/201954). **Hennes & Mauritz** (✉ Hamng. 22; Drottningg. 53 and 56; Sergelg. 1 and 22; and Sergels Torg 12; all ☎ 08/7965500) is one of the few Swedish-owned clothing stores to have achieved international success. **Polarn & Pyret** (✉ Hamng. 10, ☎ 08/4114140; ✉ Gallerian, ☎ 08/4112247; ✉ Drottningg. 29, ☎ 08/106790) carries high-quality Swedish children's and women's clothing.

Street Markets

Hötorget is the site of a lively market every day. The **Loppmarknaden** flea market (*loppmarknad*) is held in the parking garage of the Skärholmen shopping center, a 20-minute subway ride from downtown. Market hours are weekdays 11–6, Saturday 9–3, and Sunday 10–3, with an entry fee of SKr10 on weekends. Beware of pickpockets. The best streets for bric-a-brac and antiques are **Odengatan** and **Roslagsgatan**; take Odenplan subway station.

STOCKHOLM A TO Z

Arriving and Departing

By Bus

All the major bus and coach services, like Wasatrafik and Swebus, arrive at **Cityterminalen** (City Terminal, ✉ Klarabergsviadukten 72), next to the central railway station. Reservations to destinations all over Sweden on **Swebus/Vasatrafik** can be made by calling ☎ 020/640640.

By Car

You will approach the city by either the E20 or E18 highway from the west, or the E4 from the north or south. The roads are clearly marked and well sanded and plowed during winter. Signs for downtown read CENTRUM.

By Plane

Initially opened in 1960 solely for international flights, Stockholm's **Arlanda International Airport** (✉ 41 km/26 from city center) also contains a domestic terminal. A freeway links the city and airport.

Between the Airport and City Center: Buses leave both the international and domestic terminals every 10 to 15 minutes from 6:30 AM to 11 PM and run to the Cityterminalen at Klarabergsviadukten, next to the central railway station. The trip costs SKr60. For more information, call ☎ 08/6001000.

A **bus-taxi combination package** (☎ 08/6701010) is available. The bus lets you off by the taxi stand at Jarva Krog or Cityterminalen and you present your receipt to the taxi driver, who takes you to your final destination. The cost is SKr160 if your destination is within city limits, SKr220 to anywhere in the Stockholm area.

For **taxis,** the *fast pris* (fixed price) between Arlanda and the city is SKr350. For information and bookings, call ☎ 08/7973700. The best bets for cabs are **Taxi Stockholm** and **Taxi Kurir.** Watch out for unregistered cabs, which charge high rates.

SAS operates a shared **limousine** service to any point in central Stockholm for SKr263 per person; the counter is in the arrivals hall, just past customs. If two or more people travel to the same address together in a limousine, only one is charged the full rate; the others pay SKr140.

By Train

All trains arrive at Stockholm's **Central Station** (✉ Vasag., ☎ 08/7622000) in downtown Stockholm. From here regular commuter trains serve the suburbs, and an underground walkway leads to the central subway station.

Getting Around

The cheapest way to travel around the city by public transport is to purchase **Stockholmskortet** (Stockholm Card). In addition to unlimited transportation on city subway, bus, and rail services, it offers free admission to more than 60 museums and several sightseeing trips. The card costs SKr185 for 24 hours, SKr350 for two days, and SKr425 for three days and can be purchased from the tourist center at Sweden House on Hamngatan, from the Hotellcentralen accommodations bureau at Central Station, and from the tourist center at Kaknäs Tower.

By Boat

Waxholmsbolaget (Waxholm Ferries, ☎ 08/6795830) offers the *Båtluffarkortet* (Inter-Skerries Card), a discount pass for its extensive commuter network of archipelago boats; the price is SKr250 for 16 days of unlimited travel. The **Strömma Canal Company** (☎ 08/233375) operates a fleet of archipelago boats that provide excellent sightseeing tours and excursions.

By Bus and Subway

Stockholm has an excellent bus and subway network operated by **SL** (☎ 08/6001000). Tickets for the two networks are interchangeable. The subway system, known as **T-banan** (*Tunnelbanan,* stations marked by a blue-on-white T), is the easiest and fastest way to get around. Servicing over 100 stations and covering more than 96 km (60 mi) of track, trains run frequently between 5 AM and 2 AM. Late-night bus service connects certain stations when trains stop running. The comprehensive bus network serves out-of-town points of interest, such as Waxholm and Gustavsberg.

Maps and timetables for all city transportation networks are available from the SL information desks at Sergels Torg, Central Station, and Slussen.

Bus and subway fares are based on zones, starting at SKr14, good for travel within one zone, such as downtown, for one hour. You pay more if you travel in more than one zone. Single tickets are available at station ticket counters and on buses, but it's cheaper to buy a **SL Tourist Card** from one of the many Pressbyrån newsstands. A coupon is valid for both subway and buses and costs SKr95; it's good for a fixed number of trips (approximately 10) within the greater Stockholm area during an unlimited period of time. If you plan to travel within the greater Stockholm area extensively during a 24-hour period, you can purchase a one-day pass for SKr60; a 72-hour pass costs SKr120. The 24-hour pass includes transportation on the ferries between Djurgården, Nybroplan, and Slussen. The 72-hour pass also entitles the holder to admission to Skansen, Gröna Lund Tivoli, and Kaknäs Tower. People younger than 18 or older than 65 years pay SKr36 for a one-day pass and SKr72 for a two-day pass.

By Car
Driving in Stockholm is often deliberately frustrated by city planners, who impose many restrictions to keep traffic down. Get a good city map, called a **Trafikkarta,** available at most service stations for around SKr75.

By Taxi
Stockholm's taxi service is efficient but overpriced. If you call a cab, ask the dispatcher to quote you a price, which is usually lower than the meter fare. Reputable cab companies are **Taxi Stockholm** (☎ 08/150000), **Taxi 020** (☎ 020/850400), or **Taxikurir** (☎ 08/300000). **Taxi Stockholm** has an immediate charge of SKr25 whether you hail a cab or order one by telephone. A trip of 10 km (6 mi) should cost about SKr97 between 6 AM and 7 PM, SKr107 at night, and SKr114 on weekends.

Contacts and Resources

Car Rentals
Rental cars are readily available in Sweden and are relatively inexpensive. Because of the availability and efficiency of public transport, there is little point in using a car within the city limits. However, if you are traveling elsewhere in Sweden, roads are uncongested and well marked, but gasoline is expensive (SKr8 per liter). All major car-rental firms are represented, including **Avis** (⊠ Ringv. 90, ☎ 08/6449980) and **Hertz** (⊠ Vasag. 2224, ☎ 08/240720).

Doctors and Dentists
There is a 24-hour national health-service **emergency number** (☎ 08/6449200). Private care is available via **City Akuten** (☎ 08/4117177). Contact the emergency dental clinic at **Sankt Erik's Hospital** (☎ 08/6541117, 8 AM–9 PM; ☎ 08/6449200, 9 PM–8 AM).

Embassies
U.S. (⊠ Strandv. 101, ☎ 08/7835300). **Canada** (⊠ Tegelbacken 4, ☎ 08/4533000). **U.K.** (⊠ Skarpög. 68, ☎ 08/6719000).

Emergencies
Dial ☎ 112 for emergencies—this covers police, fire, ambulance, and medical help, as well as sea and air rescue services.

English-Language Bookstores
Many bookshops stock English-language books. For newspapers and magazines, try one of the newsstands at the Central Station or the **Press Center** (⊠ Gallerian shopping center, Hamng., ☎ 08/7230191). **Hedengren's** (⊠ Sturegallerian shopping complex, ☎ 08/6115132) has one of the best English-book selections. **Akademibokhandeln** (⊠ Mäster Samuelsg. 32, near the city center, ☎ 08/6136100) is another good bet.

Guided Tours
BOAT AND BUS SIGHTSEEING TOURS
A bus tour in English and Swedish covering all the main points of interest leaves each day at 9:45 AM from the tourist center at Sweden House (⊠ Hamng. 27, Box 7542, S103 93 Stockholm, ☎ 08/7892490); it costs SKr250. Other, more comprehensive tours, taking in museums,

Gamla Stan, and City Hall, are also available at the tourist center.
Strömma Kanalbolaget and **Stockholm Sightseeing** (⊠ Skeppsbron
22, ☎ 08/233375) run a variety of sightseeing tours of Stockholm. Boats
leave from the quays outside the Royal Dramatic Theater, Grand
Hotel, and City Hall.

GUIDED TOURS

You can hire your own guide from Stockholm Information Service's
Guide Centralen (⊠ Sweden House, Hamng. 27, Box 7542, S103 93
Stockholm, ☎ 08/7892496, FAX 08/7892496). In summer, but be sure
to book guides well in advance.

WALKING TOURS

City Sightseeing (☎ 08/4117023 or 08/240470) runs several tours, including the "Romantic Stockholm" tour of the Cathedral and City Hall;
the "Royal Stockholm" tour, which features visits to the Royal Palace
and the Treasury; and the "Old Town Walkabout," which strolls
through Gamla Stan in just over one hour.

Late-Night Pharmacies

C. W. Scheele (⊠ Klarabergsg. 64, ☎ 08/4548130) is open around-
the-clock.

Travel Agencies

For a complete listing, see the Yellow Pages under *Resor-Resebyråer.*

Contact **American Express** (⊠ Birger Jarlsg. 1, ☎ 08/6795200, 020/
793211 toll-free). **SJ** (Statens Järnvägar, ⊠ Vasag. 1, ☎ 020/757575),
the state railway company, has its main ticket office at Central Station.
For air travel, contact **SAS** (⊠ Klarabergsviadukten 72, accessible
from Central Station, ☎ 020/727000).

Visitor Information

Stockholm Information Service: Sweden House (Sverigehuset, ⊠ Hamng.
27, Box 7542, S103 93 Stockholm, ☎ 08/7892490). **Stockholm Central Station** (⊠ Vasag., ☎ 020/757575). **City Hall** (summer only, ⊠
Hantverkarg. 1, ☎ 08/5082900). **Kaknästornet** (Kaknäs TV Tower, ⊠
Ladugårdsgärdet, ☎ 08/7892435). **Fjäderholmarna** (☎ 08/7180100).

Swedish Travel and Tourism Council (⊠ Box 3030, Kungsg. 36, 103
61 Stockholm, ☎ 08/7255500, FAX 08/7255531).

3 Side Trips from Stockholm

SURROUNDING STOCKHOLM is a latticework of small, historic islands, most of them crowned with castles straight out of a storybook world. Set aside a day for a trip to any of these; half the pleasure of an island outing is a leisurely boat trip to get there. (However, the castles can all be reached by alternative overland routes, if you prefer the bus or train.) Farther afield is the island of Gotland, whose medieval festival, Viking remains, and wilderness reserves will take you back in time. The cathedral town of Uppsala is another popular day trip from Stockholm, its quiet atmosphere providing an enlightening contrast to the mood of the city.

Drottningholm

★ ㉝ *1 km (½ mi) west of Stockholm.*

★ Occupying an island in Mälaren (Sweden's third-largest lake) some 45 minutes from Stockholm's center, **Drottningholms Slott** (Queen's Island Castle) is a miniature Versailles dating from the 17th century. The royal family once used this property only as a summer residence, but, tiring of the Royal Palace back in town, they moved permanently to one wing of Drottningholm in the 1980s. Today it remains one of the most delightful of European palaces, embracing all that was best in the art of living practiced by mid-18th century royalty. The interiors date to the 17th, 18th, and 19th centuries, and most are open to the public. ✉ *Drottningholm,* ☎ *08/4026280.* 💳 *SKr40.* ☉ *May–Aug., daily 11–4:30; Sept., weekdays 1–3:30, weekends noon–3:30.*

The lakeside gardens of Drottningholms Slott are its most beautiful asset, containing **Drottningholms Slottsteater** (Court Theater), the only complete theater to survive from the 18th century anywhere in the world. Built by Queen Lovisa Ulrika in 1766 as a wedding present for her son Gustav III, the theater fell into disuse after his assassination at a masked ball in 1792 (dramatized in Verdi's opera *Un Ballo in Maschera*). In 1922, the theater was rediscovered; there is now a small theater museum here as well. To get performance tickets, book well in advance at the box office; the season runs from late May to early September. A word of caution: the seats are extremely hard—take a cushion. ✉ *Drottningholm,* ☎ *08/7590406, box office 08/6608225.* 💳 *SKr40.* ☉ *May–Aug., daily noon–4:30; Sept., daily 1–3:30. Guided tours in English at 12:30, 1:30, 2:30, 3:30, and 4:30. Closed for 10 days at beginning of July.*

Arriving and Departing
Boats bound for Drottningholms Slott leave from Klara Mälarstrand, a quay close to City Hall. Call **Strömma Kanalbolaget** (☎ 08/233375) for schedules and fares.

Mariefred

㉞ *63 km (39 mi) southwest of Stockholm.*

The most delightful way to experience the true vastness of Mälaren is the trip to Mariefred—an idyllic little town of mostly timber houses—aboard the coal-fired steamer of the same name, built in 1903 and still going strong.

Mariefred's principal attraction is **Gripsholm Slott.** First built in 1540, the castle contains fine Renaissance interiors, a superbly atmospheric theater commissioned in 1781 by the ill-fated Gustav III, and Sweden's royal portrait collection. ☎ *0159/10194.* 💳 *SKr40.* ☉ *Guided tours*

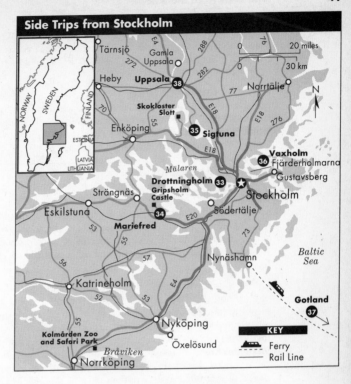

only, May–June and Aug., daily 10–4; July, daily 9–5; Apr. and Sept., Tues.–Sun. 10–3; Oct.–Mar., weekends noon–3.

The **S.S. Mariefred** departs from Klara Mälarstrand, near Stockholm's City Hall. The journey takes 3½ hours each way, and there is a restaurant on board. You can also travel by narrow-gauge steam railway from Mariefred to a junction on the main line to Stockholm, returning to the capital by ordinary train. Contact the Mariefred Tourist Office for details. ☎ 08/6698850. 🎫 SKr160 round-trip. ☉ Departures at 10 AM May, weekends only; mid-June–late Aug., Tues.–Sun. Return trip departs from Mariefred at 4:30.

Visitor Information
The **Mariefred tourist office** (☎ 0159/29790) is open only in the summer; the rest of the year, call Mälarturism (☎ 0152/29690) for information for all of Lake Mälaren.

Sigtuna

㉟ 48 km (30 mi) northwest of Stockholm.

An idyllic, picturesque town situated on a northern arm of Lake Mälar, Sigtuna was the principal trading post of the Svea, the tribe that settled Sweden after the last Ice Age; its Viking history is still apparent in the many runic stones preserved all over town. After it was ransacked by Estonian pirates, its merchants founded Stockholm sometime in the 13th century. Little remains of Sigtuna's former glory, beyond parts of the principal church. The town hall dates from the 18th century, the main part of town from the early 1800s, and there are two houses said to date from the 15th century.

About 20 km (12 mi) northeast of Sigtuna and accessible by the same ferry boat is **Skokloster Slott,** an exquisite Baroque castle. Commissioned in 1654 by a celebrated Swedish soldier, Field Marshal Carl Gustav Wrangel, the castle is furnished with the spoils of Wrangel's successful campaigns in Europe in the 17th century. The castle can be reached by boat from Sigtuna. ☒ *Bålsta,* ☎ *018/386077.* 🎫 *SKr60.* ☉ *Daily noon–6.*

Arriving and Departing

From June to mid-August Sigtuna can be reached by boat from the quay near City Hall (Strömma Kanalbolaget, ☎ 08/233375); round-trip fare is SKr140. Another option is to take a commuter train from Stockholm's Central Station to Märsta, where you change to Bus 570 or 575.

Vaxholm and the Archipelago

36 *32 km (20 mi) northeast of Stockholm.*

Skärgården (the archipelago) is Stockholm's greatest natural asset: more than 25,000 islands and skerries, many uninhabited, spread across an almost tideless sea of clean, clear water. To sail lazily among these islands aboard an old steamboat on a summer's night is a timeless delight.

For the tourist with limited time, one of the simplest ways to get a taste of the archipelago is the one-hour ferry trip to Vaxholm, an extremely pleasant, though sometimes crowded, mainland seaside town of small, red-painted wooden houses. Here, a fortress guarding what was formerly the main sea route into Stockholm now houses a small museum, **Vaxholms Kastell Museum,** showing the defense of Stockholm over the centuries. You have to take a small boat from the town landing, in front of the Tourist Bureau, over to the castle. ☎ *08/54172157.* 🎫 *SKr50, including boat fare.* ☉ *Mid-May–Aug., daily noon–4. Group admission at other times by arrangement.*

An even quicker trip into the archipelago is the 20-minute ferry ride to **Fjäderholmarna** (the Feather Islands), a group of four secluded islands. After 50 years as a military zone, the islands were opened to the public in the early 1980s. Today they are crammed with arts-and-crafts studios, shops, an aquarium, a small petting farm, a boat museum, a large cafeteria, an ingenious "shipwreck" playground, and even a smoked-fish shop.

For an in-depth tour of the archipelago, seek out the **Blidösund.** A coal-fired steamboat built in 1911 that has remained in almost continuous regular service, it is now run by a small group of enthusiasts who take parties of around 250 on evening music-and-dinner cruises. The *Blidösund* leaves from a berth close to the Royal Palace in Stockholm. ☒ *Skeppsbron,* ☎ *08/4117113.* 🎫 *SKr120.* ☉ *Departures early May–late Sept., Mon.–Thurs. 7 PM (returns at 10:45).*

Among the finest of the archipelago steamboats is the **Saltsjön,** which leaves from Nybrokajen, close to the Strand Hotel. Tuesday through Thursday evenings you can take a jazz-and-dinner cruise for SKr120; Saturday and Sunday from late June to late August, pay SKr175 to go to Utö, an attractive island known for its bike paths, bakery, and restaurant. In December, there are three daily Julbord cruises, serving a Christmas smörgåsbord. ☒ *Saltsjön, Strömma Kanalbolaget, Skeppsbron 22,* ☎ *08/233375.* ☉ *Departures July–early Aug. and Dec.*

Dining

$$$ ✕ **Fjäderholmarnas Krog.** A crackling fire on the hearth in the bar area welcomes the sailors who frequent this place. Lacking your own sailboat, you can time your dinner to end before the last ferry returns to the mainland. The food here is self-consciously Swedish: fresh, light, and beautifully presented; the service is professional, and the ambience relaxed. It's a great choice for a quiet, special night out in Stockholm. ✉ *Fjäderholmarna,* ☎ *08/7183355. AE, DC, MC, V. Closed Oct.–Apr.*

$ ✕ **Gröna Caféet.** A grassy garden terrace and an appealing selection of fresh open sandwiches on hearty brown bread make this small, old-fashioned Vaxholm café a hit. It's on Rådhusgatan, by the town square. ✉ *Rådhusg. 26,* ☎ *08/54131510. No credit cards.*

Vaxholm and the Archipelago A to Z

ARRIVING AND DEPARTING

Regular ferry services to the archipelago depart from Strömkajen, the quayside in front of the Grand Hotel. Cruises on a variety of boats leave from the harbor in front of the Royal Palace or from Nybrokajen, across the road from the Royal Dramatic Theater. Ferries to the Feather Islands run almost constantly all day long in the summer (April 29–September 17), from Slussen, Strömkajen, and Nybroplan. Contact **Strömma Canal Co.** (☎ 08/233375; ✉ Waxholmsbolaget, ☎ 08/6795830; ✉ Fjäderholmarna, ☎ 08/7180100).

VISITOR INFORMATION

The **Vaxholms Tyristbyrå** (Vaxholm Tourist Bureau; ✉ Söderhamnen, 185 83 Vaxholm, ☎ 08/54131480) is in a large kiosk at the bus terminal, adjacent to the marina and ferry landing.

Gotland

㊲ *85 km (53 mi) southwest of Stockholm.*

Gotland is Sweden's main holiday island, a place of wide, sandy beaches and wild cliff formations called *raukar.* Measuring 125 kilometers (78 mi) long and 52 km (32 mi) at its widest point, Gotland is where Swedish sheep-farming has its home. In its charming glades, 35 different varieties of wild orchids thrive, attracting botanists from all over the world.

The first record of people living on Gotland dates from around 5000 BC. By the Roman Iron Age, it had become a leading Baltic trading center. When the German marauders arrived in the 13th century, they built most of its churches and established close trading ties with the Hanseatic League in Lübeck. They were followed by the Danes, and Gotland finally became part of Sweden in 1645.

Gotland's capital, **Visby,** is a delightful, hilly town of about 20,000 people in which medieval houses, ruined fortifications, and churches blend with cobbled lanes of fairy-tale cottages, their facades covered with roses that bloom even in November because the climate is so gentle.

In its heyday Visby was protected by a wall, of which 3 km (2 mi) survive today, along with 44 towers and numerous gateways. It is considered the best-preserved medieval city wall in Europe after that of Carcassonne in southern France. The north gate provides the best vantage point for an overall view of the wall.

Visby's cathedral, **St. Maria Kyrka,** is the only one of the town's 13 medieval churches that is still intact and in use. Near the harbor is the **Gamla Apoteket** (Old Apothecary), a late-medieval four-story merchant's house. ✉ *Strandg. 28,* ☎ *0498/273184.* ⊡ *Free.* ☉ *Daily 9–5.*

Burmeisterska Huset, the home of the Burmeister, or principal German merchant, offers exhibitions and artisans. Call the tourist office in Visby to arrange for viewing. ✉ *Strandg. 9, no phone.* ⊡ *Free.*

Fornsalen (the Fornsal Museum) contains examples of medieval artwork, hoards of silver from Viking times, and impressive picture stones that predate the Viking runic stones. ✉ *Mellang. 19,* ☎ *0498/247010.* ☎ *SKr30.* ☉ *Mid-May–Sept., daily 11–6; Oct.–mid-May, Tues.–Sun. noon–4.*

The stalactite caves at **Lummelunda,** about 18 km (11 mi) north of Visby on the coastal road, are unique in this part of the world and are worth visiting. A pleasant stop along the way to Lummelunda is the **Krus-myntagården** (☎ 0498/70153), a garden with more than 200 herbs, 8 km (5 mi) north of Visby.

There are approximately 100 old churches on the island that are still in use today, dating from Gotland's great commercial era. **Barlingbo,** from the 13th century, has vault paintings, stained-glass windows, and a remarkable 12th-century font. The exquisite **Dalhem** was constructed in about 1200. **Gothem,** built during the 13th century, has a notable series of paintings of that period. **Grötlingbo** is a 14th-century church with stone sculptures and stained glass (note the 12th-century reliefs on the facade). **Tingstäde** is a mix of six building periods dating from 1169 to 1300. The massive ruins of a Cistercian monastery founded in 1164 are now called the **Roma Kloster Kyrka** (Roma Cloister Church). **Öja,** a medieval church decorated with paintings, houses a famous holy rood from the late 13th century.

Curious rock formations dot the coasts of Gotland, and two **bird sanctuaries, Stora** and **Lilla Karlsö,** stand off the coast south of Visby. The bird population consists mainly of guillemots, which look like penguins. Visits to these sanctuaries are permitted only in the company of a recognized guide. ✉ *Stora Karlsö,* ☎ *0498/241113;* ✉ *Lilla Karlsö,* ☎ *0498/241139.* ☎ *SKr180 for guided tour of one sanctuary.* ☉ *May–Aug., daily.*

Dining

$$ ✗ **Gutekällaren.** Despite the name, which means cellar in Swedish, this restaurant is above ground in a building that dates from the 12th century. Mediterranean dishes are the draw. ✉ *Stora Torget 3,* ☎ *0498/210043. DC, MC.*

$$ ✗ **Lindgården.** This atmospheric restaurant specializes in both local dishes and French cuisine. ✉ *Strandg. 26,* ☎ *0498/218700. Reservations essential. AE, DC, MC, V. Closed Sun. No lunch weekends.*

Nightlife and the Arts

Medeltidsveckan (Medieval Week), celebrated in Visby during early August, is a citywide festival marking the invasion of the prosperous island by the Danish King Valdemar on July 22, 1361. Beginning with Valdemar's grand entrance parade, events include jousting, an open-air market on Strandgatan, and a variety of street-theater performances re-creating the period.

Outdoor Activities and Sports

Bicycles, tents, and camping equipment can be rented from **Gotlands Cykeluthyrning** (✉ Skeppsbron 8, ☎ 0498/214133). **Gotlandsleden** is a 200-km (120-mi) bicycle route around the island; contact the tourist office for details.

Gotland A to Z

ARRIVING AND DEPARTING

Car ferries sail from Nynäshamn, a small port on the Baltic an hour by car or rail from Stockholm; commuter trains leave regularly from Stockholm's Central Station for Nynäshamn. Ferries depart at 11:30 AM year-round. From June through mid-August there's an additional ferry at 12:30 PM. A fast ferry operates from mid-April until mid-September, departing three times a day. The regular ferry takes about five hours;

the fast ferry takes 2½ hours. Boats also leave from Oskarshamn, farther down the Swedish coast and closer to Gotland by about an hour. *Gotland City Travel* (✉ Kungsg. 57, ☎ 08/236170 or 08/233180; ✉ Nynäshamn, ☎ 08/5206400; ✉ Visby, ☎ 0498/247065).

GUIDED TOURS

Sightseeing Tours: Guided tours of the island and Visby, the capital, are available in English by arrangement with the tourist office.

VISITOR INFORMATION

The main tourist office is **Gotlands Turistservice** (☎ 0498/206000, FAX 0498/249059), at Österport in Visby. You can also contact **Gotland City AB** in Stockholm for lodging (☎ 08/233180) or ferry reservations (☎ 08/236170).

Uppsala

38 *67 km (41 mi) north of Stockholm.*

Sweden's principal university town vies for that position with Lund in the south of the country. August Strindberg, the nation's leading dramatist, studied here—and by all accounts hated the place. Ingmar Bergman, his modern heir, was born here. It is a historic site where pagan (and extremely gory) Viking ceremonies persisted into the 11th century. Uppsala University, one of the oldest and most highly respected institutions in Europe, was established here in 1477 by Archbishop Jakob Ulfson. As late as the 16th century, nationwide *tings* (early parliaments) were convened here. Today it is a quiet home for about 170,000 people, built along the banks of Fyris River, a pleasant jumble of old buildings dominated by its cathedral, which dates from the early 13th century.

Ideally you should start your visit with a trip to **Gamla Uppsala** (Old Uppsala), 5 km (3 mi) north of the town. Here under three huge mounds lie the graves of the first Swedish kings—Aun, Egil, and Adils—of the 6th-century Ynglinga dynasty. Close by in pagan times was a sacred grove containing a legendary oak from whose branches animal and human sacrifices were hung. By the 10th century, Christianity had eliminated such practices. A small church, which was the seat of Sweden's first archbishop, was built on the site of a former pagan temple. Today the archbishopric is in Uppsala itself, and the church, **Gamla Uppsala Kyrka,** is largely for the benefit of tourists.

To sample a mead brewed from a 14th-century recipe, stop at the **Odinsborg Restaurant** (☎ 018/323525), near the burial mounds of Gamla Uppsala. A small open-air museum in Gamla Uppsala, **Disagården,** features old farm buildings, most of them dating from the 19th century. ▣ *Free.* ◔ *June–Aug., daily 9–5.*

Back in Uppsala, your first visit should be to **Uppsala Domkyrka** (Uppsala Cathedral), whose twin towers—at 362 ft the same height as the length of the nave—dominate the city. Work on the cathedral began in the early 13th century; it was consecrated in 1435 and restored between 1885 and 1893. Still the seat of Sweden's archbishop, the cathedral is also the site of the tomb of Gustav Vasa, the king who established Sweden's independence in the 16th century. Inside is a silver casket containing the bones of Saint Erik, Sweden's patron saint. ▣ *Free.* ◔ *Daily 8–6.*

The **Domkyrka Museet** in the north tower has handicrafts, church vestments, and church vessels on display. ▣ *SKr10.* ◔ *May–Aug., daily 9–5; Sept.–Apr., Sun. 12:30–3.*

Work on **Uppsala Slott** (Uppsala Castle) was started in the 1540s by Gustav Vasa, who intended it to symbolize the dominance of the monarchy over the church. It was completed under Queen Christina nearly a century later. Students gather here every April 30 to celebrate the Feast of Valborg and optimistically greet the arrival of spring. ⌂ *Castle SKr40. ☉ Guided tours of castle mid-Apr.–Sept., daily at 11 and 2 (additional tours late June–mid-Aug., weekends at 10 and 3).*

In the excavated Uppsala Slott ruins, the **Vasa Vignettes,** scenes from the 16th century, are portrayed with effigies, costumes, light, and sound effects. ⌂ *SKr40 ☉ Mid-Apr.–Aug., daily 11–4; Sept., weekends 10–5.*

One of Uppsala's most famous sons, Carl von Linné, also known as Linnaeus, was a professor of botany at the university during the 1740s and created the Latin nomenclature system for plants and animals. The **Linné Museum** is dedicated to his life and works. ⌂ *Svartbäcksg. 27,* ☏ *018/136540.* ⌂ *SKr10. ☉ Late May and early Sept., weekends noon–4; June–Aug., Tues.–Sun. 1–4.*

The botanical treasures of Linné's old garden have been re-created and are now on view in **Linnéträdgården.** The garden's orangery houses a pleasant cafeteria and is used for concerts and cultural events. ⌂ *Svartbäcksg. 27,* ☏ *018/109490.* ⌂ *SKr10. ☉ May–Aug., daily 9–9; rest of yr, daily 9–7.*

Uppsala Universitetet (Uppsala University, ☏ 018/182500), founded in 1477, is known for its **Carolina Rediviva** (university library), which contains a copy of every book published in Sweden, in addition to a large collection of foreign literature. One of its most interesting exhibits is the *Codex Argentus,* a Bible written in the 6th century.

Completed in 1625, the **Gustavianum,** which served as the university's main building for two centuries, is easy to spot by its remarkable copper cupola, now green with age. The building houses the ancient anatomical theater where lectures on human anatomy and public dissections took place. The Victoria Museum of Egyptian Antiquities and the Museums for Classical and Nordic Archeology are also in the building. ⌂ *Akademig. 3,* ☏ *018/182500.* ⌂ *SKr20 (SKr10 to anatomical theater only). ☉ June–Aug., daily 11–3. Anatomical Theater also Sept.–May, weekends noon–3.*

Dining

$$$ ✕ **Domtrappkällaren.** In a 14th-century cellar near the cathedral, Domtrappkällaren serves excellent French and Swedish cuisines. Game is the specialty, and the salmon and reindeer are delectable. ⌂ *Sankt Eriksgränd 15,* ☏ *018/130955. Reservations essential. AE, DC, MC, V.*

Uppsala A to Z

GUIDED TOURS

Sightseeing Tours: You can explore Uppsala easily by yourself, but English-language guided group tours can be arranged through the tourist office; the guide service number is ☏ 018/274818.

VISITOR INFORMATION

The main **tourist office** (⌂ Fyris Torg 8, ☏ 018/117500 or 018/274800) is in town center; in summer, a small tourist information office is also open at Uppsala Castle (☏ 018/554566).

4 Göteborg

IF YOU ARRIVE IN GÖTEBORG (Gothenburg) by car, don't
drive straight through the city in your haste to reach your
coastal vacation spot; it is well worth spending a day or
two exploring this attractive port. A quayside jungle of cranes and warehouses attests to the city's industrial might, yet within a 10-minute walk
of the waterfront is an elegant, modern city of broad avenues, green
parks, and gardens. This is not to slight the harbor: it comprises 22
km (14 mi) of quays with warehouses and sheds covering more than
1.5 million square ft and spread along both banks of the Göta Älv (river),
making Göteborg Scandinavia's largest port. The harbor is also the home
of Scandinavia's largest corporation, the automobile manufacturer
Volvo (which means "I roll" in Latin), as well as of the roller-bearing
manufacturer SKF and the world-renowned Hasselblad camera company.

Historically, Göteborg owes its existence to the sea. Tenth-century
Vikings sailed from its shores, and a settlement was founded here in
the 11th century. Not until 1621, however, did King Gustav II Adolf
grant Göteborg a charter to establish a free-trade port on the model
of others already thriving on the Continent. The west-coast harbor would
also allow Swedish shipping to avoid Danish tolls exacted for passing
through Öresund, the stretch of water separating the two countries.
Foreigners were recruited to make these visions real: the Dutch were
its builders—hence the canals that thread the city—and many Scots-
men worked and settled here, though they have left little trace.

Today Göteborg resists its second-city status by being a leader in attractions and civic structures: the Scandinavium was until recently Europe's largest indoor arena; the Ullevi Stadium stages some of the
Nordic area's most important concerts and sporting events; Nordstan
is one of Europe's biggest indoor shopping malls; and Liseberg, Scandinavia's largest amusement park in area, attracts some 2.5 million visitors a year. Over the Göta River is Älvsborgsbron, at 3,060 ft the longest
suspension bridge in Sweden, and under a southwestern suburb runs
the Gnistäng Tunnel, which at 62 ft claims the odd distinction of being
the world's widest tunnel cut through rock for motor vehicles.

EXPLORING GÖTEBORG

Göteborg is an easy city to explore: most of the major attractions are
within walking distance of one another, and the streetcar network is
excellent—in summer you can take a sightseeing trip on an open-air
streetcar. The heart of Göteborg is Avenyn (the Avenue; actually
Kungsportsavenyn, but over the years shortened to simply Avenyn), a
60-ft-wide, tree-lined boulevard that bisects the center of the city in a
south–north direction, linking its cultural heart, Götaplatsen, at the
southern end, with the main commercial area, now dominated by the
modern Nordstan shopping center. Beyond lies the waterfront, busy
with all the traffic of the port, as well as some of Göteborg's newer
cultural developments.

Cultural Göteborg

A pleasant stroll will take the visitor from Götaplatsen's modern architecture down the Avenyn—the boulevard Kungsportsavenyn lined with
elegant shops, cafés, and restaurants—and across both canals to finish
at the State Museum building. The street slopes gently up from the canal
at Kungsportsplats and ends at Poseidon's fountain in Götaplatsen.

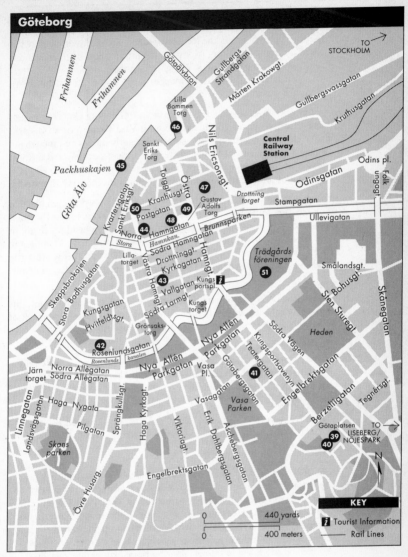

Göteborg

Börshuset, **49**
Domkyrkan, **43**
Feske Körkan, **42**
Götaplatsen, **39**
Konstmuseet, **40**
Kronhuset, **50**

Maritima
Centrum, **46**
Nordstan, **47**
Rådhuset, **48**
Röhsska Museet, **41**
Stadsmuseet, **44**
Utkiken, **45**
Trädgarn, **51**

A Good Walk

Start your tour in **Götaplatsen** ㊴, a square dominated by a statue of Poseidon; behind him is the **Konstmuseet** ㊵. Stroll downhill past the cafés and restaurants along Avenyn to the intersection with Vasagatan. A short way to the left down Vasagatan, at the junction with Teatergatan, you can visit the **Röhsska Museet** ㊶, the country's only museum of Swedish design.

Continue down Vasagatan to Folkhögskolan, Göteborg Universitet, and, if the weather's good, to the neighboring Vasa Parken, or Vasa Park. Turn right to go north on Viktoriagatan, cross the canal, and then make an immediate left to visit one of the city's most peculiar attractions, **Feske Körkan** ㊷, an archaic spelling of *Fisk Kyrkan,* the Fish Church. It resembles a place of worship but is actually an indoor fish market.

Following this you may feel inspired to visit the city's principal place of worship, **Domkyrkan** ㊸. To get here from Feske Körkan, follow the canal eastward until you come to Västra Hamngatan; then head north about four blocks to the church. Continue northward on Västra Hamngatan to the junction with Norra Hamngatan, where you'll find the **Stadsmuseet** ㊹, housed in the 18th-century Swedish East India Company.

TIMING

Depending on how much time you want to spend in each museum, this walk may take anywhere from a couple of hours to the better part of a day. Note that many sites close Monday off-season.

Sights to See

㊸ **Domkyrkan** (Göteborg Cathedral). The cathedral, in neoclassic yellow brick, dates from 1802; though disappointingly plain from the outside, the interior is impressive. ⊠ *Kungsg. 20,* ☎ *031/130479.* ⊙ *Weekdays 8–5, Sat. 8–3, Sun. 10–3.*

㊷ **Feske Körkan** (Fish Church). Built in 1872, this covered fish market gets its nickname for its Gothic-style architectural details. ⊠ *Fisktorget-Rosenlundsg.*

OFF THE BEATEN PATH   **FISKHAMNEN –** An excellent view of **Älvsborgsbron** (Älvsborg Bridge), the longest suspension bridge in Sweden, is available from Fiskhamnen, the Fish Docks west of Stigbergstorget. Built in 1967, the bridge stretches 3,060 ft across the river and is built high so that ocean liners can pass beneath. The government is considering plans to turn this part of the harbor into a scenic walkway with parks and cafés. Also look toward the sea to the large container harbors, Skarvikshamnen, Skandiahamnen (where boats depart for England), and Torshamnen, which bring most of the cargo and passengers to the city today.

★ ㊴ **Götaplatsen** (Göta Place). The cultural center of Göteborg was built in 1923 in celebration of the city's 300th anniversary. In the center is the Swedish-American sculptor Carl Milles' fountain statue of Poseidon choking an enormous shark. Behind the statue of Poseidon stands the **Konstmuseet** (Art Museum), flanked by the **Konserthuset** (Concert Hall) and the **Stadsteatern** (Municipal Theater), three contemporary buildings in which the city celebrates its important contribution to Swedish cultural life. The **Stadsbiblioteket** (Municipal Library) maintains a collection of more than 550,000 books, many in English.

OFF THE BEATEN PATH   **LISEBERG NÖJESPARK –** Göteborg proudly claims Scandinavia's largest amusement park. The city's pride is well earned: Liseberg is one of the best-run, most efficient parks in the world. In addition to a wide selection of carnival rides, Liseberg also has numerous restaurants and theaters, all set amid beautifully tended gardens. It's about a 30-minute walk east from the city center or a 10-minute ride by bus or tram; in summer a vintage open streetcar makes frequent runs to Liseberg from Brunnsparken in the middle of town. ☒ Örgrytev., ☎ 031/400100. ☒ SKr40. ☉ Late Apr.–June and late Aug., daily 3–11; July–mid-Aug., daily noon–11; Sept., Sat. 11–1, Sun. noon–8.

40 Konstmuseet. After an extensive renovation, the Art Museum reopened in January 1996 with a new, more accessible entrance and expanded facilities; one of these is the Hasselblad Center, devoted to progress in the art of photography. The museum continues to display an impressive collection of the works of leading Scandinavian painters and sculptors, encapsulating some of the moody introspection of the artistic community in this part of the world. Among the artists represented are Swedes such as Carl Milles, Johan Tobias Sergel, the Impressionist Anders Zorn, the Victorian idealist Carl Larsson, and Prince Eugen. The 19th- and 20th-century French art collection is the best in Sweden, and there's also a small collection of old masters. ☒ Götaplatsen, S412 56, ☎ 031/612980. ☒ SKr35. ☉ Weekdays 11–4 (Wed. until 9), weekends 11–5. Closed Mon. Sept.–May.

41 Röhsska Museet (Museum of Arts and Crafts). Fine collections of furniture, books and manuscripts, tapestries, and pottery are on view. ☒ Vasag. 3739, Box 53178, S400 15, ☎ 031/613850. ☒ SKr40. ☉ Year-round, weekends noon–5; May–mid-June, weekdays noon–4; mid-June–Aug., Mon. and Wed.–Fri. noon–6, Tues. noon–9; Apr. and Sept., Tues. noon–9, Wed.–Fri. noon–4.

44 Stadsmuseet (City Museum). Once the warehouse and auction rooms of the Swedish East India Company, a major trading firm founded in 1731, this palatial structure dates from 1750. Today it contains exhibits on the Swedish west coast, with a focus on Göteborg's nautical and trading past. One interesting exhibit deals with the East India Company and its ship the Göteborg, which in 1745, returning from China, sank just outside the city while members of the crew's families watched from shore. ☒ Norra Hamng. 12, S411 14, ☎ 031/612770. ☒ SKr40. ☉ Weekdays noon–6, weekends 11–4. Closed Mon. Sept.–Apr.

| NEED A BREAK? | In the cellar of Stadsmuseet, the **Ostindiska Huset Krog & Kafé** (☎ 031/135750) re-creates an 18th-century atmosphere. The dagenslunch, priced at SKr65, is available from 11:30 to 2. |

Commercial Göteborg

Explore Göteborg's portside character, both historic and modern, at the waterfront development near town center, where an array of markets and boutiques may keep you busy for hours.

A Good Walk

Begin at the harborside square known as Lilla Bomen, where the **Utkiken** ㊹ offers a bird's-eye view of the city and harbor. The waterfront development here includes the training ship Viking, the Opera House, and the **Maritima Centrum** ㊻.

From Lilla Bomen Torg, take the pedestrian bridge across the highway to **Nordstan** ㊼. Leave the mall at the opposite end, which puts you at Brunnsparken, the hub of the city's streetcar network. Turn right and cross the street to Gustav Adolfs Torg, the city's official center, dominated by **Rådhuset** ㊽. On the north side of the square is the **Börshuset** ㊾, built in 1849.

Head north from the square along Östra Hamngatan and turn left onto Postgatan to visit **Kronhuset** ⑤⓪, the city's oldest secular building, dating from 1643. The **Kronhusbodarna** are carefully restored turn-of-the-century shops and handicrafts boutiques that surround the entrance to Kronhuset.

Return to Gustaf Adolfs Torg and follow Östra Hamngatan south across the Stora Hamnkanal to Kungsportsplats, where the Saluhall, or Market Hall, has stood since 1888. A number of pedestrian-only shopping streets branch out through this neighborhood on either side of Östra Hamngatan. Crossing the bridge over Rosenlunds Kanalen from Kungsportsplats brings you onto Kungsportsavenyn and the entrance to **Trädgarn** ⑤①.

TIMING

The walk itself will take about two hours; allow extra time to explore the sites and for shopping. Note that Kronhuset is always closed weekends, and Utkiken is closed weekdays off-season. The Kronhusbodarna is closed Sunday. Trädgarn is closed Monday off-season.

Sights to See

⓪ **Börshuset** (Stock Exchange). Completed in 1849, the former Stock Exchange building houses city administrative offices as well as facilities for large banquets. ✉ *Gustaf Adolfs Torg 5.*

Kronhusbodarna (Historical Shopping Center). Glassblowing and watchmaking are among the handicrafts offered in the adjoining Kronhuset; there is also a nice, old-fashioned café. ✉ *Kronhusg. 1D.* ☉ *Closed Sun.*

⑤⓪ **Kronhuset** (Crown House). The city's oldest secular building, dating from 1643, was originally the city's armory. In 1660 Sweden's Parliament met here to arrange the succession for King Karl X Gustav, who died suddenly while visiting the city. ✉ *Postg. 68,* ☎ *031/7117377.* ⌚ *SKr30.* ☉ *Weekends 11–4.*

④⑥ **Maritima Centrum** (Marine Center). Here modern naval vessels, including a destroyer, submarines, lightship, cargo vessel, and various tugboats, provide an insight into Göteborg's historic role as a major port. ✉ *Packhuskajen, S411 04,* ☎ *031/101035 or 031/101290 for English recording.* ⌚ *SKr50.* ☉ *May–June, daily 10–6; July and Aug., daily 10–9; Mar.–Apr. and Sept.–Nov., daily 10–4.*

④⑦ **Nordstan.** Sweden's largest indoor shopping mall—open daily—includes a huge parking garage, 24-hour pharmacy, post office, several restaurants, entertainment for children, the department store Åhlens, and a tourist information kiosk. ✉ *Entrances on Köpmansg., Nils Ericsonsg., Kanaltorgsg., and Östra Hamng.*

④⑧ **Rådhuset.** Though the Town Hall dates from 1672, when it was designed by Nicodemus Tessin Senior, its controversial modern extension by Swedish architect Gunnar Asplund dates from 1937. ✉ *Gustaf Adolfs Torg 1.*

⑤① **Trädgarn** (Botanic Gardens). Trädgårdsföreningen comprises beautiful open green spaces, a magnificent Rose Garden, Butterfly House, and Palm House. ✉ *Just off Kungsportsavenyn.,* ☎ *031/611911 for Butterfly House.* ☉ *Park 7–8; Palm House 10–4; Butterfly House Oct.–Mar., Tues.–Sun. 10–3; Apr., Tues.–Sun. 10–4; May and Sept., daily 10–4; June–Aug., daily 10–5.*

④⑤ **Utkiken** (Lookout Tower). This red-and-white-striped skyscraper towers 282 ft above the waterfront, offering an unparalleled view of the city and skyscrapers. ⊠ *Lilla Bomen.* ☎ *SKr25.* ⊙ *May–Aug., daily 11–7; Oct.–Apr., weekends 11–4.*

GASVERKSKAJEN – For an interesting tour of the docks, head east from Lilla Bomen about 1½ km (1 mi) along the riverside to the Gas Works Quay, just off Gullbergsstrandgatan. Today, this is the headquarters of a local boating association, its brightly colored pleasure craft contrasting with the old-fashioned working barges either anchored or being repaired at Ringön, just across the river.

NYA ELFSBORGS FÄSTNING – Boats leave regularly from Lilla Bomen to the Elfsborg Fortress, built in 1670 on a harbor island to protect the city from attack. ⊠ *Börjessons, Lilla Bommen, kajskul 205, Box 31084, S400 32,* ☎ *031/800750.* ☎ *SKr65.* ⊙ *6 departures per day early May–Aug., daily; Sept., weekends.*

VIKING – This four-masted schooner, built in 1907, was among the last of Sweden's sailing cargo ships. The Hotel and Restaurant School of Göteborg opened a hotel and restaurant inside the ship in February 1995. Visitors are welcome. ⊠ *Lilla Bommen,* ☎ *031/635800.* ☎ *SKr25.*

DINING

You can eat well in Göteborg, but expect to pay dearly for the privilege. Fish dishes are the best bet here. Call ahead to be sure restaurants are open, as many close for a month in summer.

$$$ ✕ **A Hereford Beefstouw.** Probably as close as you come to an American steak house in Sweden, this restaurant has gained popularity in a town dominated by fish restaurants. Diners' beef selections are cooked by chefs at grills in the center of the three dining rooms (one of which is set aside for nonsmokers). The rustic atmosphere is heightened by thick wooden tables, pine floors, and landscape paintings. ⊠ *Linnég. 5,* ☎ *031/7750441. AE, DC, MC, V. No lunch weekends or July.*

$$$ ✕ **Åtta Glas.** This casual, lively restaurant in what was formally a barge offers excellent views of the river and of the Kungsportsbron, a bridge spanning the canal in town center. Swedish-style fish and meat dishes are the focus, and a children's menu is available. The second-floor bar gets crowds on weekends. ⊠ *Kungsportsbron 1,* ☎ *031/136015. AE, DC, MC, V.*

$$$ ✕ **The Place.** Possibly Göteborg's finest dining establishment, the Place
★ offers a warm, intimate atmosphere created by terra-cotta ceilings, pastel-yellow walls, and white linen tablecloths. A wide selection of exotic dishes, from smoked breast of pigeon to beef tartare with caviar, are prepared with quality ingredients. This is also the home of one of the best wine cellars in Sweden, with Mouton Rothschild wines dating from 1904. An outdoor terrace is open during summer. ⊠ *Arkivg. 7,* ☎ *031/160333. Reservations essential. AE, DC, MC, V.*

$$$ ✕ **Räkan.** This informal and popular place makes the most of an unusual gimmick: the tables are arranged around a long tank, and if you order shrimp, the house specialty, they arrive at your table in radio-controlled boats you navigate yourself. ⊠ *Lorensbergsg. 16,* ☎ *031/169839. Reservations essential. AE, DC, MC, V. No lunch weekends.*

$$$ ✕ **Sjömagasinet.** Seafood is the obvious specialty at this waterfront restaurant. In a 200-year-old renovated shipping warehouse, the dining room has views of the harbor and suspension bridge. An outdoor terrace opens up in summer. ⊠ *Klippans Kulturreservat,* ☎ *031/246510. Reservations essential. AE, DC, MC, V.*

$$ ✕ **Fiskekrogen.** Its name means Fish Inn, and it has more than 30 fish and seafood dishes to choose from. Lunches are particularly good, and it's just across the canal from the Stadsmuseet. ⊠ *Lilla Torget 1,* ☎ *031/7112184. AE, DC, MC, V. Closed Sun.*

$ ✕ **Amanda Boman.** This little restaurant in one corner of the market hall at Kungsportsplats keeps early hours, so unless you eat an afternoon dinner, plan on lunch instead. The cuisine is primarily Swedish, including fish soup and gravlax (marinated salmon). ⊠ *Saluhallen,* ☎ *031/137676. AE, DC, MC, V. Closed Sun.*

$ ✕ **Gabriel.** A buffet of fresh shellfish and the fish dish of the day draw crowds to this restaurant on a balcony above the fish hall. You can eat lunch and watch all the trading. ⊠ *Feske Körkan,* ☎ *031/139051. AE, DC, MC, V. Closed Sun. and Mon. No dinner.*

LODGING

$$$$ 🏨 **Park Avenue (Radisson SAS).** Though a 1991 renovation failed to give this modern luxury hotel the ambience it so sorely lacks, all the facilities are in place, including a SAS check-in counter. The well-equipped rooms are decorated in earth tones and have good views of the city. ⊠ *Kungsportsavenyn 3638, Box 53233, S400 16,* ☎ *031/176520,* ⨳ *031/169568. 318 rooms. 2 restaurants, bar, 2 no-smoking floors, indoor pool, sauna, meeting room. AE, DC, MC, V.*

$$$$ 🏨 **Sheraton Hotel and Towers.** Opened in 1986 across Drottningtorget from the picturesque central train station, the Sheraton Hotel and Towers is Göteborg's most modern and spectacular international-style hotel. The attractive atrium lobby is home to two restaurants: Frascati, which serves international cuisine, and the Atrium piano bar with a lighter menu. Rooms are large and luxurious and decorated in pastels. Guests receive a 20% discount at the well-appointed health club on the premises. ⊠ *Södra Hamng. 5965, S401 24,* ☎ *031/806000,* ⨳ *031/ 159888. 344 rooms. Restaurant, piano bar, no-smoking rooms, beauty salon, health club, shops, casino, convention center, travel services. AE, DC, MC, V.*

$$$ 🏨 **Eggers.** Dating from 1859, Best Western's Eggers has more Old
★   World character than any other hotel in the city. It is a minute's walk from the train station and was probably the last port of call in Sweden for many emigrants to the United States. Rooms vary in size, and all are beautifully appointed, often with antiques. Only breakfast is served. ⊠ *Drottningtorget, Box 323, S401 25,* ☎ *031/806070,* ⨳ *031/154243. 65 rooms. No-smoking rooms, meeting rooms. AE, DC, MC, V.*

$$$ 🏨 **Europa.** Large and comfortable, this hotel is part of the Nordstan
★   mall complex, very close to the central train station. ⊠ *Köpmansg. 38, S401 24,* ☎ *031/801280,* ⨳ *031/154755. 475 rooms, 5 suites. Restaurant, piano bar, no-smoking floors, indoor pool, sauna, conference center, parking. AE, DC, MC, V.*

$$$ 🏨 **Liseberg Heden.** Not far from the famous Liseberg Amusement Park, Liseberg Heden is a popular family hotel. Rooms are modern and are done in light colors; most have wood floors, and all have a satellite television, minibar, and large desk. Perks include a sauna and a gourmet restaurant. ⊠ *Sten Stureg., S411 38,* ☎ *031/200280,* ⨳ *031/ 165283. 160 rooms. Restaurant, no-smoking rooms, minibars, sauna, meeting rooms. AE, DC, MC, V.*

$$$ 🏨 **Opalen.** If you are attending an event at the Scandinavium stadium, or if you have children and are heading for the Liseberg Amusement Park, this Reso hotel is ideally located. Rooms are bright and modern. ⊠ *Engelbrektsg. 73, Box 5106, S402 23,* ☎ *031/810300,* ⨳ *031/ 187622. 241 rooms. Restaurant, bar, 2 no-smoking floors, sauna. AE, DC, MC, V.*

$$$ 🏨 **Panorama.** Within reach of all downtown attractions and close to Liseberg, this Best Western hotel nevertheless manages to provide a quiet, relaxing atmosphere. ✉ *Eklandag. 5153, Box 24037, S400 22,* ☎ *031/810880,* 𝖥𝖠𝖷 *031/814237. 339 rooms. Restaurant, no-smoking floors, hot tub, sauna, nightclub, meeting rooms, free parking. AE, DC, MC, V.*

$$$ 🏨 **Riverton.** Convenient for people arriving in the city by ferry, this hotel is close to the European terminals and overlooks the harbor. Built in 1985, it has a glossy marble floor and reflective ceiling in the lobby. Rooms are decorated with abstract-pattern textiles and whimsical prints. ✉ *Stora Badhusg. 26, S411 21,* ☎ *031/101200,* 𝖥𝖠𝖷 *031/130866. 190 rooms. Restaurant, bar, no-smoking rooms, hot tub, sauna, meeting rooms, free parking. AE, DC, MC, V.*

$$$ 🏨 **Royal.** Göteborg's oldest hotel, built in 1852, is small, family owned,
  ★ and traditional. Rooms, most with new parquet floors, are individually decorated with reproductions of elegant Swedish traditional furniture. It's in the city center a few blocks from the central train station. ✉ *Drottningg. 67, S411 07,* ☎ *031/806100,* 𝖥𝖠𝖷 *031/156246. 82 rooms. Breakfast room, no-smoking floor. AE, DC, MC, V.*

$$$ 🏨 **Rubinen.** The central location on Avenyn is a plus, but this Reso hotel can be noisy in summer. ✉ *Kungsportsavenyn 24, Box 53097, S400 14,* ☎ *031/810800,* 𝖥𝖠𝖷 *031/167586. 185 rooms. Restaurant, bar, no-smoking rooms, meeting rooms. AE, DC, MC, V.*

$ 🏨 **Ostkupans Vandrarhem.** Situated in a modern apartment block, this hostel is 5 km (3 mi) from the train station. Rooms are contemporary, with Swedish-designed furnishings. Breakfast (SKr40) is not included in the rates. ✉ *Mejerig. 2, S412 76,* ☎ *031/401050,* 𝖥𝖠𝖷 *031/401151. 250 beds, 6- to 8-bed apartments. MC, V. Closed Sept.–May.*

$ 🏨 **Partille Vandrarhem.** This hostel is in a pleasant old house 15 km (9 mi) outside the city, next to a lake for swimming. You can order meals or prepare them yourself in the guest kitchen. ✉ *Landvetterv., Box 214, S433 24, Partille,* ☎ *031/446501,* ☎ 𝖥𝖠𝖷 *031/446163. 120 beds, 2- to 6-bed rooms. No credit cards.*

Camping

If camping is your bag, then **Uddevalla** (Hafstens Camping, ☎ 0522/644117), **Göteborg** (Kärralund, ☎ 031/840200, 𝖥𝖠𝖷 031/840500), and **Askim** (Askim Strand, ☎ 031/286261, 𝖥𝖠𝖷 031/681335) have fine sites.

NIGHTLIFE AND THE ARTS

Music, Opera, and Theater

Home of the highly acclaimed Göteborg Symphony Orchestra, **Konserthuset** (✉ Götaplatsen, S412 56, ☎ 031/167000) features a mural by Sweden's Prince Eugen in the lobby. **Operan** (✉ Packhuskajen, ☎ 031/131300), home of the Göteborg's Opera Company, was completed in 1994 and incorporates a 1,250-seat auditorium with a glassed-in dining area overlooking the harbor. **Stadsteatern** (✉ Götaplatsen, Box 5094, S402 22, ☎ 031/819960 tickets, 031/7786600 information) has a good reputation in Sweden. The vast majority of its productions are in Swedish.

OUTDOOR ACTIVITIES AND SPORTS

Beaches

There are several excellent local beaches. The two most popular—though you'll be unlikely to find them crowded—are Näset and Askim.

Fishing

Mackerel fishing is popular here. Among the boats that take expeditions into the archipelago is the **M.S. Daisy** (☎ 031/963018 or 010/2358017), which leaves from Hjuvik on the Hisingen side of the Göta River.

SHOPPING

Department Stores

Try the local branch of **NK** (⊠ Östra Hamng. 42 (☎ 031/107000). **Åhléns** (☎ 031/800200) is in the Nordstan mall (☞ Exploring Göteborg, *above*).

Specialty Stores

Antiques
Antikhallarna (Antiques Halls, ⊠ Västra Hamng. 6, ☎ 031/7111324) claims to be the largest of its kind in Scandinavia. You'll find Sweden's leading auction house, **Bukowskis** (⊠ Kungsportsavenyn 43, ☎ 031/200360), on Avenyn.

Crafts
If you are looking to buy Swedish handicrafts and glassware in a suitably atmospheric setting then visit the various shops in **Kronhusbodarna.** Excellent examples of local handicrafts can also be bought at **Bohusslöjden** (⊠ Kungsportsavenyn 25, ☎ 031/160072).

Men's Clothing
Ströms (⊠ Kungsg. 2729, ☎ 031/177100) has occupied its street corner location for two generations, offering clothing of high quality and good taste. The fashions at **Gillblads** (⊠ Kungsg. 44, ☎ 031/108846) suit a younger, somewhat trendier customer.

Women's Clothing
Gillblads (⊠ Kungsg. 44, ☎ 031/108846) has the most current fashions. **Ströms** (⊠ Kungsg. 2729, ☎ 031/177100) offers clothing of high quality and mildly conservative style. **Hennes & Mauritz** (⊠ Kungsg. 5557, ☎ 031/7110011) sells clothes roughly comparable to the standard choices at Sears or Marks & Spencer.

GÖTEBORG A TO Z

Arriving and Departing

By Bus
All buses arrive in the central city area and the principal bus company is **Swebus** (☎ 031/103285).

By Car
Göteborg is reached by car either via the E20 or the E4 highway from Stockholm (495 km/307 mi) and the east, or on the E6/E20 coastal highway from the south (Malmö is 290 km/180 mi away). Markings are excellent, and roads are well sanded and plowed in winter.

By Plane
Landvetter (☎ 031/941100), is approximately 26 km (16 mi) from the city. Among the airlines operating from the airport are **SAS** (☎ 031/942000 or 020/727000), **British Airways** (☎ 020/781144), **Air France** (☎ 031/941180), and **Lufthansa** (☎ 031/941325 or 020/228800).

Between the Airport and City Center: Landvetter is linked to Göteborg by freeway. Buses leave Landvetter every 15 to 30 minutes and arrive

30 minutes later at Nils Ericsonsplatsen by the central train station, with stops at Lisebergsstationen, Korsvägen, the SAS Park Avenue Hotel, and Kungsportsplatsen; weekend schedules include some non-stop departures. The price of the trip is SKr50. For more information, call **GL** (Göteborg Bus and Tram, ☏ 031/801235).

The **taxi** ride to the city center should cost no more than SKr250. A shared **SAS limousine** for up to four people to the same address costs SKr215 (SAS Limousine Service, ☏ 031/942424).

By Train

There is regular service from Stockholm, taking a little over 4½ hours, as well as frequent high-speed (X2000) train service, which takes about three hours. All trains arrive at the **central train station** (☏ 031/805000) in Drottningtorget, downtown Göteborg. For schedules, call **SJ** (☏ 031/104445 or 020/757575). Streetcars and buses leave from here for the suburbs, but the hub for all streetcar traffic is a block down Norra Hamngatan, at Brunnsparken.

Getting Around

By Boat

Traveling the entire length of the Göta Canal by passenger boat to Stockholm takes between four and six days. For details, contact the **Göta Canal Steamship Company** (✉ Hotellplatsen 2, Box 272, S401 24, Göteborg, ☏ 031/806315; ✉ N. Riddarholshamnen 5, S111 28, Stockholm, ☏ 08/202728). For information about sailing your own boat on the Göta Canal, contact **AB Göta Kanalbolaget** (☏ 0141/53510).

By Bus and Tram

Göteborg has an excellent transit service, called Stadstrafiken; pick up a brochure in English at a TidPunkten office (✉ Drottningtorget, Brunnsparken, Nils Ericsonsplatsen, and Folkungabron, ☏ 031/801235), which explains the various discount passes and procedures.

The best bet for the tourist, however, is the **Göteborg Card,** which covers free use of public transport, various sightseeing trips, and admission to Liseberg and local museums, among other benefits. The card costs SKr125 for one day, SKr225 for two days, and SKr275 for three days; there are lower rates for children younger than 18 years from mid-June to mid-September. You can buy the Göteborg Card as well as regular tram and bus passes at Pressbyrån shops, camping sites, and the tourist information offices.

By Car

Avis has offices at the airport (☏ 031/946030) and the central railway station (☏ 031/805780). Also try **Hertz** (✉ Spannmålsg. 16, ☏ 031/803730).

By Taxi

To order a taxi, call **Taxi Göteborg** (☏ 031/650000); for advance bookings, call ☏ 031/500504.

Contacts and Resources

Doctors and Dentists

Dial ☏ 031/7031500 day or night for information on medical services. Emergencies are handled by the **Sahlgrenska Hospital** (☏ 031/601000), **Östrasjukhuset** (☏ 031/374000), and **Mölndalssjukhuset** (☏ 031/861000). There is a private medical service at **City Akuten** weekdays 8–6 (✉ Drottningg. 45, ☏ 031/101010). There is a 24-hour children's emergency service at Östrasjukhuset as well.

The national dental-service emergency number is ☎ 031/807800; the private dental-service emergency number is ☎ 031/800500. Both are available 8 AM–9 PM only; for emergencies after hours, call ☎ 031/7031500.

Embassies and Consulates

U.K. Consulate (⊠ Götg. 15, ☎ 031/151327).

Emergencies

Dial ☎ 112.

English-Language Bookstores

Nearly all bookshops stock English-language books. The broadest selection is at **Eckersteins Akademibokhandeln** (⊠ Södra Larmg. 11, ☎ 031/171100).

Guided Tours

Boat and Bus Sightseeing Tours: A 90-minute bus tour and a two-hour combination boat-and-bus tour of the chief points of interest leave from outside the main tourist office at Kungsportsplatsen every day from mid-May through August and on Saturday in April, September, and October. Call the tourist office for schedules.

For a view of the city from the water and an expert commentary on its sights and history in English and German, take one of the **Paddan** sightseeing boats. *Paddan* means "toad" in Swedish, an apt commentary on the vessels' squat appearance. The boats pass under 20 bridges and take in both the canals and part of the Göta River. ⊠ *Kungsportsbron*, ☎ *031/133000.* 🎫 *SKr70.* ☉ *Late Apr.–late June and mid-Aug.–early Sept., daily 10–5; late June–mid-Aug., daily 10–9; early Sept.–Oct. 1, daily noon–3.*

Late-Night Pharmacy

Vasen (⊠ Götg. 12, ☎ 031/804410), in the Nordstan shopping mall, is open 24 hours.

Travel Agencies

See the Yellow Pages under *Resor-Resebyråer.* **Ticket Travel Agency** (⊠ Östra Hamng. 35, ☎ 031/176860). **STF** (⊠ Drottningtorget 6, Box 305, S401 24, ☎ 031/150930).

Visitor Information

The main tourist office is **Göteborg's Turistbyrå** (⊠ Kungsportsplatsen 2, S411 10 Göteborg, ☎ 031/100740, FAX 031/132184). There are also offices at the Nordstan shopping center (⊠ Nordstadstorget, S411 05 Göteborg, ☎ 031/150705) and in front of the central train station at Drottningtorget.

A free visitor's guide called *Göteborgarn* is available in English during the summer; you can pick it up at tourist offices, shopping centers, and some restaurants, as well as on the streetcars.

The Friday edition of the principal morning newspaper, *Göteborgs Posten*, includes a weekly supplement called "Aveny"—it's in Swedish but is reasonably easy to decipher.

5 Side Trips from Göteborg

BOHUSLÄN

The Bohuslän coastal region north of Göteborg, with its indented, rocky coastline, provides a foretaste of Norway's fjords farther north. It was from these rugged shores that the 9th-and 10th-century Vikings sailed southward on their epic voyages. Today small towns and attractive fishing villages nestle among the distinctively rounded granite rocks and the thousands of skerries and islands that form Sweden's western archipelago, best described by Prince Vilhelm, brother of the late King Gustav V, as "an archipelago formed of gneiss and granite and water that eternally stretches foamy arms after life." The ideal way to explore the area is by drifting slowly north of Göteborg, taking full advantage of the uncluttered beaches and small, picturesque fishing villages. Painters and sailors haunt the region in summer.

Kungälv

⓹ *15 km (9 mi) north of Göteborg.*

Strategically placed at the confluence of the two arms of the Göta River, Kungälv was an important battle grounds in ancient times. Though today it is something of a bedroom suburb for Göteborg, the town still has several ancient sights, including a white wooden church dating from 1679, with an unusual Baroque interior.

For a sense of Kungälv's military past, visit **Bohus Fästning,** now a ruined fortress built by the Norwegians in 1308, where many battles between Swedish, Norwegian, and Danish armies took place. ⊠ *Kungalv.* ☎ *0303/99200.* ☒ *SKr15.* ☉ *May–June and Aug., daily 10–7; July, daily 10–8; Sept., weekends 11–5.*

Outdoor Activities and Sports

Skärhamn on the island of Tjörn offers excellent **deep-sea fishing,** Mackerel is the prized catch. You can drive over the road bridge from Stenungsund.

Uddevalla

⓼ *64 km (40 mi) north of Kungälv, 79 km (49 mi) north of Göteborg.*

A former shipbuilding town located at the head of a picturesque fjord, Kungälv is best known in history for a battle in which heavy rains doused musketeers' tinder boxes, effectively ending hostilities.

En Route Lysekil, off the E6 highway on a promontory at the head of the Gullmarn Fjord, has been one of Sweden's most popular summer resorts since the 19th century. It specializes in boat excursions to neighboring islands and deep-sea fishing trips. The best bathing is at Pinnevik Cove. A little to the north lies the Sotenäs Peninsula and the attractive island of **Smögen,** which can be reached by road bridge. It is renowned locally for its shrimp.

Before the E6 highway reaches Strömstad, stop at **Tanumshede** to see Europe's largest single collection of Bronze Age rock carvings at **Vitlycke.** They cover 673 square ft of rock and depict battles, hunting, and fishing. The carvings are close to the main road and are well marked.

Strömstad

⓾ *90 km (56 mi) northwest of Uddvalla, 169 km (105 mi) north of Göteborg.*

This popular Swedish resort claims to have more summer sunshine than any other town north of the Alps. Formerly Norwegian, it has been

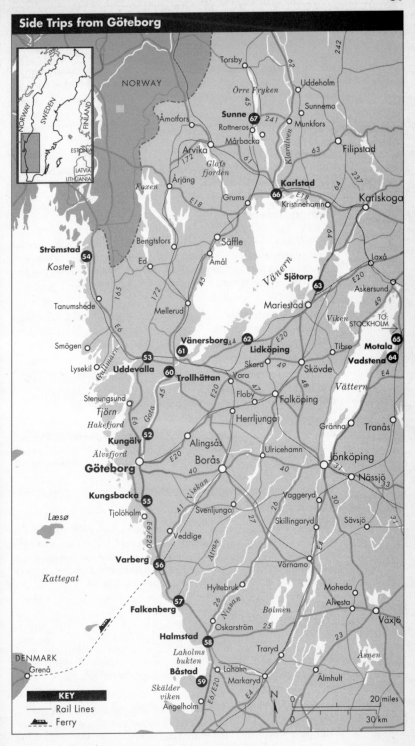

Side Trips from Göteborg

the site of many battles between warring Danes, Norwegians, and Swedes. A short trip over the Norwegian border takes you to Halden, where Sweden's warrior king, Karl XII, died in 1718.

OFF THE   **KOSTER ISLANDS –** There are regular ferry boats from Strömstad to the
BEATEN PATH   Koster Islands, a favorite holiday spot, with uncluttered beaches and
                trips to catch prawn and lobster.

Bohuslän A to Z

Arriving and Departing

Buses leave from behind the central train station in Göteborg; the main bus lines are **GL** (☎ 031/801235) and **Bohus Trafiken** (☎ 0522/ 14030). The trip to Strömstad takes between two and three hours.

Getting Around

BY CAR

The best way to explore Bohuslän is by car. The E6 highway runs the length of the coast from Göteborg north to Strömstad, close to the Norwegian border, and for campers there are numerous well-equipped and uncluttered camping sites along the coast's entire length.

BY TRAIN

There is regular service along the coast between all the major towns of Bohuslän. The trip from Göteborg to Strömstad takes about two hours, and there are several trains each day. For schedules, call **SJ** (✉ Göteborg, ☎ 031/103000 or 020/757575).

Visitor Information

REGIONAL TOURIST OFFICE

Göteborg Turistbyrå (☞ Göteborg A to Z *in* Chapter 4).

LOCAL TOURIST OFFICES

Kungälv (✉ Fästningsholmen, ☎ 0303/99200). **Kungshamn** (✉ Hamng. 6, ☎ 0523/37150). **Öckerö** (✉ Stranden 2, ☎ 031/965080). **Strömstad** (✉ Tullhuset, Norra Hamnen, ☎ 0526/13025). **Uddevalla** (✉ Kampenhof, ☎ 0522/511787).

SWEDISH RIVIERA

The coastal region south of Göteborg, Halland—locally dubbed the Swedish Riviera—is the closest that mainland Sweden comes to having a resort area. Fine beaches abound, and there are plenty of opportunities for many sporting activities. The region stretches down to Båstad in the country's southernmost province, Skåne.

Kungsbacka

⑤ *25 km (15 mi) south of Göteborg.*

This bedroom suburb of Göteborg holds a market on the first Thursday of every month. A break in a high ridge to the west, the **Fjärås Crack,** offers a fine view of the coast. On the slopes of the ridge are Iron Age and Viking graves.

En Route At **Tjolöholm,** 12 km (7 mi) down the E6/E20 highway from Kungsbacka, you'll encounter Tjolöholms Slott (Tjolöholm Castle), a manor house built by a Scotsman at the beginning of this century in mock English Tudor style. ✉ S430 33 Fjärås, ☎ 0300/44200. ☞ SKr40. ☼ June–Aug., daily 11–4; Apr.–May and Sept., weekends 11–4; Oct., Sun. 11–4.

In case you want to be welcomed there.

We're here to see that you're always welcomed at establishments everywhere. That's why millions of people carry the American Express® Card — for peace of mind, confidence, and security, around the world or just around the corner.

do more ®

Cards

In case you're running low.

We're here to help with more than 118,000 Express Cash locations around the world. In order to enroll, just call American Express before you start your vacation.

do more

Express Cash

And just in case.

We're here with American Express® Travelers Cheques and Cheques *for Two*® They're the safest way to carry money on your vacation and the surest way to get a refund, practically anywhere, anytime.

Another way we help you...

do more ®

Travelers Cheques

Near Tjolöholm is the tiny 18th-century village of **Äskhult,** the site of an open-air museum, the Gamla By. ☎ *0300/42159. ⊡ SKr20. ☉ May–Aug., daily 10–6; Sept., weekends 10–6.*

Varberg

56 *40 km (25 mi) south of Kungsbacka, 65 km (40 mi) south of Göteborg.*

Varberg is a busy port with connections to Grenå in Denmark. The town boasts some good beaches, but is best known for a suit of medieval clothing preserved in the museum in the 13th-century **Varbergs Fästning** (Varberg Fortress). The suit belonged to a man who was murdered and thrown into a peat bog. The peat preserved his body, and his clothes are the only suit of ordinary medieval clothing in existence. The museum also contains a silver bullet said to be the one that killed Karl XII. ☎ *0340/18520. ⊡ SKr20. ☉ Weekdays 10–4, weekends noon–4. Hourly guided tours mid-June–mid-Aug., daily 10–7; May–mid-June and mid-Aug.–Sept., Sun. 10–7.*

Falkenberg

57 *29 km (18 mi) south of Varberg, 94 km (58 mi) south of Göteborg.*

With its fine beaches and plentiful salmon in the Ätran River, Falkenberg is one of Sweden's most attractive resorts. Its Gamla Stan (Old Town) is full of narrow, cobblestone streets and quaint old wooden houses.

Shopping
Here you'll find **Törngren's** (⊠ Krukmakareg. 4, ☎ 0346/16920, ☎ 0346/10354 pottery) a pottery shop, probably the oldest still operating in Scandinavia, owned and run by the seventh generation of the founding family. It's open normal business hours, but you might have to call ahead to view pottery.

Halmstad

58 *40 km (25 mi) south of Falkenberg, 143 km (89 mi) south of Göteborg.*

With a population of 50,000, including Per Gestle of Roxette, Halmstad is the largest seaside resort on the west coast. The Norreport town gate, all that remains of the town's original fortifications, dates from 1605. The modern Town Hall has interior decorations by the so-called Halmstad Group of painters, formed here in 1929. A 14th-century church in the main square contains fragments of medieval murals and a 17th-century pulpit.

Båstad

59 *35 km (22 mi) south of Halmstad, 178 km (111 mi) south of Göteborg.*

In the southernmost province of Skåne, Båstad is regarded by locals to be Sweden's most fashionable resort, where ambassadors and local captains of industry have their summer houses. Aside from this, it is best known for its tennis. In addition to the **Båstad Open,** a Grand Prix tournament in late summer, there is the annual **Donald Duck Cup** in July for children ages 11 to 15; it was the very first trophy won by Björn Borg, who later took the Wimbledon men's singles title an unprecedented five times in a row. Spurred on by Borg and other Swedish champions, such as Stefan Edberg and Mats Wilander, thousands of youngsters take part in the Donald Duck Cup each year. For details, contact the **Svenska Tennisförbundet** (Swedish Tennis Association, ⊠ Lidingöv. 75, Stockholm, ☎ 08/6679770).

Norrviken Gardens, 3 km (2 mi) northwest of Båstad, are beautifully laid out in different styles, with a restaurant, shop, and pottery studio. ☎ 0431/69040. ⌑ SKr35. ⊙ Early June–mid-Aug., daily 10–6; late Aug.–May, daily 10:30–5.

Swedish Riviera A to Z

Arriving and Departing

BY BUS

Buses leave from behind Göteborg's central train station.

BY CAR

Simply follow the E6/E20 highway south from Göteborg. It runs parallel to the coast.

BY TRAIN

Regular train services connect the Göteborg central station with all major towns. Contact **SJ** (⊠ Göteborg, ☎ 031/103000 or 020/757575).

Visitor Information

Båstad (⊠ Stortorget 1, ☎ 0431/75045). **Falkenberg** (⊠ Stortorget, ☎ 0346/17410). **Halmstad** (⊠ Lilla Torg, ☎ 035/109345). **Kungsbacka** (⊠ Storg. 41, ☎ 0300/34595). **Laholm** (⊠ Rådhuset, ☎ 0430/15216 or 0430/15450). **Varberg** (⊠ Brunnsparken, ☎ 0340/88770).

GÖTA CANAL

Stretching 614 km (382 mi) between Stockholm and Göteborg, the Göta Canal is actually a series of interconnected canals, rivers, lakes, and even a stretch of sea. Bishop Hans Brask of Linköping in the 16th century was the first to suggest the idea; in 1718, King Karl XII ordered the canal to be built, but work was abandoned when he was killed in battle the same year. Not until 1810 was the idea again taken up in earnest. The driving force was a Swedish nobleman, Count Baltzar Bogislaus von Platen (1766–1829), and his motive was commercial. Von Platen saw in the canal a way of beating Danish tolls on shipping that passed through the Öresund and of enhancing the importance of Göteborg by linking the port with Stockholm on the east coast. At a time when Swedish fortunes were at a low ebb, the canal was also envisaged as a means of reestablishing faith in the future and boosting national morale.

The building of the canal took 22 years and involved a total of 58,000 men. The linking of the various stretches of water required 87 km (54 mi) of man-made cuts through soil and rock, and the building of 58 locks, 47 bridges, 27 culverts, and 3 dry docks. Unfortunately, the canal never achieved the financial success hoped for by von Platen. By 1857 the Danes had removed shipping tolls, and in the following decade the linking of Göteborg with Stockholm by rail effectively ended the canal's commercial potential. The canal has come into its own as a 20th-century tourist attraction, however.

Drifting lazily down this lovely series of waterways, across the enormous lakes, Vänern and Vättern, through a microcosm of all that is best about Sweden—abundant fresh air; clear, clean water; pristine nature; well-tended farmland—it is difficult to conceive of the canal's industrial origins. A bicycle path runs parallel to the canal, offering another means of touring the country.

En Route   The trip from Göteborg takes you first along the Göta Älv, a wide waterway that 10,000 years ago, when the ice cap melted, was a great fjord.

Some 30 minutes into the voyage the boat passes below a rocky escarpment, topped by the remains of **Bohus Fästning** (Bohus Castle), distinguished by two round towers known as Father's Hat and Mother's Bonnet. It dates from the 14th century and was once the mightiest fortress in western Scandinavia, commanding the confluence of the Göta and Nordre rivers. It was strengthened and enlarged in the 16th century and successfully survived 14 sieges. From 1678 onward, the castle began to lose its strategic and military importance and fell into decay, until 1838, when King Karl XIV passed by on a river journey, admired the old fortress, and ordered its preservation.

Just north of Kungälv along the Göta Canal, you'll come to the quiet village of **Lödöse,** once a major trading settlement and a predecessor of Göteborg. From here, the countryside becomes wilder, with pines and oaks clustered thickly on either bank between cliffs of lichen-clad granite.

Trollhättan

60 *70 km (43 mi) north of Göteborg.*

In this pleasant industrial town of about 50,000 inhabitants, a spectacular waterfall was rechanneled in 1906 to become Sweden's first hydroelectric plant. In most years, on specific days the waters are allowed to follow their natural course, a fall of 106 ft in six torrents. This sight is well worth seeing. The other main point of interest is the area between what were the falls and the series of locks that allowed the canal to bypass them. Here are disused locks from 1800 and 1844 and a strange Ice Age grotto where members of the Swedish royal family have carved their names since the 18th century. Trollhättan also has a fine, wide marketplace and pleasant waterside parks.

En Route Soon after leaving Trollhättan, the Göta Canal takes you past Hunneberg and Halleberg, two strange, flat-topped hills, both more than 500 ft high; the woods surrounding them are extraordinarily rich in elk, legend, and Viking burial mounds. It then proceeds through **Karls Grav**, the oldest part of the canal, begun early in the 17th century; its purpose was to bypass the Ronnum Falls on the Göta River, which have been harnessed to power a hydroelectric project.

Vänersborg

61 *15 km (9 mi) north of Trollhättan, 85 km (53 mi) north of Göteborg.*

Eventually, the canal enters **Vänern**, Sweden's largest and Europe's third-largest lake: 3,424 square km (1,322 square mi) of water, 145 km (90 mi) long and 81 km (50 mi) wide at one point.

At the southern tip of the lake is Vänersborg, a town of about 30,000 inhabitants that was founded in the mid-17th century. The church and the governor's residence date from the 18th century, but the rest of the town was destroyed by fire in 1834. Vänersborg is distinguished by its fine lakeside park, the trees of which act as a windbreak for the gusts that sweep in from Vänern.

Lidköping

62 *55 km (34 mi) east of Värnersberg, 140 km (87 mi) northeast of Göteborg.*

On an inlet at the southernmost point of Vänern's eastern arm lies the town of Lidköping, which received its charter in 1446 and is said to have the largest town square in Sweden.

OFF THE **LÄCKÖ SLOTT –** Lying 24 km (15 mi) to the north of Lidköping, on an
BEATEN PATH island off the point dividing the eastern arm of Vänern from the western,
is Läckö Castle, one of Sweden's finest 17th-century Renaissance
palaces. Its 250 rooms were once the home of Magnus Gabriel de la
Gardie, a great favorite of Queen Christina. Only the Royal Palace in
Stockholm is larger. In 1681 Karl XI, to curtail the power of the nobility,
confiscated it, and in 1830 all its furnishings were auctioned. Many of
them have since been restored to the palace.

En Route On a peninsula to the east of Lidköping, the landscape is dominated
by the great hill of **Kinnekulle,** towering 900 ft above the lake. The hill
is rich in colorful vegetation and wildlife and was a favorite hike for
the botanist Linnaeus.

Sjötorp

⑥³ *67 km (42 mi) northeast of Lidköping, 207 km (129 mi) northeast of
Göteborg.*

At the lakeside port of Sjötorp, the Göta Canal proper begins: a cut
through earth and granite with a series of locks raising the steamer to
Lanthöjden, at 304 ft above sea level the highest point on the canal.
The boat next enters the narrow, twisting lakes of Viken and Botten-
sjön and continues to Forsvik through the canal's oldest lock, built in
1813. It then sails out into **Vättern,** Sweden's second-largest lake,
nearly 129 km (80 mi) from north to south and 31 km (19 mi) across
at its widest point. Its waters are so clear that in some parts the bot-
tom is visible at a depth of 50 ft. The lake is subject to sudden storms
that can whip its normally placid waters into choppy waves.

Vadstena

⑥⁴ *249 km (155 mi) northeast of Göteborg (via Jönköping).*

This little-known historic gem of a town grew up around the monastery
founded by Saint Birgitta, or Bridget (1303–73), who wrote in her *Revelations* that she had a vision of Christ in which he revealed the rules
of the religious order she went on to establish. These rules seem to have
been a precursor for the Swedish ideal of sexual equality, with both
nuns and monks sharing a common church. Her order spread rapidly
after her death, and at one time there were 80 Bridgetine monasteries
in Europe. Little remains of the Vadstena monastery, however; in 1545
King Gustav Vasa ordered its demolition, and its stones were used to
build **Vadstena Slott** (Vadstena Castle), the huge fortress dominating
the lake. Swedish royalty held court here until 1715. It then fell into
decay and was used as a granary. Today it houses part of the National
Archives and is also the site of an annual summer opera festival. ☏
0143/15123. ⌁ SKr30. ☉ *Mid-May–June and late Aug., daily noon–
4; July–mid-Aug., daily 11–4. Guided tours mid-May–mid-Aug. at
12:30 and 1:30, late Aug. also at 2:30.*

Also worth a visit is **Vadstena Kyrka.** The triptych altarpiece on the
south wall features Saint Birgitta presenting her book of revelations
to a group of kneeling cardinals. There is also a fine wood carving of
the Madonna and Child from 1500.

Lodging

$$ ⛨ **Kungs-Starby Wärdshus.** This functional guest house, reached via
Route 50, adjoins a renovated manor house and restaurant, surrounded
by a park on the outskirts of town. ✉ *S592 01 Vadstena,* ☏ *0143/
75100,* FAX *0143/75170. 61 rooms. Restaurant, no-smoking rooms, in-
door pool, sauna, meeting rooms. AE, DC, MC, V.*

$$ 🖫 **Vadstena Klosterhotel.** This hotel is housed in Sweden's oldest secular building, parts of which date from the 13th century. Rooms are modern and well appointed, and there are three comfortable lounges. ✉ *Klosterområdet, off Lasarettsg., S592 30 Vadstena,* ☎ *0143/11530,* FAX *0143/13648. 29 rooms. Restaurant, no-smoking rooms, meeting rooms. AE, DC, MC, V.*

Motala

⑥⑤ *13 km (8 mi) north of Vadstena, 262 km (163 mi) northeast of Göteborg.*

Before reaching Stockholm, the canal passes through Motala, where Baltzar von Platen is buried close to the canal. He had envisaged the establishment of four new towns along the waterway, but only Motala fulfilled his dream. He designed the town himself, and his statue is in the main square.

En Route At Borenshult a series of locks take the boat down to **Boren,** a lake in the province of Östergötland. On the southern shore of the next lake, Roxen, lies the city of **Linköping,** capital of the province and home of Saab, the aircraft and automotive company. Once out of the lake, you follow a new stretch of canal past the sleepy town of **Söderköping.** A few miles east, at the hamlet of Mem, the canal's last lock lowers the boat into Slätbaken, a Baltic fjord presided over by the ruins of the ancient **Stegeborg Fortress.** The boat then steams north along the coastline until it enters **Mälaren** through the Södertälje Canal and finally anchors in the capital at Riddarholmen.

Göta Canal A to Z

Arriving and Departing

BY BOAT

For details about cruises along the Göta Canal, *see* Getting Around in Göteborg A to Z *in* Chapter 4.

BY CAR

From Stockholm, follow E18 west; from Göteborg, take Route 45 north to E18.

BY TRAIN

Call **SJ** (✉ Göteborg, ☎ 054/102160) for information about service.

Visitor Information

REGIONAL TOURIST OFFICES

Uddevalla (Bohusturist, ✉ Skansg. 3, ☎ 0522/14055). **Skövde** (Västergötlands Turistråd, ✉ Kyrkog. 11, ☎ 0500/418050).

LOCAL TOURIST OFFICES

Karlsborg (✉ N. Kanalg. 2, ☎ 0505/17350). **Vadstena** (✉ Rådhustorget, ☎ 0143/15125).

VÄRMLAND

Close to the Norwegian border on the north shores of Vänern, this province is rich in folklore. It was also the home of Alfred Nobel and the birthplace of other famous Swedes, among them the Nobel Prize–winning novelist Selma Lagerlöf, the poet Gustaf Fröding, former prime minister Tage Erlander, and present-day opera star Håkan Hagegård. Värmland's forested, lake-dotted landscape attracts artists seeking refuge and Swedes on holiday.

Karlstad

66   *255 km (158 mi) northeast of Göteborg.*

Värmland's principal city (population 74,000) is situated on Klaraäl-ven (Klara River) at the point where it empties into Vänern. Founded in 1684, when it was known as Tingvalla, the city was totally rebuilt after a fire in 1865. Its name was later changed to honor King Karl IX—Karlstad, meaning Karl's Town. In **Stortorget,** the main square, there is a statue of Karl IX by the local sculptor Christian Eriksson.

The **Värmlands Museum** has rooms dedicated to both Eriksson and the poet Fröding. ⊠ *Sandgrun, Box 335, S651 08, Karlstad,* ☎ *054/ 211419.* 🎫 *SKr20.* ☉ *Thurs.–Tues. noon–4, Wed. noon–8.*

The **Marieberg Skogspark** (Marieberg Forest Park) is worth visiting. A delight for the whole family, the park has restaurants and an out-door theater. ☉ *Early June–late Aug., Thurs.–Tues. 11–5, Wed. 11–8; late Aug.–early June, Tues.–Sun. noon–4, Wed. noon–8.*

Karlstad is the site of the **Emigrant Registret** (Emigrant Registry), which maintains detailed records of the Swedes' emigration to America. Vis-itors of Swedish extraction can trace their ancestors at the center's re-search facility. ⊠ *Norra Strandg. 4, Box 331, S651 08, Karlstad,* ☎ *054/159272.* 🎫 *Free.* ☉ *May–Sept., daily 8–4; rest of yr, Tues.–Sun. 8–4:30, Mon. 8–7.*

Dining and Lodging

$$$ ✕ **Inn Alstern.** Overlooking Lake Alstern, this elegant restaurant offers Swedish and continental cuisine, with fish dishes as the specialty. Reser-vations are advised. ⊠ *Morgonv. 4,* ☎ *054/834900. AE, MC, V.*

$$$ 🏨 **Stadshotellet.** On the banks of Klarälven (Klara River), this hotel built in 1870 is steeped in tradition. All of the rooms are decorated differently, some in modern Swedish style, others evoking their origi-nal look. You can dine at the gourmet Matsalon or in the more casual atmosphere of the Cafeet Statt. ⊠ *Kungsg. 22, S651 08,* ☎ *054/ 215220,* 🖷 *054/188211. 143 rooms. Restaurant, pub, no-smoking rooms, sauna, nightclub, meeting rooms. AE, DC, MC, V.*

$$ 🏨 **Gösta Berling.** In town center, this small hotel, named for the hero of the Selma Lagerlöf novel, offers nondescript common rooms but invit-ing, plushly carpeted guest rooms. ⊠ *Drottningg. 1, S652 24,* ☎ *054/ 150190,* 🖷 *054/154826. 66 rooms. No-smoking rooms, sauna, meet-ing rooms. AE, DC, MC, V.*

En Route   Värmland is, above all, a rural experience. Drive along the **Klaräl-ven,** through the beautiful Fryken Valley, to Ransater, where author Erik Gustaf Geijer was born in 1783 and where Erlander, the former prime minister, also grew up. The rural idyll ends in **Munkfors,** where some of the best-quality steel in Europe is manufactured.

OFF THE BEATEN PATH   **SUNNEMO AND UDDEHOLM –** Ten kilometers (6 miles) north of Munkfors lies the little village of **Sunnemo,** with its beautiful wooden church. At the northern end of Lake Råda, the town of **Uddeholm** is home of the Udde-holm Corporation, which produces iron and steel, forestry products, and chemicals.

Sunne

 63 km (39 mi) north of Karlstad, 318 km (198 mi) northeast of Göteborg.

Straddling the long, narrow Fryken Lake, Sunne is best known as a jumping-off point for Mårbacka, a stone's throw southeast. Here the estate where Nobel Prize winner Selma Lagerlöf was born in 1858 has been kept much as she left it at the time of her death in 1940; it can be seen by guided tour. ⊠ *Östra Ämtervik, S686 26 Sunne,* ☎ *0565/ 31027.* 🎫 *SKr40.* ⊙ *Mid-May–June and Aug.–early Sept., daily 10– 5, tours every hr; July, daily 9:30–5, tours every half hr.*

OFF THE BEATEN PATH

ROTTNEROS HERRGÅRDS PARK – On the western shore of Fryken Lake, 5 km (3 mi) south of Sunne, you'll find Rottneros Manor, the inspiration for Ekeby, the fictional estate in Lagerlöf's *Gösta Berlings Saga* (*The Tale of Gösta Berling*). The house is privately owned, but visitors are invited to admire its park, with its fine collection of Scandinavian sculpture—including works by Carl Milles, Norwegian artist Gustav Vigeland, and Wäinö Aaltonen of Finland. The entrance fee covers both the sculpture park and the Nils Holgerssons Adventure Park, an elaborate playground for children. ⊠ *S686 02 Rottneros,* ☎ *0565/60295.* 🎫 *SKr50.* ⊙ *Mid-May–early June and late Aug., weekdays 10–4, weekends 10–6; rest of June, weekdays 10–5, weekends 10–6; July–Aug., daily 10–6.*

Värmland A to Z

Arriving and Departing

BY CAR

From Stockholm, follow E18 west; from Göteborg, take Route 45 north to E18.

BY TRAIN

There is regular service to Karlstad from Stockholm and Göteborg on **SJ** (⊠ Göteborg, ☎ 031/103000 or 020/757575).

Visitor Information

REGIONAL TOURIST OFFICE

Värmlands Turistbyrå (⊠ Tage Erlanderg. 10, Karlstad, ☎ 054/102160).

LOCAL TOURIST OFFICES

Karlstad (Karlstad Conference Center, ☎ 054/149055). **Sunne** (Turistbyrå, ⊠ Mejerig. 2, ☎ 0565/13530).

6 The South and the Kingdom of Glass

SOUTHERN SWEDEN is a world of its own, clearly distinguished from the rest of the country by its geography, culture, and history. Skåne (pronounced *skoh*-neh), the southernmost province, is known as the granary of Sweden. It is a comparatively small province of beautifully fertile plains, sand beaches, thriving farms, medieval churches, and summer resorts. These gently rolling hills and fields are broken every few miles by lovely castles, chronologically and architecturally diverse, that have given this part of Sweden the name Château Country; often they are surrounded by beautiful grounds and moats. A significant number of the estates have remained in the hands of the original families and are still inhabited.

The two other southern provinces, Blekinge and Halland, are also fertile and rolling and edged by seashores. Historically, these three provinces are distinct from the rest of Sweden: they were the last to be incorporated into the country, having been ruled by Denmark until 1658. They retain the influences of the continental culture in their architecture, language, and cuisine, viewing the rest of Sweden—especially Stockholm—with some disdain. Skåne even has its own independence movement, and the dialect here is so akin to Danish that many Swedes from other parts of the country have trouble understanding it.

Småland, to the north, is larger than the other provinces, with a harsh countryside of stone and woods, the so-called Kingdom of Glass. It is an area of small glassblowing firms, such as Kosta Boda and Orrefors, that are world-renowned for the quality of their products. In addition to visiting these works (and perhaps finding some bargains), the traveler forms an insight into a poorer, harsher way of life that led thousands of peasants to emigrate from Småland to the United States in search of a better life. Those who stayed behind developed a reputation for their inventiveness in setting up small industries to circumvent the region's traditional poverty and are also notorious for being extremely careful—if not downright mean—with money.

Your itinerary should follow the coast from the western city of Helsingborg around the southern loop and up the eastern shore, taking a side trip to the Baltic island province of Öland before heading inland to finish at Växjo. The entire route can be followed by train, with the exception of Öland and most of the glassworks in Småland—the Orrefors factory is the only one on the railway line. It's easy to continue your trip in any direction from Växjö, as it lies at a main crossroads for both highways and railway lines.

Helsingborg

68 *221 km (137 mi) south of Göteborg, 186 km (116 mi) southwest of Växjö, 64 km (40 mi) north of Malmö.*

Helsingborg (still sometimes spelled the old way, Hälsingborg), with a population of 108,000, seems to the first-time visitor little more than a nondescript though modern ferry terminal (it has connections to Denmark, Norway, and Germany). Actually, it has a rich history, having first been mentioned in 10th-century sagas and later the site of many battles between the Danes and the Swedes. Together with its twin town, Helsingör (Elsinore in William Shakespeare's *Hamlet*), across the Öresund, it controlled shipping traffic in and out of the Baltic for centuries. Helsingborg was officially incorporated into Sweden in 1658 and totally destroyed in a battle with the Danes in 1710. It was then

The South and the Kingdom of Glass

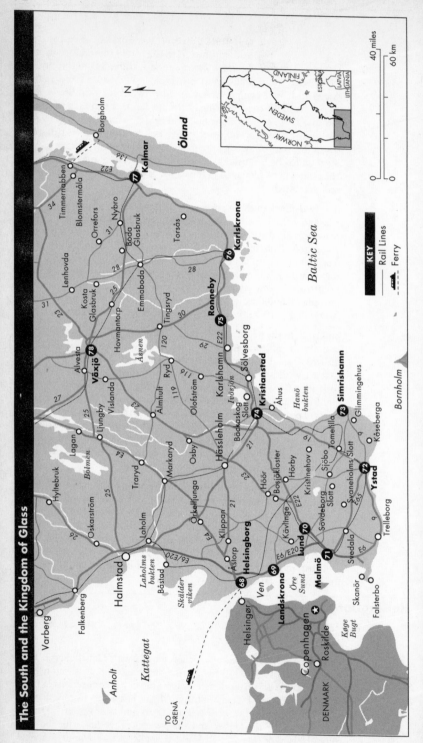

KEY
— Rail Lines
- - - Ferry

Baltic Sea

Kattegat

Öland

Bornholm

DENMARK

Copenhagen

Roskilde

Køge Bugt

Skanör

Falsterbo

Malmö 71

Lund 70

69 **Landskrona**

68 Helsingborg

Ven

Öre Sund

Helsingør

Anholt

TO GRENÅ

Laholms bukten

Båstad

Skälder viken

Halmstad

Varberg

Falkenberg

Hyltebruk

Oskarström

Lagan

Bolmen

Ljungby

Vislanda

Traryd

Markaryd

Laholm

Örkelljunga

Klippan

Åstorp

Ängelholm

Höör

Bosjökloster

Hörby

Kristinehov

Sjöbo

Tomelilla

Glimmingehus

Kåseberga

Ystad 72

73 **Simrishamn**

Svaneholms Slott

Sövdeborg Slott

Skedala

Trelleborg

E6

E65

Kävlinge

E6/E20

E22

Svedala

Almhult

Osby

Hässleholm

Bäckaskog Slott

Ivösjön

Kristianstad 74

Åhus

Hanö bukten

Sölvesborg

75 **Ronneby**

76 **Karlskrona**

Karlshamn

Olofström

Ryd

119

116

120

Växjö 78

Alvesta

Åsnen

Hovmantorp

Emmaboda

Tingsryd

Kosta Glasbruk

Lenhovda

Boda Glasbruk

Orrefors

Nybro

Blomstermåla

Timmernabben

Borgholm

Kalmar 77

Bornholm

34

136

E22

31

28

25

30

29

E22

28

62

31

27

25

26

E4

21

23

16

9

25

32

Landskrona

40 miles

60 km

SWEDEN

NORWAY

FINLAND

ESTONIA

LATVIA

LITHUANIA

rebuilt, and Jean-Baptiste Bernadotte, founder of the present Swedish royal dynasty, landed here in 1810.

The Helsingborg **Stadshuset** (Town Hall) has a small museum of exhibits on the city and the region. ⊠ *Södra Storg. 31,* ☎ *042/105963.* 🎫 *SKr20.* ⊘ *May–Aug., Tues.–Sun. noon–5; Sept.–Apr., Tues.–Sun. noon–4.*

All that remains of Helsingborg's castle is **Kärnan** (the Keep). The surviving center tower, built to provide living quarters and defend the medieval castle, is the most remarkable relic of its kind in the north. The interior is divided into several floors, where there is a chapel, kitchen, and other medieval fittings. It stands in a park and offers fine views over the Öresund from the top. ⊠ *Slottshagen,* ☎ *042/105991.* 🎫 *SKr20.* ⊘ *June–Aug., daily 10–7; Apr.–May and Sept., daily 9–4; Oct.–Mar., daily 10–2.*

Sofiero Slott (Sofiero Castle), 5 km (3 mi) outside the town, was, until very recently, a royal summer residence. It opened to the public for the first time in May 1995. Built in 1865 in the Dutch Renaissance style, it has a fine park designed by Crown Princess Margareta. ⊠ *Sofierov. (on the road to Laröd),* ☎ *042/137400.* 🎫 *SKr30.* ⊘ *May–mid-Sept., daily 10–6; guided tours only. Park open year-round.*

Lodging

$$$ 🏨 **Grand Hotel.** One of Sweden's oldest hotels has been completely renovated, maintaining its long-standing reputation for excellence. Antiques and fresh flowers fill the hotel, and the well-equipped guest rooms have cable TV, a hair dryer, minibar, and trouser press. The hotel is conveniently close to the railway station and ferry terminals. The bar offers a good selection of wines at reasonable prices. ⊠ *Stortorget 812, S251 11,* ☎ *042/120170,* 🖷 *042/118833. 117 rooms. Restaurant, bar, no-smoking rooms, sauna, meeting rooms. AE, DC, MC, V.*

$$$ 🏨 **Marina Plaza.** This modern hotel, with its enormous central glass atrium, is right next to the Knutpunkten ferry, rail, and bus terminal. Relaxing and stylish, the Marina Plaza has spacious, elegantly decorated rooms with air conditioning, minibars, trouser presses, and cable TV. ⊠ *Kungstorget 6, S251 11,* ☎ *042/192100,* 🖷 *042/149616. 190 rooms. Restaurant, bar, no-smoking rooms, sauna, conference rooms. AE, DC, MC, V.*

$ 🏨 **Villa Thalassa.** This youth hostel has fine views over Öresund. One large building contains 140 bunks in two-, four-, and six-bunk rooms. There are also 12 cottages near the water, each with two bedrooms (with double bed and bunk bed), bathroom with shower, and kitchen. The SKr40 breakfast is not included. ⊠ *Dag Hammarskjölds väg, S-254 33,* ☎ *042/210384,* 🖷 *042/128792. 140 beds, 4- to 6-bed rooms (in winter 2-bed rooms also available). Meeting rooms. No credit cards.*

Landskrona

⑥⑨ *26 km (16 mi) south of Helsingborg (via E6/E20), 41 km (25 mi) north of Malmö, 204 km (127 mi) southwest of Växjö.*

The 17th-century Dutch-style fortifications of Landskrona are among the best preserved of their kind in Europe. Though it appears to be just another modern town, Landskrona actually dates from 1413, when it received its charter. In 1888, author Selma Lagerlöf worked at Landskrona's elementary school, where she began her novel *Gösta Berlings Saga.*

Landskrona's **Citadellet** (castle) was built under orders of the Danish King Christian III in 1549 and is all that remains of the original town, which was razed in 1747 by decree of the Swedish Parliament to make way for extended fortifications. The new town was then built on land reclaimed from the sea. ⊠ *Slottsg.*, ☎ *0418/16980.* ☑ *SKr20.* ☉ *Early June–late Aug., daily 11–4.*

**OFF THE
BEATEN PATH**

VEN – From Landskrona Harbor there are regular 25-minute boat trips to the island of Ven (☒ SKr60 round-trip); there are departures every 90 minutes 6 AM–9 PM). The Danish astronomer Tycho Brahe conducted his pioneering research here from 1576 to 1597. The foundations of his Renaissance castle, **Uranienborg**, can be visited, as can **Stjärneborg**, his reconstructed observatory. The small **Tycho Brahe Museet** is dedicated to Brahe and his work. Landsv., Ven, ☎ *0418/79557.* ☑ *SKr20.* ☉ *May–Sept., daily 10–4:30.*

Outdoor Activities and Sports

Three kilometers (2 miles) north of Landskrona lies the **Borstahusen recreation area** (⊠ 261 61 Landskrona, ☎ 0418/10837), with long stretches of beach, a marina, and a holiday village with 74 summer chalets. Ven is ideal for **camping;** check with the local tourist office. There are special paths across Ven for **bicycling;** rentals are available from Bäckviken, the small harbor.

Lund

 34 km (21 mi) southeast of Landskrona (via E6/E20 and Route 16), 25 km (15 mi) northeast of Malmö, 183 km (113 mi) southwest of Växjö.

One of the oldest towns in Europe, Lund was founded in 990. In 1103 Lund became the religious capital of Scandinavia and at one time had 27 churches and eight monasteries—until King Christian III of Denmark ordered most of them razed to use their stones for the construction of Malmöhus Castle in Malmö. Lund lost its importance until 1666, when its university was established. It is now one of Sweden's two chief university towns and one of the nicest of Swedish towns, having managed to preserve its historic character.

Lund's monumental gray stone Romanesque **cathedral** is the oldest in Scandinavia, consecrated in 1145. Its crypt features 23 finely carved pillars, but its main attraction is an astrological clock, *Horologum Mirabile Lundense* (the miraculous Lund clock), dating from 1380 and restored in 1923. It depicts an amazing pageant of knights jousting on horseback, trumpets blowing a medieval fanfare, and the Magi walking in procession past the Virgin and Child as the organ plays *In Dulci Jubilo.* The clock plays at noon and 3 PM on weekdays and at 1 and 3 PM on Sunday.

One block east of the cathedral is the **Botaniska Trädgården** (Botanical Gardens), which contains 7,500 specimens of plants from all over the world—very pleasant on a summer's day. ⊠ *Östra Vallg. 20,* ☎ *046/2227320.* ☑ *Free.* ☉ *Gardens daily 6 AM–8 PM, greenhouses noon–3.*

Esaias Tegnér, the Swedish poet, lived from 1813 to 1826 in a little house immediately behind the cathedral. The house has since been turned into the **Tegnér Museet,** providing insight into his life and works. ⊠ *Gråbrödersg.,* ☎ *046/691319.* ☑ *SKr10.* ☉ *First Sun. each month noon–3.*

On the southern side of the main square is **Drottens Kyrkoruin** (the Church Ruins of Drotten), an "underground" museum showing life as it was in Lund in the Middle Ages. The foundations of three Catholic churches are here: the first and oldest was built of wood in approximately AD 1000. It was torn down to make room for one of stone built in about 1100; this was replaced by a second stone church built around 1300. ⊠ *Kattensund 6*, ☎ *046/141328.* ▣ *SKr10.* ☉ *Tues.–Fri. and Sun. noon–4, Sat. 10–2.*

Kulturen (the Museum of Cultural History) is both an outdoor and an indoor museum, including 20 old cottages, farms, and manor houses from southern Sweden plus an excellent collection of ceramics, textiles, weapons, and furniture. ⊠ *Karolinsplats,* ☎ *046/350400.* ▣ *SKr30.* ☉ *May–Sept., Fri.–Wed. 11–5, Thurs. 11–9; rest of yr, Tues.–Sun. noon–4.*

Lodging

$$$ 🏨 **Djingis Khan.** This English colonial–style Best Western hotel is in a quiet part of town. ⊠ *Margarethev. 7, S222 40,* ☎ *046/140060,* 𝖥𝖠𝖷 *046/143626. 55 rooms. No-smoking rooms, hot tub, sauna, exercise room, bicycles, meeting rooms. AE, DC, MC, V. Closed July.*

$$$ 🏨 **Grand.** This elegant red-stone hotel is in the heart of the city, close to the railway station in a pleasant square. Renovated rooms have vintage turn-of-the-century decor and charm. The elegant restaurant offers an alternative vegetarian menu. ⊠ *Bantorget 1, S221 04,* ☎ *046/2117010,* 𝖥𝖠𝖷 *046/147301. 80 rooms. Restaurant, no-smoking rooms, hot tub, meeting rooms. AE, DC, MC, V.*

$$$ 🏨 **Hotel Lundia.** Only 330 ft from the train station, Hotel Lundia is ideal for those who want to be within walking distance of the city center. Built in 1968, the modern, four-story square building has transparent glass walls on the ground floor. Rooms are decorated with Scandinavian fabrics and lithographs. ⊠ *Knut den Stores torg 2, Box 1136, S221 04,* ☎ *046/124140,* 𝖥𝖠𝖷 *046/141995. 97 rooms. Restaurant, no-smoking rooms, nightclub, meeting rooms. AE, DC, MC, V.*

$$ 🏨 **Concordia.** This center-city Sweden Hotel property is in an elegant former home built in 1890. A 1990 renovation gave the rooms a modern and clean, if somewhat colorless, look. ⊠ *Stålbrog. 1, S222 24,* ☎ *046/135050,* 𝖥𝖠𝖷 *046/137422. 49 rooms. No-smoking rooms, sauna, meeting rooms. AE, DC, MC, V.*

$ 🏨 **STF Vandrarhem Tåget.** So named because of its proximity to the train station (*tåget* means "train"), this youth hostel faces a park in central Lund. ⊠ *Bjerredsparken, Vävareg. 22, S222 37 Lund,* ☎ *046/142820. 108 beds. No credit cards.*

OFF THE BEATEN PATH **BOSJÖKLOSTER –** About 30 km (19 mi) northeast of Lund via E22 and Route 23, Bosjökloster is an 11th-century, white Gothic castle with lovely grounds on Ringsjön, the second-largest lake in southern Skåne. The castle's original owner donated the estate to the church, which turned it over to the Benedictine order of nuns. They founded a convent school for the daughters of Scandinavian nobility, no longer in existence, and built the convent church with its tower made of sandstone. The 300-acre castle grounds, with a 1,000-year-old oak tree, a network of pathways, a children's park, a rose garden, and an indoor-outdoor restaurant, are ideal for picnics. ⊠ *Höör,* ☎ *0413/25048.* ▣ *SKr40.* ☉ *Castle grounds May–Oct., daily 8–8, restaurant and exhibition halls May–Sept., Tues.–Sun. 10–6.*

Malmö

🌐 *25 km (15 mi) southwest of Lund (via E22), 198 km (123 mi) southwest of Växjö.*

Malmö is very different from Lund. Capital of the province of Skåne, with a population of about 250,000, this is Sweden's third-largest city. The city's castle, **Malmöhus,** completed in 1542, was for many years used as a prison (James Bothwell, husband of Mary, Queen of Scots, was one of its notable inmates). Today it houses a variety of museums, including the City Museum, the Museum of Natural History, and the Art Museum with a collection of Nordic art. Across the street you will find the Science and Technology Museum, the Maritime Museum, and a toy museum. ⊠ *Malmöhusv.,* ☎ *040/341000.* 🖭 *SKr40.* ☉ *June–Aug., daily 10–4; Sept.–May, Tues.–Sun. noon–4.*

On the far side of the castle grounds from Malmöhus, **Aq-va-kul** is a water park that offers a wide variety of bathing experiences for children and their parents, from water slides to bubble baths. ⊠ *Regementsg. 24,* ☎ *040/300540.* 🖭 *SKr58 adults.* ☉ *Weekdays 9–9, weekends 9–6; Mon. and Wed. evening adult sessions 7–9:30.*

There's a clutch of tiny red-painted shacks called the **Fiskehodderna** (Fish Shacks), adjoining a dock where the fishing boats come in every morning to unload their catch. The piers, dock, and huts were restored in 1991 and are now a government-protected district. You can buy fresh fish directly from the fishermen Tuesday through Saturday mornings.

In Gamla Staden, the Old Town, look for the **St. Petri Church** on Kalendegatan; dating from the 14th century, it is an impressive example of the Baltic Gothic style, with its distinctive stepped gables. Inside there is a fine Renaissance altar.

Rådhuset (Town Hall), dating from 1546, dominates Stortorget, a huge, cobbled market square in Gamla Staden, and makes an impressive spectacle when illuminated at night. In the center of the square stands an equestrian statue of Karl X, the king who united this part of the country with Sweden in 1658. Off the southeast corner of Stortorget is Lilla Torg, an attractive small cobblestone square surrounded by restored buildings from the 17th and 18th centuries.

The **Museum of Sport** occupies **Baltiska Hallen,** next to Malmö Stadium. It traces the history of sports, including soccer and wrestling, from antiquity to the present. ☎ *040/342688.* 🖭 *Free.* ☉ *Weekdays 8–4.*

Also downtown, the **Rooseum,** in a turn-of-the-century brick building that was once a power plant, is one of Sweden's most outstanding art museums, with exhibitions of contemporary art and a quality selection of Nordic art. ⊠ *Gasverksg. 22,* ☎ *040/121716.* 🖭 *SKr30.* ☉ *Tues.–Sun. 11–5. Guided tours weekends at 2.*

Dining and Lodging

$$$ ✗ **Johan P.** This extremely popular restaurant specializes in seafood and shellfish prepared in Swedish and Continental styles. White walls and crisp white tablecloths give it an elegant air, which contrasts with the generally casual dress of the customers. An outdoor section opens during the summer. ⊠ *Saluhallen, Lilla Torg,* ☎ *040/971818. AE, DC, MC, V. Closed Sun.*

$$$ ✗ **Kockska Krogen Årstiderna.** Marie and Wilhelm Pieplow's former
★ Årstiderna had merged with the Kockska Krogen. The new spot still has a pleasant, intimate atmosphere and serves large portions from a good, medium-price bistro menu and wine list. ⊠ *Stortorget,* ☎ *040/230910. AE, DC, MC, V.*

$$ ✗ **Anno 1900.** Here is a curiosity: a charming little restaurant located in a former working-class area of Malmö. It is a popular local luncheon place with a cheerful outdoor garden terrace for summer eating. ⊠ *Norra Bulltoftav. 7,* ☎ *040/184747. Reservations essential. AE, MC, V.*

$$ ✗ **B & B.** It stands for *Butik och Bar* (Bar Shop) because of its location in the market hall in central Malmö. There's always good home

cooking, and sometimes even entertainment at the piano. The restaurant is extremely popular with a young crowd on weekday nights. ⊠ *Saluhallen, Lilla Torg*, ☎ 040/127120. *AE, DC, MC, V.*

$$ ✕ **Glorias.** This friendly little restaurant usually offers extremely good value. The special menu, *Kvartersmenyn*, is an excellent bet, with a three-course prix fixe for SKr175. Reservations are advised. ⊠ *Foreningsg. 37*, ☎ 040/116816. *AE, DC, MC, V.*

$$ ✕ **Valvet.** Centrally located in the St. Jörgen hotel, this restaurant was expanded in 1992. Although the wine list has been deemphasized, the restaurant still offers good Swedish cuisine with a French accent and excels at grilled meats and fish. ⊠ *Stora Nyg. 35*, ☎ 040/77300. *AE, DC, MC, V. Closed Sun. and mid-June–mid-Aug.*

$$$$ 🏨 **Mäster Johan Hotel.** The unpretentious exterior of this Best Western hotel disguises a plush and meticulously crafted interior. The 1990
★ top-to-bottom redesign of a 19th-century building, with the focal point an Italianate atrium breakfast room, is unusually personal in tone for a chain hotel. The rooms are impressive, with exposed Dutch brick walls, recessed lighting, oak floors, Oriental carpets, and French cherrywood furnishings. ⊠ *Mäster Johansg. 13, S211 22*, ☎ 040/71560, ℻ 040/127242. 68 *rooms. Breakfast room, no-smoking rooms, room service, sauna, meeting rooms. AE, DC, MC, V.*

$$$$ 🏨 **Radisson SAS Hotel.** Only a five-minute walk from the train station, this modern luxury hotel has rooms decorated in several styles: Scandinavian, Asian, and Italian. There are even special rooms for guests with pets. Service is impeccable. The restaurant serves Scandinavian and continental cuisine, and there's a cafeteria for quick meals. ⊠ *Österg. 10, S211 25*, ☎ 040/239200, ℻ 040/112840. 221 *rooms. Restaurant, no-smoking rooms, sauna, exercise room, meeting rooms. AE, DC, MC, V.*

$$$$ 🏨 **Sheraton.** Ultramodern, in steel and glass, the Sheraton is the city's only skyscraper—at a modest 20 floors. It provides excellent views all the way to Copenhagen on a clear day. Rooms are standard Sheraton style. The hotel is connected to the Triangeln shopping center. ⊠ *Triangeln 2, S200 10*, ☎ 040/74000, ℻ 040/232020. 214 *rooms. Restaurant, bar, no-smoking rooms, sauna, exercise room, meeting rooms. AE, DC, MC, V.*

$$ 🏨 **Baltzar.** A turn-of-the-century house in central Malmö was converted
★ in 1920 into a small, comfortable hotel. Rooms are modern, with thick carpets. ⊠ *Söderg. 20, S211 34*, ☎ 040/72005, ℻ 040/236375. 41 *rooms. No-smoking rooms. AE, DC, MC, V.*

$ 🏨 **Prize Hotel.** In a rejuvenated part of Malmö Harbor, this low-overhead, minimal-service hotel has small but comfortable rooms equipped with satellite TV, telephone, and radio. The large front entrance and lobby atrium are inventively created out of a narrow strip of empty space between two buildings. Though the hotel doesn't add a surcharge to the telephone bill, it also doesn't include the SKr65 breakfast in the room rate: you get exactly what you pay for. ⊠ *Carlsg. 10C, S211 20*, ☎ 040/112511, ℻ 040/112310. 109 *rooms. Breakfast room. AE, DC, MC, V.*

OFF THE **FALSTERBRO AND SKANÖR** – The idyllic towns of Falsterbo and Skanör
BEATEN PATH are two popular summer resorts located on a tiny peninsula, 32 km (20 mi) away from Mälmö at the country's southwesternmost corner. Falsterbo is popular among ornithologists who flock there every fall to watch the spectacular migration of hundreds of raptors.

TORUP SLOTT – Built around 1550 near a beautiful beech forest, Torup Castle is a great example of the classic, square fortified stronghold.

From Malmö, drive 10 km (6 mi) southeast on E65, then head north for another 6 km (4 mi) to Torup. ⊠ *Torup.* ▣ *SKr30.* ⊙ *May–June, weekends 1–4:30. Group tours available at other times through Malmö Turistbyrå,* ☎ *040/341270.*

En Route   One of Skåne's outstanding Renaissance strongholds, **Svaneholms Slott** lies 30 km (19 mi) east of Malmö, on E65. First built in 1530 and rebuilt in 1694, the castle today features a museum occupying four floors with sections depicting the nobility and peasants. On the grounds are a noted restaurant (Gästgiveri, ☎ 0411/40540), walking paths, and a lake for fishing and rowing. ⊠ *Skurup,* ☎ *0411/40012.* ▣ *SKr30.* ⊙ *May–Aug., Tues.–Sun. 11–5; Sept.–mid-Oct., Wed.–Sun. 11–4.*

Ystad

②②   *64 km (40 mi) southeast of Malmö (via E65), 205 km (127 mi) southwest of Växjö.*

A smuggling center during the Napoleonic Wars, Ystad has preserved its medieval character with winding, narrow streets and hundreds of half-timber houses dating from four or five different centuries. The principal ancient monument is **St. Maria Kyrka,** begun shortly after 1220 as a basilica in the Romanesque style but with later additions.

OFF THE
BEATEN PATH   **SÖVDEBORG SLOTT** – Twenty-one kilometers (13 miles) north of Ystad on Route 13 is Sövdeborg Slott (Sövdeborg Castle). Built in the 16th century and restored in the mid-1840s, the castle, now a private home, consists of three two-story brick buildings and a four-story-high crenellated corner tower. The main attraction is the Stensal (Stone Hall), with its impressive stuccowork ceiling. It's open for tours booked in advance for groups of at least 10. ⊠ *Sjöbo,* ☎ *0416/16012.* ▣ *SKr50.*

En Route   Eighteen kilometers (11 miles) east of Ystad, on the coastal road off of Route 9, is the charming fishing village of Kåseberga. On the hill behind it stand the impressive **Ales stenar** (Ale's stones), an intriguing 251-ft arrangement of 58 Viking stones in the shape of a ship. The stones are still something of a puzzle to anthropologists.

About 28 km (17 mi) east of Ystad and 10 km (6 mi) southwest of Simrishamn just off Route 9 lies **Glimmingehus** (Glimminge House), Scandinavia's best-preserved medieval stronghold. Built between 1499 and 1505 to defend the region against invaders, the late-Gothic castle was lived in only briefly. The walls are 8 ft thick at the base, tapering to 6½ ft at the top of the 85-ft-high building. On the grounds are a small museum and a theater. There are concerts and lectures throughout the summer and a medieval festival at the end of August. ⊠ *Hammenhög,* ☎ *0414/32089.* ▣ *SKr40.* ⊙ *Apr. and Sept., daily 10–4; May–Aug., daily 9–6; Oct., weekends 11–4.*

Simrishamn

②③   *41 km (25 mi) northeast of Ystad (via Route 9), 105 km (65 mi) east of Malmö, 190 km (118 mi) southwest of Växjö.*

This bustling fishing village of 25,000 swells to many times that number during the summer. Built in the mid-1100s, the town has cobblestone streets lined with tiny brick houses covered with white stucco. The medieval St. Nicolai's Church, which dominates the town's skyline, was once a landmark for local sailors. Inside are models of sailing ships.

The **Frasses Musik Museum** contains an eclectic collection of music oddities, such as self-playing barrel organs, antique accordions, children's gramophones, and the world's most complete collection of Edison phonographs. ⊠ *Peder Mörksv. 5,* ☎ *0414/14520.* ☜ *SKr10.* ☉ *Early June–late Aug., Sun. 2–6; July, Sun.–Wed. 2–6.*

En Route If you're in the area between July 1 and August 10, you might want to stop off at **Kristinehov,** about 8 km (5 mi) west of Brösarp and 35 km (22 mi) north of Simrishamn, via Route 9. A summer wine festival is presented at the castle by a local Swedish wine producer, **Åkersson & Sons** (☎ 0417/19700). Known as the pink castle, Kristinehov was built in 1740 by Countess Christina Piper in the late Caroline style. Although closed to the public since 1989, the castle is occasionally used for rock concerts and other summer programs.

Kristianstad

74 *73 km (45 mi) north of Simrishamn (via Routes 9/19 and E22), 95 km (59 mi) northeast of Malmö (via E22), 126 km (78 mi) southwest of Växjö.*

Kristianstad was founded by Danish King Christian IV in 1614 as a fortified town to keep the Swedes at bay. Its former ramparts and moats are today wide, tree-lined boulevards.

About 17 km (11 mi) east of Kristianstad is **Bäckaskog Slott** (Bäckaskog Castle), located on a strip of land between two lakes, just north of the E22 highway. Originally founded as a monastery by a French religious order in the 13th century, it was turned into a fortified castle by Danish noblemen during the 16th century and later appropriated by the Swedish government and used as a residence for the cavalry. The castle was a favorite of the Swedish royalty until 1900. ⊠ *Fjälkinge,* ☎ *044/53250.* ☜ *SKr30.* ☉ *May 15–Aug. 15, daily 10–6; open off-season to groups by appointment only.*

Ronneby

75 *86 km (53 mi) east of Kristianstad (via E22), 181 km (112 mi) northeast of Malmö, 86 km (53 mi) southeast of Växjö.*

The spa town of Ronneby has a picturesque waterfall and rapids called **Djupadal,** where a river runs through a cleft in the rock just 5 ft wide but 50 ft deep. There are boat trips on the river each summer.

Karlskrona

76 *111 km (69 mi) east of Kristianstad (via E22), 201 km (125 mi) northeast of Malmö, 107 km (66 mi) southeast of Växjö.*

A small city built on the mainland and five nearby islands, Karlskrona achieved great notoriety in 1981, when a Soviet submarine ran aground a short distance from its naval base. The town dates from 1679, when it was laid out in the Baroque style on the orders of Karl XI. In 1790 it was severely damaged by fire.

The **Admiralitetskyrkan** (Admiralty Church) is Sweden's oldest wooden church. Two other churches, **Holy Trinity** and **Frederiks,** were designed by the 17th-century architect Nicodemus Tessin. The **Marinmuseum** (Naval Museum), dating from 1752, is one of the oldest museums in Sweden. ⊠ *Admiralitetsslatten,* ☎ *0455/84000.* ☜ *SKr20.* ☉ *June and Aug., daily 10–4; July, daily 10–6; Sept.–May, daily noon–4.*

Kalmar

77 *91 km (57 mi) northeast of Karlskrona (via E22), 292 km (181 mi) northeast of Malmö, 109 km (68 mi) east of Växjö.*

★ The attractive coastal town of Kalmar, opposite the Baltic island of Öland, is dominated by the imposing **Kalmar Slott,** Sweden's best-preserved Renaissance castle, part of which dates from the 12th century. The living rooms, chapel, and dungeon can be visited. ⊠ *Slottsv.,* ☎ *0480/ 56450.* ⊡ *SKr60.* ☉ *Mid-June–mid-Aug., Mon.–Sat. 10–6, Sun. noon– 6; Apr.–mid-June and mid-Aug.–Oct., weekdays 10–4, weekends noon– 4; Nov.–Mar., Sun. 1–3.*

The **Kalmar Läns Museum** (Kalmar District Museum), with good archaeological and ethnographic collections, contains the remains of the royal ship *Kronan,* which sank in 1676. Consisting primarily of cannons, wood sculptures, and old coins, they were raised from the seabed in 1980. Another exhibit focuses on Jenny Nystrom, a painter famous for popularizing the *tomte,* a rustic Christmas elf. ⊠ *Skeppsbrog. 51,* ☎ *0480/15350.* ⊡ *SKr40.* ☉ *Mid-June–mid-Aug., Mon.–Sat. 10–6, Sun. noon–6; rest of yr, weekdays 10–4, Wed. until 8, weekends noon–4.*

Lodging

$$$ 🏨 **Slottshotellet.** Occupying a gracious old house on a quiet street, Slottshotellet faces a waterfront park, a few minutes' walk from both the train station and Kalmar Castle. Guest rooms are charmingly individual, with carved-wood bedsteads, old-fashioned chandeliers, pretty wallpaper, wooden floors, and antique furniture. The bathrooms are spotlessly clean. Only breakfast is served year-round, but in summer, full restaurant service is offered on the terrace. ⊠ *Slottsv. 7, S392 33,* ☎ *0480/88260,* 𝔽𝔸𝕏 *0480/88266. 36 rooms. No-smoking rooms, sauna, meeting room. AE, DC, V.*

$$ 🏨 **Stadshotellet.** In city center, Best Western's Stadshotellet is a fairly large hotel with traditional English decor. The main building dates from 1907. Guest rooms are freshly decorated and have hair dryers and radios, among other amenities. There's also a fine restaurant. ⊠ *Stortorget 14, S392 32,* ☎ *0480/15180,* 𝔽𝔸𝕏 *0480/15847. 140 rooms. Restaurant, bar, no-smoking rooms, hot tub, sauna, meeting rooms. AE, DC, MC, V.*

Öland

8 km (5 mi) east of Kalmar (via the Ölandsbron bridge).

Linked to the mainland by one of the longest bridges in Europe (6 km/4 mi), Öland is a limestone plateau 139 km (86 mi) long and 37 km (23 mi) at its widest point. First settled some 4,000 years ago, the island is fringed with fine sandy beaches and is dotted with old windmills and such archaeological remains as the massive stone walls of the 6th-century **Gråborg Fortress,** the 5th-century fortified village of **Eketorp,** and the medieval **Borgholm Castle.** In spring and fall, Öland is a way station for hundreds of species of migrating birds.

The royal family has a summer home at **Solliden** on the outskirts of Borgholm, the principal town, 25 km (16 mi) north of the bridge via Route 136.

Lodging

$$ 🏨 **Halltorps Gästgiveri.** This manor house dating from the 17th century has modernized duplex rooms decorated in Swedish landscape tones and an excellent restaurant. Drive north from Ölandsbron, and it's on the left-hand side of the road.⊠ *S387 92 Borgholm,* ☎ *0485/85000,*

FAX 0485/85001. 35 rooms. Restaurant, no-smoking rooms, 2 saunas, meeting rooms. AE, DC, MC, V.

OFF THE
BEATEN PATH

PATAHOLM AND TIMMERNABBE – On the mainland coast opposite Öland, along E22, numerous picturesque seaside towns dot the coastline, such as **Pataholm,** with its cobblestone main square, and **Timmernabbe,** which is famous for its caramel factory and from which the Borgholm-bound car ferries depart. Miles of clean, attractive, and easily accessible—if windy—beaches line this strip of the coast.

The Kingdom of Glass

Stretching roughly 109 km (68 mi) between Kalmar and Växjo.

Scattered among the rocky woodlands of Småland province are isolated villages with names synonymous with quality in crystal glassware. In the streets of Kosta, Orrefors, Boda, and Strömbergshyttan, red-painted cottages surround the actual factories, which resemble large barns. The region is the home of 16 major glassworks, and visitors may see glass being blown and crystal being etched by skilled craftspeople. *Hyttsil* evenings are also arranged, a revival of an old tradition in which Baltic herring (*sil*) is cooked in the glass furnaces of the *hytt* (literally "hut," but meaning the works). Most glassworks also have shops selling quality firsts and not-so-perfect seconds at a discount. The larger establishments have restrooms and cafeterias.

Fifteen kilometers (9 mi) north of Route 25 on Route 28 is **Kosta Glasburk,** the oldest works, dating from 1742 and named for its founders, Anders Koskull and Georg Bogislaus Stael von Holstein, two former generals. Faced with a dearth of local talent, they initially imported glassblowers from Bohemia. The Kosta works pioneered the production of crystal (to qualify for that label, glass must contain at least 24% lead oxide). You can see glassblowing off-season (August 18–June 6) between 9–3. To get to Kosta from Kalmar, drive 49 km (30 mi) west on Route 25, then 14 km (9 mi) north on Route 28. ☎ 0478/34500. ☼ *Late June–early Aug., weekdays 9–6, Sat. 9–4, Sun. 11–4; early Aug.–late June, weekdays 9–6, Sat. 10–4, Sun. noon–4.*

On Route 31, about 18 km (25 mi) east of Kosta, is **Orrefors,** one of the best known of the glass companies. Orrefors came on the scene late—in 1898—but set particularly high artistic standards. The skilled workers in Orrefors dance a slow, delicate minuet as they carry the pieces of red-hot glass back and forth, passing them on rods from hand to hand, blowing and shaping them. The basic procedures and tools are ancient, and the finished product is the result of unusual teamwork, from designer to craftsman to finisher. One of Orrefors's special attractions is a magnificent display of pieces made during the past century; younger visitors will probably be more interested in the cafeteria and playground. In summer, June 7– August 17, you can watch glassblowing at 9–10 and 11–3. ☎ 0481/34000. ☼ *Aug.–May, weekdays 10–6; June and July, weekdays 9–4, Sat. 10–4, Sun. 11–4.*

Boda Glasbruk, part of the Kosta Boda Company, is just off Route 25, 42 km (26 mi) west of Kalmar. ☎ 0481/24030. ☼ *Daily 9–4.*

Växjö

78 *109 km (68 mi) northwest of Kalmar (via Rte. 25), 198 km (123 mi) northeast of Malmö, 228 km (142 mi) southeast of Göteborg, 446 km (277 mi) southwest of Stockholm.*

Some 10,000 Americans visit this town every year, for it was from this area that their Swedish ancestors set sail in the 19th century. On the second Sunday in August, Växjö celebrates "Minnesota Day": Swedes and Swedish-Americans come together to commemorate their common heritage with American-style square dancing and other festivities. The **Utvandrarnas Hus** (Emigrants' House) in the town center tells the story of the migration, when more than a million Swedes—one quarter of the population—departed for the promised land. The museum exhibits provide a vivid sense of the rigorous journey, and an archive room and research center allow American visitors to trace their ancestry. ⊠ *Museum Park, Box 201, S351 04,* ☎ *0470/20120.* ☐ *Free.* ☉ *June–Aug., weekdays 9–5, Sat. 11–3, Sun. 1–5; Sept.–May, weekdays 9–4.*

The **Småland Museum** has the largest glass collection in northern Europe; it was reopened in summer 1996 after extensive renovation. ⊠ *Södra Järnvägsg. 2, S351 04,* ☎ *0470/45145.* ☐ *SKr40.* ☉ *Call for hrs.*

OFF THE BEATEN PATH	**KRONOBERGS SLOTT** – About 5 km (3 mi) north of Växjö, this 14th-century castle ruin lies on the edge of the Helgasjön (Holy Lake). The Småland freedom fighter Nils Dacke used the castle as a base for his attacks against the Danish occupiers during the mid-1500s; now it's an idyllic destination. In summer, you can eat waffles from the café under the shade of birch trees or take a lunch or sightseeing cruise around the lake on the toylike *Thor,* Sweden's oldest steamboat. *Castle,* ☎ *0470/45145. Boat tours,* ☎ *0470/63000. Tours offered late June–late Aug.* ☐ *Lunch cruise SKr280, 2½-hr canal trip to Årby SKr120, 1-hr around-the-lake trip SKr85.*

Lodging

$$$ ⊞ **Hotel Statt.** Now a Best Western hotel, this conveniently located, traditional property is popular with tour groups. The building dates from 1853, but the rooms themselves are modern. The hotel has a cozy pub, nightclub, bistro, and café. ⊠ *Kungsg. 6, S-351 04,* ☎ *0470/13400,* FAX *0470/44837. 130 rooms. Restaurant, café, pub, no-smoking rooms, sauna, exercise room, meeting rooms. AE, DC, MC, V.*

$ ⊞ **Esplanad.** In town center, the Esplanad is a small, family hotel offering basic amenities. ⊞ *Norra Esplanaden 21A, S-351 04,* ☎ *0470/22580,* FAX *0470/26226. 27 rooms. No-smoking rooms. MC, V.*

The South and the Kingdom of Glass A to Z

Arriving and Departing

BY BOAT

The most common way to get to southern Sweden is by boat. Several regular services run from Copenhagen to Malmö, including hovercraft that make the trip in less than an hour, and a bus-ferry service from Copenhagen Station, which also goes to Lund. There are also regular ferry connections to Denmark, Germany, and Poland from such ports as Malmö, Helsingborg, Landskrona, Trelleborg, and Ystad. **Stena Line** (⊠ Kungsg. 12–14, Stockholm, ☎ 08/141475; ⊠ Danmarksterminalen, Göteborg, ☎ 031/858000) is one of the major Swedish carriers.

Day-trippers can pick up tickets at Malmö Harbor and catch one of the hourly Copenhagen-bound hovercraft operated by the following ferry lines: **Flygbåtarna** (☎ 040/103930), **Pilen** (☎ 040/234411), and **Shopping Linje** (☎ 040/110099). **SFL Skandlines** (☎ 040/362000) runs the only car-ferry service between Dragör, Denmark, and Limhamn, Sweden, a town that adjoins Malmö's southern edge.

BY CAR

Malmö is 620 km (386 mi) from Stockholm. Take the E4 freeway to Helsingborg, then the E6/E20 to Malmö and Lund. From Göteborg, take the E6/E20.

BY PLANE

Malmö's airport, **Sturup** (☎ 040/6131100), is approximately 30 km (19 mi) from Malmö and 25 km (15 mi) from Lund. **SAS** (☎ 040/357200 or 020/727000), **KLM** (☎ 040/500530), and **Malmö Aviation** (☎ 040/502900) serve the airport. SAS offers discounts on trips to Malmö year-round; ask for the "Jackpot" discount package.

Between the Airport and City Center: Buses for Malmö and Lund meet all flights at Sturup Airport. The price of the trip is SKr60 to either destination. For more information on bus schedules, routes, and fares, call ☎ 020/616161 or the airport at ☎ 040/6131100. A **taxi** from the airport to Malmö or Lund costs about SKr250. For SAS **limousine service,** call ☎ 040/500600.

BY TRAIN

There is regular service from Stockholm to Helsingborg, Lund, and Malmö. Each trip takes about 6½ hours, and about 4½ hours by high-speed (X2000) train. All three railway stations are central.

Getting Around

A special 48-hour *Öresund Runt* (Around Öresund) pass is available from the Malmö Tourist Office: at SKr149, the ticket covers a train from Malmö to Helsingborg, a ferry to Helsingør, a train to Copenhagen, and a ferry back to Malmö.

The *Malmökortet* (Malmö Card), entitles the holder to, among other benefits, free admission or discounts to most museums, concert halls, nightclubs, theaters, the Royal Cab company, and many shops and restaurants. A one-day card costs SKr125, two-day card SKr140, and a three-day card SKr155. Cards are available from the tourist office in Malmö.

BY CAR

Roads are well marked and well maintained. Traveling around the coast counterclockwise from Helsingborg, you take the E6/E20 to Landskrona, Malmö, and Lund, then the E6/E22 to Trelleborg; Route 9 follows the south coast from there to Simrishamn and north until just before Kristianstad, where you pick up E22 all the way through Karlshamn, Ronneby, Karlskrona, and up the east coast to Kalmar. From Kalmar, Route 25 goes almost directly west through Växjö to Halmstad, on the west coast between Helsingborg and Göteborg.

BY TRAIN

The major towns of the south are all connected by rail.

Contacts and Resources

CAR RENTALS

If you are coming from Denmark and want to rent a car as soon as you arrive, several rental companies have locations at Malmö Harbor, including **Avis** (☎ 040/77830), **Hertz** (☎ 040/74955), and **Europcar/InterRent** (☎ 040/71640). Hertz car rentals are available for less than SKr600 a day on weekends (less during the summer) if you book a SAS (☎ 040/357200 or 020/727000) flight.

EMERGENCIES

As elsewhere in Sweden, call ☎ 112 for emergencies.

VISITOR INFORMATION

Regional Tourist Offices: Skånes Turistråd (Skåne Tourist Council, ✉ Skifferv. 38, Lund, ☎ 046/124350). **Jönköping** (✉ Västra Storg. 18A, ☎ 036/199570).

Local Tourist Offices: Helsingborg (✉ Knutpunkten terminal, ☎ 042/120310). **Kalmar** (✉ Larmg. 6, ☎ 0480/15350). **Karlskrona** (✉ Borgnästoreg. 68, ☎ 0455/83490). **Kristianstad** (✉ Stora Torg, ☎ 044/121988). **Landskrona** (✉ Rådhusg. 3, ☎ 0418/16980; ✉ Landsv. 2, ☎ 0418/72420). **Lund** (✉ Kyrkog. 11, ☎ 046/355040). **Malmö** (✉ Skeppsbron at the Central Station, ☎ 040/300150). **Ronneby** (✉ Kallingev. 3, ☎ 0457/17650). **Växjö** (✉ Kronobergsg. 8, ☎ 0470/41410). **Ystad** (✉ St. Knuts Torg, ☎ 0411/77681).

7 Dalarna: The Folklore District

DALARNA IS CONSIDERED to be the most typically Swedish of all the country's 24 provinces, a place of forests, mountains, and red-painted wooden farmhouses and cottages by the shores of pristine, sun-dappled lakes. It is the favorite site for Midsummer Day celebrations, in which Swedes don folk costumes and dance to fiddle and accordion music around maypoles garlanded with wildflowers.

Dalarna played a key role in the history of the nation. It was from here that Gustav Vasa recruited the army that freed the country from Danish domination during the 16th century. The region is also important artistically, both for its tradition of naive religious decoration and for producing two of the nation's best-loved painters, Anders Zorn (1860–1920) and Carl Larsson (1853–1915), and one of its favorite poets, the melancholy, mystical Dan Andersson, who sought inspiration in the remote camps of the old charcoal burners deep in the forest.

As for dining and lodging, do not expect too much in Dalarna. Traditionally, visitors to the area—many from elsewhere in Scandinavia or from Germany—make use either of the region's many well-equipped campsites or of *stugbyar* (small villages of log cabins, with cooking facilities), usually set near lakesides or in forest clearings.

Our itinerary circles Lake Siljan, the largest of the 6,000 lakes in the province and the center of Dalarna's folklore, then crosses east to the coastal town of Gävle. The main points can all be reached by train, except for the southern side of Lake Siljan.

En Route   On the route from Stockholm to Dalarna, 158 km (98 mi) from Stockholm and just south of Avesta on Route 70, stands the world's biggest *Dalahäst* (Dala horse), 43 ft tall. The bright orange-red painted monument marks a modern roadside rest stop with a spacious cafeteria and a helpful tourist information center.

Falun

㉙   *224 km (139 mi) northwest of Stockholm (via E18 and Rte. 70).*

Falun is the traditional capital of Dalarna, though in recent years the nondescript railway town of Borlänge has grown in importance. Falun's history has always been very much bound to its copper mine. This has been worked since 1230 by Stora Kopparbergs Bergslags AB (today just *Stora*), which claims to be the oldest limited company in the world. Its greatest period of prosperity was the 17th century, when it financed Sweden's "Age of Greatness," and the country became the dominant Baltic power. In 1650, Stora produced a record 3,067 tons of copper; probably as a result of such rapid extraction, 37 years later its mine shafts caved in. Fortunately, the accident was on Midsummer's Day, when most of the miners were off duty, and as a result no one was killed. Today the major part of the mine is an enormous hole in the ground that has become Falun's principal tourist attraction, with its own museum, **Stora Museum.** ☎ *023/711475.* 🖭 *Mine SKr60, museum free with mine tour.* ☉ *Mine May–Aug., daily 10–4:30; Sept.–mid-Nov. and Mar.–Apr., weekends 12:30–4:30; museum May–Aug., daily 10–4:30; Sept.–Apr., daily 12:30–4:30.*

Lodging

$$$ 🏨 **Bergmästaren.** This small, cozy hotel in town center is built in tra-
★   ditional Dalarna style and filled with antique furnishings. Some rooms share bathrooms. ⊠ *Bergskolegränd 7, S791 26,* ☎ *023/63600,* 🖷 *023/*

Dalarna

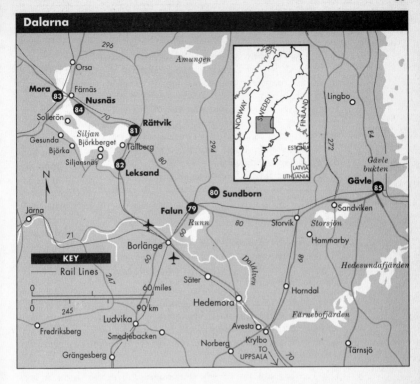

22524. 88 rooms. Restaurant, no-smoking rooms, hot tub, sauna, meeting room. AE, DC, MC, V.

$$$ 🏨 **Grand.** Now part of the First Hotel chain, this conventional, modern hotel is close to town center. The bright rooms are decorated with Chippendale-style furniture, and most have minibars. ⊠ *Trotzg. 911, S791 71,* ☎ *023/18700,* FAX *023/14143. 183 rooms. Restaurant, bar, minibars, no-smoking rooms, indoor pool, sauna, exercise room, convention center, parking. AE, DC, MC, V.*

$$$ 🏨 **Scandic.** This ultramodern, Legolike hotel is in the expanded Lugnet sports and recreation center outside Falun, where the 1993 World Skiing Championships took place. The comfortable rooms have good views. ⊠ *Svärdsjög. 51, S791 31 Falun,* ☎ *023/22160,* FAX *023/12845. 135 rooms. Restaurant, pub, snack bar, no-smoking rooms, indoor pool, sauna, meeting rooms, parking. AE, DC, MC, V.*

$$ 🏨 **Falun.** Rolf Carlsson runs this small, friendly, but bland-looking hotel just 1,300 ft from the railway station. Twelve rooms have shared baths and are offered at a lower rate. The front desk closes at 9 PM. ⊠ *Centrumhuset, Trotzg. 16, S791 30,* ☎ *023/29180,* FAX *023/13006. 27 rooms, 15 with bath. No-smoking rooms, meeting rooms. AE, DC, MC, V.*

$ 🏨 **Birgittagården.** This small hotel, 8 km (5 mi) out of town, is run by the religious order Stiftelsen Dalarnas Birgitta Systrar (the Dalarna Sisters of Birgitta). It's smoke-free and alcohol-free, and set in a fine park. There are no telephones or televisions in the rooms. ⊠ *Uddnäsv., S791 46,* ☎ *023/32147,* FAX *023/32471. 25 rooms. No-smoking rooms, meeting rooms. No credit cards.*

Sundborn

⑧⓪   *10 km (6 mi) northeast of Falun (off Rte. 80).*

In this small village you can visit **Carl Larsson Gården,** the lakeside home of the Swedish artist Carl Larsson. Larsson was an excellent textile designer and draftsman who painted scenes from his family's busy, domestic life. The house itself was creatively painted and decorated by Larsson's wife, Karin, also trained as an artist. Their home's turn-of-the-century fittings and furnishings have been carefully preserved; their great-grandchildren still use the house on occasion. Lines for guided tours can take two hours in summer. ☎ *023/60053 in summer, 023/60069 in winter.* ▨ *Guided tours only, SKr60.* ☾ *May–Sept., daily 10–5; Oct.–Apr., Tues. 11. Off-season visits by advance reservation.*

Rättvik

⑧①   *48 km (30 mi) northwest of Falun (via Rte. 80).*

Surrounded by wooded slopes, Rättvik is a pleasant town of timbered houses on the eastern tip of Lake Siljan. A center for local folklore, the town has several shops that sell handmade articles and produce from the surrounding region.

Every year in June, hundreds of people wearing traditional costumes arrive in longboats to attend Midsummer services at the town's 14th-century church, **Rättvik Kyrka,** which stands on a promontory stretching into the lake. Its interior contains some fine examples of local naive religious art.

The open-air museum **Rättvik Gammalgård** gives the visitor an idea of the peasant lifestyles of bygone days. Tours in English can be arranged through the Rättvik tourist office. ▨ *Free, guided tour SKr20.* ☾ *Mid-June–mid-Aug., daily 11–6; tours at 1 and 2:30.*

Leksand

⑧②   *18 km (11 mi) south of Rättvik (via Rte. 70), 66 km (41 mi) northwest of Falun (via Rättvik).*

Thousands of tourists converge on Leksand in June each year for the Midsummer celebrations; they also come in July for *Himlaspelet* (*The Play of the Way that Leads to Heaven*), a traditional musical with an all-local cast, staged outdoors near the town's church. It is easy to get seats; ask the local tourist office for details.

Leksand is also an excellent vantage point from which to watch the "church-boat" races on Siljan. These vessels are claimed to be successors to the Viking longboats and were traditionally used to take peasants from outlying regions to church on Sunday. On Midsummer Eve, the longboats, crewed by people in folk costumes, skim the lake.

In the hills around Leksand and elsewhere near Siljan you will find the *fäbodar,* small settlements in the forest where cattle were taken to graze during the summer. Less idyllic memories of bygone days are conjured up by **Käringberget,** a 720-ft-high mountain north of town where alleged witches were burned to death during the 17th century.

En Route   From Leksand, drive along the small road toward Mora by the southern shores of Siljan, passing through the small communities of Siljansnäs and Björka before stopping at **Gesunda,** a pleasant little village at the foot of a mountain. A chairlift will take you from there to the top where there are unbeatable views over the lake.

Near Gesunda, **Tomteland** (Santaland) claims to be the home of Santa Claus, or Father Christmas. Toys are for sale at Santa's workshop and kiosks. There are rides in horse-drawn carriages in summer and sleighs in winter. ⊠ *Gesundaberget, S792 90, Sollerön,* ☎ *0250/29000.* 🖾 *SKr95.* ⊘ *Mid-June–late Aug., daily 10–5; July, daily 10–6; late Nov.– early Jan, call ahead for daily schedule.*

The large island of **Sollerön** is connected to the mainland at Gesunda by a bridge, from which there are fine views of the mountains surrounding Siljan. Several excellent bathing places and an interesting Viking gravesite are also here. The church dates from 1775.

Mora

83 *50 km (31 mi) northwest of Leksand, 83 km (52 mi) northwest of Falun (via Rte. 70).*

To get to this pleasant and relaxed lakeside town of 20,000, you can take Route 70 directly from Rättvik along the northern shore of Lake Silja, or follow the lake's southern shore through Leksand and Gesunda to get a good sense of Dalarna.

Mora is best known as the finishing point for the world's longest cross-country ski race, the *Vasalopp,* which begins 90 km (56 mi) away at Sälen, a ski resort close to the Norwegian border. The race commemorates a fundamental piece of Swedish history: the successful attempt by Gustav Vasa in 1521 to rally local peasants to the cause of ridding Sweden of Danish occupation. Vasa, only 21 years old, had fled the capital and described to the Mora locals in graphic detail a massacre of Swedish noblemen ordered by Danish King Christian in Stockholm's Stortorget. Unfortunately, no one believed him and the dispirited Vasa was forced to abandon his attempts at insurrection and take off on either skis or snowshoes for Norway, where he hoped to evade Christian and go into exile. Just after he left, confirmation reached Mora of the Stockholm bloodbath, and the peasants, already discontented with Danish rule, relented, sending two skiers after Vasa to tell him they would join his cause. The two men caught up with the young nobleman at Sälen. They returned with him to Mora, where an army was recruited. Vasa marched south, defeated the Danes, and became king and the founder of modern Sweden. The commemorative race, held on the first Sunday in March, attracts thousands of competitors from all over the world, including the Swedish king. There is a spectacular mass start at Sälen before the field thins out. The finish is eagerly awaited in Mora, though in recent years the number of spectators has fallen thanks to the fact that the race is now usually televised live. You can get a comfortable glimpse of the race's history in the **Vasaloppsmuseet,** with its collection of past ski gear and photos, news clippings, and a short film. ⊠ *Vasag.,* ☎ *0250/39225.* 🖾 *SKr30.* ⊘ *Mid-May–Aug., daily 10–6; Sept.–mid-May, daily 11–5.*

Mora is also known as the home of Anders Zorn (1860–1920), Sweden's leading Impressionist painter, who lived in Stockholm and Paris before returning to his roots here, painting the local scenes for which he is now famous. His former **private residence,** a large, sumptuous house designed with great originality and taste by the painter himself, has retained the same exquisite furnishings, paintings, and decor it had when he lived there with his wife. The garden, also a Zorn creation, ★ is open to the public. Next door, the **Zornmuseet** (Zorn Museum), built 19 years after the painter's death, contains many of his best works. ⊠ *Vasag. 36,* ☎ *0250/16560.* 🖾 *Museum SKr30, home SKr30.* ⊘ *Museum mid-May–mid-Sept., Mon.–Sat. 9–5, Sun. 11–5; mid-Sept.–mid-*

*May, Mon.–Sat. 10–5, Sun. 1–5; home (guided tours only) mid-May–
mid-Sept., Mon.–Sat. 10–4, Sun. 11–4; mid-Sept.–mid-May, Mon.–Sat.
12:30–4, Sun. 1–4.*

On the south side of town you'll find **Zorns Gammalgård,** a fine collection of old wooden houses from local farms, brought here and donated to Mora by Anders Zorn. One of them was converted in 1995
into the **Textil Kammare** (Textile Chamber), the first exhibit of Zorn's
collection of textiles and period clothing. ⊠ *Yvradsv.,* ☎ *0250/10454
(summer only).* ⊠ *SKr25.* ☉ *June–Aug., daily 11–5.*

Lodging

$$ ⬚ **Kung Gästa.** This modern, reasonably sized hotel is 2 km (1 mi) from
town center and only 330 ft from the Mora train station. ⊠ *Kristeneberg,
S792 32,* ☎ *0250/15070,* ꜰꜱ *0250/17078. 47 rooms. Restaurant, no-
smoking rooms, indoor pool, sauna, exercise room, meeting rooms.
AE, DC, MC, V.*

$$ ⬚ **Mora.** A pleasant little Best Western chain hotel is in town center and
5 km (3 mi) from the airport. Its comfortable rooms are brightly dec-
orated and have minibars and radios. ⊠ *Strandg. 12, S792 01,* ☎
0250/71750, ꜰꜱ *0250/18981. 138 rooms. Restaurant, bar, minibars, no-
smoking rooms, indoor pool, sauna, meeting rooms. AE, DC, MC, V.*

$$ ⬚ **Siljan.** Part of the Sweden Hotel group, this small, modern hotel af-
fords views over the lake. Rooms are standard, with radio, television,
and wall-to-wall carpeting; most are single rooms with sofa beds. ⊠
Morag. 6, S792 22, ☎ *0250/13000,* ꜰꜱ *0250/13098. 45 rooms. Restau-
rant, bar, no-smoking floor, sauna, exercise room, dance club, meet-
ing room. AE, DC, MC, V.*

$ ⬚ **Moraparken.** This modern hotel sits in a park by the banks of the
Dala River, not far from town center. ⊠ *Parkgarten 1, S792 25,* ☎
0250/17800, ꜰꜱ *0250/18583. 75 rooms. Restaurant, no-smoking
rooms, sauna, convention center. AE, DC, MC, V.*

Outdoor Activities and Sports

SKIING

Dalarna's principal ski resort is **Sälen,** starting point for the Vasalopp,
about 80 km (50 mi) west of Mora.

Nusnäs

🖲 *6 km (4 mi) southeast of Mora (via Rte. 70), 28 km (17 mi) northwest
of Falun.*

The lakeside village of Nusnäs is where the small, brightly red-painted
wooden Dala horses are made. These were originally carved by the peas-
ants of Dalarna as toys for their children, but their popularity rapidly
spread with the advent of tourism in the 20th century. Mass produc-
tion of the little horses started at Nusnäs in 1928. In 1939 they achieved
international popularity after being shown at the New York World's
Fair, and since then they have become a Swedish symbol—today some
of the smaller versions available in Stockholm's tourist shops are,
however, made in East Asia. At Nusnäs you can watch the genuine ar-
ticle being made, now with the aid of modern machinery but still
painted by hand.

Shopping

Naturally you'll be able to buy some painted horses to take home; the
place to visit is **Nils Olsson** (⊠ *Edåkerv. 17,* ☎ *0250/37200*). Shops
are open every day except Sunday.

Gävle

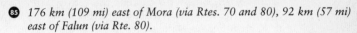

85 *176 km (109 mi) east of Mora (via Rtes. 70 and 80), 92 km (57 mi) east of Falun (via Rte. 80).*

The port town of Gävle achieved dubious renown at the time of the Chernobyl nuclear accident in 1986 by briefly becoming the most radioactive place in Europe. A freak storm dumped large amounts of fallout from the Soviet Union on the town. For a while farmers had to burn newly harvested hay and keep their cattle inside. However, the scare soon passed and today one can visit the town in perfect safety. Gävle is worth visiting for a glimpse of its two relatively new museums.

The **Joe Hill Museet** (Joe Hill Museum), dedicated to the Swedish emigrant who went on to become America's first well-known protest singer and union organizer, is in Hill's former home in the oldest section of Gävle. Once a poor, working-class district, this is now the most picturesque and highly sought-after residential part of town, with art studios and crafts workshops nearby. The museum—furnished in the same style as when Hill lived there—contains very few of his possessions but does display his prison letters. The house itself bears witness to the poor conditions that forced so many Swedes to emigrate to the United States (an estimated 850,000 to 1 million between 1840 and 1900). Hill, whose original Swedish name was Joel Hägglund, became a founder of the International Workers of the World and was executed for the murder of a Salt Lake City grocer in 1914, but he maintained his innocence right up to the end. ⊠ *Nedre Bergsg. 28,* ☎ *026/613425.* ▨ *Free.* ☉ *June–Aug., daily 11–3.*

The **Skogsmuseet Silvanum** (Silvanum Forestry Museum) is on the west end of town, by the river. Silvanum, Latin for "The Forest," was inaugurated in 1961; it was the first such museum in the world and is one of the largest. The museum provides an in-depth picture of the forestry industry in Sweden, still the backbone of the country's industrial wealth: trees cover more than 50% of Sweden's surface area, and forest products account for 20% of national exports. Silvanum includes a forest botanical park and an arboretum that contains an example of every tree and bush growing in Sweden. ⊠ *Kungsbäcksv. 32,* ☎ *026/614100.* ▨ *Free.* ☉ *Tues., Thurs.–Fri. 10–4, Wed. 10–9, weekends 1–5.*

Dalarna: The Folklore District A to Z

Arriving and Departing

BY BUS

Swebus/Vasatrafik (☎ 020/640640) runs tour buses to the area from Stockholm on weekends.

BY CAR

From Stockholm, take E18 to Enköping and follow Route 70 northwest. From Göteborg, take E20 to Örebro and Route 60 north from there.

BY PLANE

There are 11 flights daily from Stockholm to **Dala Airport** (⊠ 8 km/5 mi from Borlänge, ☎ 0243/55100). **Mora Airport** (⊠ 6 km/4 mi from Mora) is served by **Holmström Air** (☎ 0250/30175), with five flights daily from Stockholm Monday through Friday, fewer on weekends.

Between the Airport and Town: There are half-hourly bus connections on weekdays between Dala Airport and Falun, 26 km (16 mi) away. The 601 bus runs every half hour from Dala Airport to Borlänge; the trip costs SKr15. There are no buses from Mora Airport.

A **taxi** from Dala Airport to Borlänge costs around SKr100, to Falun approximately SKr215. A taxi into Mora from Mora Airport costs SKr90. Order taxis in advance through your travel agent or when you make an airline reservation. Book the **DalaFalun** taxi service by calling ☎ 0243/229290.

BY TRAIN

There is regular daily train service from Stockholm to both Mora and Falun.

Contacts and Resources

CAR RENTALS

Avis has offices in Borlänge (☎ 0243/87080) and Mora (☎ 0250/16711). **Hertz** has offices in Falun (☎ 023/58872) and Mora (☎ 0250/28800). **Europcar/InterRent** has its office in Borlänge (☎ 0243/19050).

DOCTORS AND DENTISTS

Falun Hospital (☎ 023/82000). **Mora Hospital** (☎ 0250/25000). **24-hour medical advisory service** (☎ 023/82900).

EMERGENCIES

For emergencies dial ☎ 112.

GUIDED TOURS

Sightseeing Tours: Call the Falun tourist office for English-speaking guides to Falun and the region around Lake Siljan; guides cost about SKr900.

LATE-NIGHT PHARMACIES

There are no late-night pharmacies in the area, but doctors called to emergencies can supply medication. **Vasen** pharmacy in Falun (✉ Åsg., ☎ 023/20000) is open until 7 PM weekdays.

VISITOR INFORMATION

Falun (✉ Stora Torget, ☎ 023/83637). **Leksand** (✉ Norsg., ☎ 0247/80300). **Ludvika** (✉ Sporthallen, ☎ 0240/86050). **Mora** (✉ Ångbåtskajn, ☎ 0250/26550). **Rättvik** (✉ Railway Station House, ☎ 0248/70200). **Sälen** (✉ Sälen Centrum, ☎ 0280/20250).

8 Norrland and Norbotten

THE NORTH OF SWEDEN, Norrland, is a place of wide-open spaces where the silence is almost audible. Golden eagles soar above snowcapped crags; huge salmon fight their way up wild, tumbling rivers; rare orchids bloom in Arctic heathland; and wild rhododendrons splash the land with color.

In the summer the sun shines at midnight above the Arctic Circle. In the winter it hardly shines at all. The weather can change with bewildering speed: a June day can dawn sunny and bright; then the skies may darken and the temperature drop to around zero as a snow squall blows in. Just as suddenly, the sun comes out again and the temperature starts to rise.

Here live the once-nomadic Lapps, or Sami as they prefer to be known. They carefully guard what remains of their identity, while doing their best to inform the public of their culture. Many of the 17,000 Sami who live in Sweden still earn their living herding reindeer, but as open space shrinks, the younger generation is turning in greater numbers toward the allure of the cities. Often the Sami exhibit a sad resignation to the gradual disappearance of their way of life as the modern world makes incursions. This is best expressed in one of their folk poems: "Our memory, the memory of us vanishes/We forget and we are forgotten."

Yet there is a growing struggle, especially among younger Sami, to maintain their identity, and, thanks to their traditional closeness to nature, they are now finding allies in Sweden's Green movement. They refer to the north of Scandinavia as *Sapmi,* their spiritual and physical home, making no allowance for the different countries that now rule it.

Nearly all Swedish Sami now live in ordinary houses, having abandoned the *kåta* (Lapp wigwam), and some even herd their reindeer with helicopters. Efforts are now being made to protect and preserve their language, which is totally unlike Swedish and bears far greater resemblance to Finnish. The language reflects their closeness to nature. The word *goadnil,* for example, means "a quiet part of the river, free of current, near the bank or beside a rock."

Nowadays many Sami depend on the tourist industry for their living, selling their artifacts, such as expertly carved bone-handled knives, wooden cups and bowls, bark bags, silver jewelry, and leather straps embroidered with pewter thread.

The land that the Sami inhabit is vast. Norrland stretches 1,000 km (560 mi) from south to north, making up more than half of Sweden; its size is comparable to that of Great Britain. On the west there are mountain ranges, to the east a wild and rocky coastline, and in between boundless forests and moorland. Its towns are often little more than a group of houses along a street, built around a local industry such as mining, forestry, or hydropower utilities. However, thanks to Sweden's excellent transportation infrastructure, Norrland and the northernmost region of Norbotten are no longer inaccessible and even travelers with limited time can get at least a taste of the area. Its wild spaces are ideal for open-air vacations. Hiking, climbing, canoeing, river rafting, and fishing are all popular in summer, skiing, skating, and dogsledding in winter.

A word of warning: In summer mosquitoes are a constant nuisance, even worse than in other parts of Sweden, so be sure to bring plenty of repellent (you won't find anything effective in Sweden). Fall is perhaps the best season to visit Norrland. Roads are well maintained, but be careful of *gupp* (holes) following thaws. Highways are generally traffic free, but keep an eye out for the occasional reindeer.

Dining and lodging are on the primitive side in this region. Standards of cuisine and service are not nearly as high as prices—but hotels are usually exceptionally clean and staff scrupulously honest. Accommodations are limited, but the various local tourist offices can supply details of bed-and-breakfasts and holiday villages equipped with housekeeping cabins. The area is also rich in campsites—but with the highly unpredictable climate, this may appeal only to the very hardy.

Norbotten is best discovered from a base in Kiruna, in the center of the alpine region that has been described as Europe's last wilderness. You can tour south and west to the mountains and national parks, east and south to Sami villages, and farther south still to Baltic coastal settlements.

Kiruna

🟤 *1,239 km (710 mi) north of Stockholm.*

About 145 kilometers (90 mi) north of the Arctic Circle, and 1,670 ft above sea level, Kiruna is the most northerly city in Sweden. Although its inhabitants number only around 26,000, Kiruna is one of Sweden's largest cities—it spreads over the equivalent of half the area of Switzerland. Until an Australian community took the claim, Kiruna was often called "the world's biggest city." With 20,000 square km (7,722 square mi) within the municipal limits, Kiruna boasts that it could accommodate the entire world population with 150 square ft of space per person.

Kiruna lies at the eastern end of Lake Luossajärvi, spread over a wide area between two mountains, Luossavaara and Kirunavaara, that are largely composed of iron ore—its raison d'être. Here is the world's largest underground iron mine, with reserves estimated at 500 million tons. Automated mining technology has largely replaced the traditional miner in the Kirunavaara underground mines, which are some 500 km (280 mi) long. Of the city's 26,000 inhabitants, an estimated fifth are Finnish immigrants who came to work in the mine.

The city was established in 1890 as a mining town, but true prosperity came only with the building of the railway to the Baltic port of Luleå and the northern Norwegian port of Narvik in 1902.

Like most of Norrland, Kiruna is full of remarkable contrasts, from the seemingly pitch-black, months-long winter to the summer, when the sun never sets and it is actually possible to play golf round-the-clock for 50 days at a stretch. Here, too, the ancient Sami culture exists side by side with the high-tech culture of cutting-edge satellite research. In recent years the city has diversified its economy and now supports the Esrange Space Range, about 40 km (24 mi) east, which sends rockets and balloons to probe the upper reaches of the earth's atmosphere, and the Swedish Institute of Space Physics, which has pioneered the investigation of the phenomenon of the northern lights. The city received a boost in 1984 with the opening of Nordkalottvägen, a 170-km-long (106-mi-long) road to Narvik.

One of Kiruna's few buildings of interest is **Kiruna Kyrka** (Kiruna Church), on Gruvvägen, near the center of the city. It was built in 1921, its inspiration a blending of a Sami kåta with a Swedish stave church. The altarpiece is by Prince Eugen (1863–1947), Sweden's painter prince.

Norrland and Norbotten

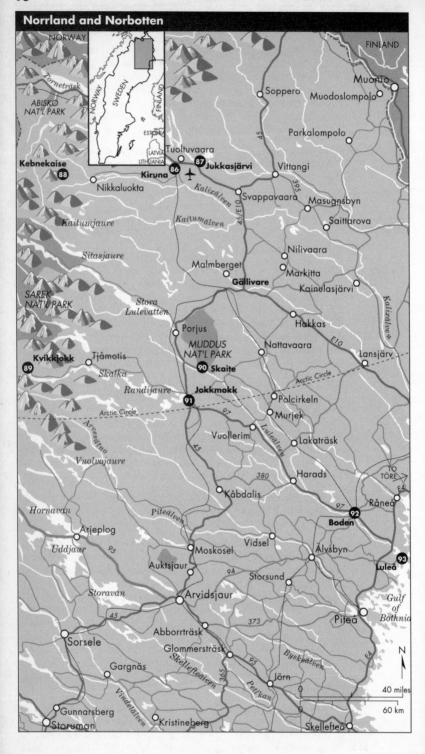

NORWAY

FINLAND

Torneträsk

ABISKO NAT'L PARK

NORWAY SWEDEN FINLAND

ESTONIA

LATVIA

LITHUANIA

Muonio

Soppero

Muodoslompolo

Parkalompolo

Tuoltuvaara

87 Jukkasjärvi

Vittangi

86 **Kiruna**

Kebnekaise **88**

Nikkaluokta

Kalixälven

Svappavaara

Masugnsbyn

Saittarova

Kaitumjaure

Kaitumälven

Nilivaara

Malmberget

Markitta

Sitasjaure

Gällivare

Kainulasjärvi

SAREK NAT'L PARK

Stora Lulevatten

Porjus

Hakkas

Kalixälven

MUDDUS NAT'L PARK

Nattavaara

E10

Lansjärv

Kvikkjokk **89**

Tjåmotis

90 Skaite

Arctic Circle

Skalka

Randijaure

91 **Jokkmokk**

Pålcirkeln

Arctic Circle

Arvesjåkno

Murjek

Vuollerim

Lakaträsk

Vuolvojaure

Luleälven

Harads

TO TÖRE

Hornavan

Piteälven

380

Kåbdalis

92

Rånea

Uddjaur

Arjeplog

95

Boden

97

Luleå **93**

Moskosel

Vidsel

Älvsbyn

Storavan

Auktsjaur

94

Gulf of Bothnia

45

Arvidsjaur

Storsund

Piteå

Sorsele

Abborrträsk

373

Gargnäs

Glommersträsk

95

Skellefteälven

365

Byskeälven

Jörn

Vindelälven

Petikån

N

Gunnarsberg

Kristineberg

0   40 miles

Storuman

0   60 km

Skellefteå

Lodging

$$$ 🏨 **Ferrum.** Part of the Reso Hotels chain, this late-1960s-vintage hotel is near the railway station. Rooms have wall-to-wall carpeting and modern, standard furniture. ⊠ *Lars Janssonsg. 15, Box 22, S981 21,* ☎ *0980/18600,* 🆒 *0980/14505. 169 rooms. 2 restaurants, bar, no-smoking rooms, sauna, exercise room, dance club, meeting rooms. AE, DC, MC, V.*

$$ 🏨 **Kebne och Kaisa.** These twin modern hotels—named after the local mountain, Kebnekaise (☞ *below*)—are close to the railway station and the airport bus stop. Rooms are bland but modern and comfortable. The restaurant is one of the best in Kiruna; it's open for breakfast and dinner. ⊠ *Konduktörsg. 3 and 7, S981 34,* ☎ *0980/12380,* 🆒 *0980/82111. 54 rooms. Restaurant, no-smoking rooms, sauna. AE, DC, MC, V.*

$ 🏨 **Fyra Vindar.** Dating from 1903, this small hotel has the advantage of being close to the railway station. ⊠ *Bangårdsv. 9, S981 34,* ☎ *0980/ 12050. 18 rooms. Restaurant, no-smoking rooms. DC, MC, V.*

$ 🏨 **STF Vandrarhem.** Formerly a hospital for the aged, this modernized, 1926 building now serves as a youth hostel. It faces a large park near the railway station. ⊠ *Skytteg. 16A, S981 34,* ☎ *0980/17195 or 0980/ 12784. 35 2- to 5-bed rooms. No credit cards. Closed mid-Aug.–mid-June.*

En Route Driving south from Kiruna toward Muddus National Park, you'll pass several small former mining villages before coming into the **Kalixälv** (Kalix River) valley, where the countryside becomes more settled, with small farms and fertile meadows replacing the wilder northern landscape.

Jukkasjärvi

㊲ *16 km (10 mi) east of Kiruna.*

The history of Jukkasjärvi, a Sami village by the shores of the fast-flowing Torneälven (Torne River), dates from 1543 when a market was recorded here. There is a wooden church from the 17th century and a small open-air museum that gives a feeling of Sami life in times gone by.

Here, if you are gastronomically adventuresome you may want to sample one of the most unusual of all Sami delicacies: *kaffeost,* a cup of thick black coffee with small lumps of goat cheese. After the cheese sits in the coffee for a bit, you fish it out with a spoon and consume it, then drink the coffee.

Dining and Lodging

$ ✕🏨 **Jukkasjärvi Wärdshus och Hembygdsgård.** The restaurant spe-
★ cializes in Norrland cuisine—characterized by reindeer, wild berries, mushrooms, dried and smoked meats, salted fish, fermented herring, rich sauces using thick creams—and is the lifework of its manager, Yngve Bergqvist. The manor has one large honeymoon suite with wood floors and antique furniture; there are 45 cabins around it, 30 with bathroom, kitchen, and two bedrooms with bunk beds. Fifteen "camping cabins" are simple shelters that share the use of a common house with toilets, showers, sauna, kitchen, and washing machine. Breakfast is not included. River-rafting and canoeing trips can be arranged. ⊠ *Jukkasjärvi, Marknadsv. 63, S981 91,* ☎ *0980/21190,* 🆒 *0980/21406. 1 suite, 45 cabins. Restaurant, sauna, meeting rooms. AE, DC, MC, V.*

$$$ 🏨 **Ice Hotel.** At the peak of winter, tourists are drawn by the annual construction of the world's largest igloo, which opens for business as a hotel from December through April, after which it melts away. Made of snow, ice, and sheet metal, the Ice Hotel offers rooms for 40 guests, who spend the night in specially insulated sleeping bags on top of layers of reindeer skins and spruce boughs. The bar is called In the Rocks, and colored electric lights liven up the solid ice walls. Breakfast is served in the sauna, with a view of the (nonelectric) northern lights. The entire hotel is designated nonsmoking, as it takes only a few puffs to tarnish the snow-white interiors. ✉ *Marknadsv. 63, S981 91 Jukkasjärvi,* ☎ *0980/21190,* 🗚 *0980/21406. 40 beds, 1 suite. Restaurant, bar, sauna, cross-country skiing, snowmobiling, chapel, meeting rooms. AE, DC, MC, V. Closed May–Nov.*

Outdoor Activities and Sports

A challenging local activity is riding the rapids of the Torne River in an inflatable boat. In winter Jukkasjärvi also offers dogsled rides and snowmobile safaris. Call the Gällivare tourist office (☞ Norrland and Norbotten A to Z, *below*).

Kebnekaise

🔠 *85 km (53 mi) west of Kiruna.*

At 7,000 ft above sea level, Kebnekaise is Sweden's highest mountain, but you'll need to be in good physical shape just to get to it. From Kiruna you travel about 66 km (41 mi) west to the Sami village of Nikkaluokta. (There are two buses a day from Kiruna in the summer.) From Nikkaluokta it is a hike of 19 km (12 mi) to the Fjällstationen (mountain station) at the foot of Kebnekaise, though you can take a boat 5 km (3 mi) across Lake Ladtjojaure. Kebnekaise itself is easy to climb provided there's good weather and you're in shape; mountaineering equipment is not necessary. If you feel up to more walking, the track continues past the Kebnekaise Fjällstationen to become part of what is known as Kungsleden (the King's Path), a 500-km (280-mi) trail through the mountains and Abisko National Park to Riksgränsen on the Norwegian border.

Lodging

$ 🔠 **Kebnekaise Fjällstation.** This rustic, wooden mountain station consists of seven separate buildings. Choose between the main building, with its heavy wood beams, wood floors, and wood bunk beds—five per room—and the newer annex, where more modern rooms each contain two or four beds. All guests share the use of a service house, with toilets, men's and women's showers, and sauna. The facility is 19 km (12 mi) from Nikkaloukta and can be reached by footpath, a combination of boat and hiking, or helicopter. Guided mountain tours are available. ✉ *S981 29 Kiruna,* ☎ *0980/55042,* 🗚 *0980/55048; off-season, contact Abisko tourist office (☞ Norrland and Norbotten A to Z, below). 200 beds. Restaurant, bar, sauna. AE, V. Closed mid-Aug.–mid-Mar.*

Outdoor Activities and Sports

All the regional tourist offices can supply details of skiing holidays, but never forget the extreme temperatures and weather conditions. For the really adventuresome, the Kebnekaise mountain station offers combined skiing and climbing weeks at SKr3,795. It also offers weeklong combined dogsledding, skiing, and climbing holidays on the mountains, which vary in price from SKr4,225 to SKr5,395. Because of the extreme cold and the danger involved, be sure to have proper equipment. Consult the **mountain station** (☎ 0980/55000) well in advance for advice.

Kvikkjokk and Sarek National Park

89 *310 km (193 mi) southwest of Kiruna (via Rte. 45).*

Sarek is Sweden's largest high mountain area and was molded by the last Ice Age. The mountains have been sculpted by glaciers, of which there are about 100 in the park. The mountain area totals 487,000 acres, a small portion of which is forest, bogs, and waterways. The remainder is bare mountain. The park has 90 peaks some 6,000 ft above sea level.

The Rapaätno River, which drains the park, runs through the lovely, desolate Rapadalen (Rapa Valley). The area is marked by a surprising variety of landscapes—luxuriant green meadows contrasting with the snowy peaks of the mountains. Elk, bears, wolverines, lynx, ermines, hare, Arctic foxes, red foxes, and mountain lemmings inhabit the terrain. Birdlife includes ptarmigan, willow grouse, teal, wigeon, tufted ducks, bluethroat, and warblers. Golden eagles, rough-legged buzzards, and merlins have also been spotted here.

Visiting Sarek demands a good knowledge of mountains and a familiarity with the outdoors. The park can be dangerous in winter because of avalanches and snowstorms. However, in summer, despite its unpredictable, often inhospitable climate, it attracts large numbers of experienced hikers. At Kvikkjokk, hikers can choose between a trail through the Tarradalen (Tarra Valley), which divides the Sarek from the Padjelanta National Park to the west, or part of the Kungsleden trail, which crosses about 15 km (9 mi) of Sarek's southeastern corner.

Skaite and Muddus National Park

90 *192 km (119 mi) south of Kiruna (via E10 and Rte. 45).*

Established in 1942, Muddus National Park is less mountainous and spectacular than Sarek, its 121,770 acres comprising mainly virgin coniferous forest, some of whose trees may be up to 600 years old. The park's 3,680 acres of water are composed primarily of two huge lakes at the center of the park and the Muddusjåkkå River, which tumbles spectacularly through a gorge with 330-ft-high sheer rock walls and includes a waterfall crashing 140 ft down. The highest point of Muddus is Sör-Stubba mountain, 2,158 ft above sea level. From Skaite, where you enter the park, a series of well-marked trails begins. There are four well-equipped overnight communal rest huts and two tourist cabins. The park shelters bears, elk, lynx, wolverines, moose, ermines, weasels, otters, and many bird species. A popular pastime is picking cloudberries in autumn.

Jokkmokk

91 *205 km (127 mi) south of Kiruna (via E10 and Rte. 45).*

Jokkmokk is an important center of Sami culture. Each February it is the scene of the region's largest market, nowadays an odd event featuring everything from stalls selling frozen reindeer meat to Sami handcrafted wooden utensils. If you're an outdoor enthusiast, Jokkmokk makes perhaps the best base in Norrland for you. The village has three campsites and is surrounded by wilderness. The local tourist office (☞ Norrland and Norbotten A to Z, *below*) sells fishing permits, which cost SKr50 for 24 hours, SKr100 for three days, SKr150 for one week, and SKr300 for the entire year. The office can also supply lists of camping and housekeeping cabins.

Lodging

$$$ ⊡ **Hotel Jokkmokk.** A modern hotel of this level of luxury seems in-
★ congruous in this remote region but is welcome nevertheless. Rooms

are carpeted, and six of them are designated as "Ladies' Rooms," basically all with pastels and florals. The hotel is in town center, but the staff can arrange dogsled rides and helicopter trips to the Sarek and Muddus national parks; there is excellent fishing nearby. ⊠ *Solg. 45, S962 23,* ☎ *0971/55320,* FAX *0971/55625. 75 rooms. Restaurant, no-smoking rooms, indoor pool, sauna, meeting rooms. AE, DC, MC, V.*

$ ☒ **Gästis.** This small hotel in central Jokkmokk opened in 1915. Rooms are standard, with television, shower, and either carpeted or vinyl floors. ⊠ *Herrev. 1, S962 31,* ☎ *0971/10012,* FAX *0971/10044. 30 rooms. Restaurant, no-smoking rooms, sauna, meeting rooms. AE, DC, MC, V.*

$ ☒ **Jokkmokks Turistcenter.** This complex is in a pleasant forest area, near Luleälven, 3 km (2 mi) from the railway station. Rooms have bunk beds, a small table, and chairs; showers, toilets, and a common cooking area are in the hall. ⊠ *Box 75, S962 22,* ☎ *0971/12370,* FAX *0971/ 12476. 26 rooms, 84 cabins. 4 pools, sauna, meeting rooms. MC, V.*

Boden

92 *290 km (180 mi) southeast of Kiruna, 130 km (81 mi) southeast of Jokkmokk (on Route 97).*

Boden, the nation's largest garrison town, dates from 1809, when Sweden lost Finland to Russia and feared an invasion of its own territory. The **Garnisonsmuseet** (Garrison Museum), contains exhibits from Swedish military history, with an extensive collection of weapons and uniforms. ⊠ *Garnisonsmuseet, Sveav. 10, Boden,* ☎ *0921/68399.* ☒ *Free.* ☉ *Mid-June–late Aug., Tues.–Sat. 11–4, Sun. 1–4.*

Luleå

93 *340 km (211 mi) southeast of Kiruna (via E10 and E4).*

The most northerly major town in Sweden, Luleå is an important port at the top of the Gulf of Bothnia, at the mouth of the Luleälv (Lule River). The town was some 10 km (6 mi) farther inland when it was first granted its charter in 1621, but by 1649 trade had grown so much that it was moved closer to the sea. The development of Kiruna and the iron trade is linked, by means of a railway, with the fortunes of Luleå, where a steelworks was set up in the 1940s. Like its fellow port towns—Piteå, Skellefteå, Umeå, and Sundsvall—farther south, Luleå is a very modern and nondescript city, but it has some reasonable hotels. A beautiful archipelago of hundreds of islands hugs the coastline.

The **Norrbottens Museet** (Norbotten Museum) has one of the best collections of Sami ethnography in the world. ⊠ *Hermelinsparken 2,* ☎ *0920/220355.* ☒ *Free.* ☉ *Mid-June–mid-Aug., Thurs.–Tues. 10–6, Wed. 10–8.*

Dining and Lodging

$$$ ×☒ **Arctic.** Right in town center, the Arctic is known locally for its restaurant, which serves local specialties. The hotel is warm and cozy, with tastefully decorated, rustic rooms. ⊠ *Sandviksg. 80, S972 34,* ☎ *0920/ 10980,* FAX *0920/60980. 94 rooms. Restaurant, no-smoking rooms, hot tub, sauna, meeting rooms. AE, DC, MC, V.*

$$$$ ☒ **Luleå Hotel.** As you might expect of a Radisson SAS hotel, this one is large, modern, and central. Each floor is different: the third floor is done in blue tones; the English colonial–style second floor has ceiling fans and dried flowers; and the ground floor is art deco. ⊠ *Storg. 17, S971 28,* ☎ *0920/94000,* FAX *0920/88222. 216 rooms. Restaurant, no-*

smoking rooms, indoor pool, sauna, exercise room, nightclub, meeting rooms. AE, DC, MC, V.

$$$$ 🏨 **Luleå Stads Hotell.** This large, central Best Western hotel has nightly—sometimes boisterous—dancing. Rooms in the building dating back to 1901 are spacious and carpeted, with turn-of-the-century furnishings. ⊠ *Storg. 15, S972 32,* ☎ *0920/67000,* 𝔉𝔄𝔛 *0920/67092. 135 rooms, 3 suites. Restaurant, café, no-smoking rooms, sauna, dance club, meeting rooms. AE, DC, MC, V.*

$$$ 🏨 **Scandic.** This hotel on Lake Sjö has an extremely pleasant setting and is 2 km (1 mi) from the railway station. ⊠ *Banv. 3, S973 46,* ☎ *0920/ 228360,* 𝔉𝔄𝔛 *0920/69472. 157 rooms. Restaurant, no-smoking rooms, indoor pool, sauna, exercise room, meeting rooms. AE, DC, MC, V.*

$$ 🏨 **Amber.** A particularly fine old building, listed on the historic register, houses this hotel close to the railway station. Rooms are modern, with plush carpeting, minibars, and satellite television. ⊠ *Stationsg. 67, S972 34,* ☎ *0920/10200,* 𝔉𝔄𝔛 *0920/87906. 16 rooms. No-smoking rooms. AE, DC, MC, V.*

$$ 🏨 **Aveny.** Rooms are of varying sizes and colors, but all are spotless and fresh. It's close to the railway station. ⊠ *Hermelinsg. 10, S973 46,* ☎ *0920/221820,* 𝔉𝔄𝔛 *0920/220122. 24 rooms. No-smoking rooms. AE, DC, MC, V.*

Norrland and Norbotten A to Z

Arriving and Departing

BY PLANE

There are two nonstop SAS flights a day from Stockholm to **Kiruna Airport** (⊠ 5 km/3 mi from Kiruna, ☎ 0980/84810) and three additional flights via Luleå. Check **SAS** (☎ 020/727000) for specific times.

Between the Airport and Town: In summer, **buses** connect the airport and Kiruna; the fare is about SKr50. A **taxi** from the airport to the center of Kiruna costs about SKr75; book through the airline or call ☎ 0980/12020.

BY TRAIN

The best and cheapest way to get to Kiruna is to take the evening sleeper from Stockholm on Tuesday, Wednesday, or Saturday, when the fare is reduced to SKr595 for a single. The regular one-way price is SKr695 plus SKr90 for the couchette, double for return. You'll arrive at around lunchtime the next day.

Getting Around

Since public transportation is nonexistent in this part of the country, having a car is essential. The few roads are well built and maintained, although spring thaws can present potholes. Keep in mind that habitations are few and far between in this wilderness region.

CAR RENTALS

Kiruna: Avis (⊠ Hotel Ferrum, ☎ 0980/13080). **Hertz** (⊠ Industriv. 5, ☎ 0980/19000). **Europcar/InterRent** (⊠ Växlareg. 20, ☎ 0980/14365).

Contacts and Resources

DOCTORS AND DENTISTS

Kiruna Health Center (⊠ Thuleg. 29, ☎ 0980/73000). Medical advisory service, **Luleå** (☎ 0920/71400). **Jokkmokk Health Center** (⊠ Lappstav. 9, ☎ 0971/44444).

EMERGENCIES

For emergencies dial ☎ 112.

GUIDED TOURS

Local tourist offices have information on guided tours.

Lapland Tours: Same Laṅs Resor (⊠ c/o Rental Line I Jokkmokk, Hermelinsg. 20, 962 33, Jokkmokk, ☎ 0971/10606) arranges tours to points of interest in Lappland.

Sami Tours: Call **Swedish Sami Association** (⊠ Brog. 5, S90325, Umeå, ☎ 090/141180).

LATE-NIGHT PHARMACIES

There are no late-night pharmacies in Norbotten, but doctors called to emergencies can dispense medicine. The pharmacy at the Gallerian shopping center in Kiruna (⊠ Föreningsg. 6, ☎ 0980/18775) is open weekdays 9:30–6 and Saturdays 9:30–1.

VISITOR INFORMATION

Regional Tourist Office: Norrbottens Turistråd (⊠ Stationsg. 69, Luleå, ☎ 0920/94070) covers the entire area.

Local Tourist Offices: Abisko (⊠ S980 24 Abisko, ☎ 0980/40200). **Jokkmokk** (⊠ Stortorget 4, ☎ 0971/12140 or 0971/17257). **Kiruna** (⊠ Folkets Hus, ☎ 0980/18880). **Luleå** (⊠ Kulturcentrum Ebeneser, ☎ 0920/293500). **Gällivare** (⊠ Storg. 16, ☎ 0970/16660).

9 Portraits of Sweden

Sweden at a Glance: A Chronology

Reflections of Stockholm

Astrid Lindgren

Books and Videos

SCANDINAVIA AT A GLANCE:
A CHRONOLOGY

c 12,000 BC	The first migrations into Sweden.
2,000 BC	Southern European tribes migrate toward Denmark. The majority of early settlers in Scandinavia were Germanic.
c AD 770	The Viking Age begins. For the next 250 years, Scandinavians set sail on expeditions stretching from the Baltic to the Irish seas and to the Mediterranean as far as Sicily, employing superior ships and weapons and efficient military organization.
c 800–c 1000	Swedes control river trade routes between the Baltic and Black seas; establish Novgorod, Kiev, and other cities.
830	Frankish monk Ansgar makes one of the first attempts to Christianize Sweden and builds the first church in Slesvig, Denmark. Sweden is not successfully Christianized until the end of the 11th century, when the temple at Uppsala, a center for pagan resistance, is destroyed.
1248	Erik Eriksson appoints Birger as Jarl, in charge of military affairs and expeditions abroad. Birger improves women's rights, makes laws establishing peace in the home and church, and begins building Stockholm.
1250	Stockholm, Sweden, is officially founded.
1319	Sweden and Norway form a union that lasts until 1335.
1370	The Treaty of Stralsund gives the north German trading centers of the Hanseatic League free passage through Danish waters. German power increases throughout Scandinavia.
1397	The Kalmar Union is formed as a result of the dynastic ties between Sweden, Denmark, and Norway, the geographical position of the Scandinavian states, and the growing influence of Germans in the Baltic. Erik of Pomerania is crowned king of the Kalmar Union.
1477	University of Uppsala, Sweden's oldest university, is founded.
1520	Christian II, ruler of the Kalmar Union, executes 82 people who oppose the Scandinavian union, an event known as the "Stockholm blood bath." Sweden secedes from the Union three years later.
1523	Gustav Ericsson founds Swedish Vasa dynasty as King Gustav I Vasa.
1611–1613	The Kalmar War: Denmark wages war against Sweden in hope of restoring the Kalmar Union.
1611–1660	Gustav II Adolphus reigns in Sweden. Sweden defeats Denmark in the Thirty Years' War and becomes the greatest power in Scandinavia as well as in Northern and Central Europe.
1660	Peace of Copenhagen establishes modern boundaries of Denmark, Sweden, and Norway.
1668	Bank of Sweden, the world's oldest central bank, is founded.
1700–1721	Sweden, led by Karl XII, first broadens then loses its position to Russia as Northern Europe's greatest power in the Great Northern War.
1807	During the Napoleonic wars, Gustav III joins the coalition against France and accepts war with France and Russia.

1809 Sweden surrenders the Åland Islands and Finland to Russia, Finland becomes a Grand Duchy of the Russian Empire, and the Instrument of Government, Sweden's constitution, is adopted.

1813 Sweden takes a Frenchman as king: Karl XIV Johann establishes the Bernadotte dynasty.

1814 Sweden, after Napoleon's defeat at the Battle of Leipzig, attacks Denmark and forces the Danish surrender of Norway. The Treaty of Kiel, in 1814, calls for a union between Norway and Sweden despite Norway's desire for independence.

c 1850 The building of railroads begins in Scandinavia.

1889 The Swedish Social Democratic Party is founded.

1901 Alfred Nobel, the Swedish millionaire chemist and industrialist, initiates the Nobel prizes.

1905 Norway's union with Sweden is dissolved.

1914 At the outbreak of World War I, Sweden declares neutrality but is effectively blockaded.

1918 Women gain the right to vote.

1920 Scandinavian countries join the League of Nations.

1929–1937 The first social democratic government takes office in Sweden.

1939 Sweden declares neutrality in World War II.

1949 Sweden declines membership in NATO.

1952 The Nordic Council, which promotes cooperation among the Nordic parliaments, is founded.

1975 Sweden's Instrument of Government of 1809 is revised. This constitution reduces the voting age to eighteen and removes many of the king's powers and responsibilities.

1980 Fifty-eight percent of Sweden's voters advocate minimizing the use of nuclear reactors at Sweden's four power plants.

1986 Sweden's prime minister, Olof Palme, is assassinated for unknown reasons. Ingvar Carlsson succeeds him.

1991 The Social Democrats are voted out of office and a conservative coalition government takes over.

1992 Sweden's Riksbank (National Bank) raises overnight interest rates to a world record of 500% in an effort to defend the Swedish krona against speculation.

1995 Sweden and Finland join the EU in January.

1998 Stockholm is the 1998 Cultural Capital of Europe, hosting arts, culture, and nature events throughout the year.

REFLECTIONS OF STOCKHOLM

AT A RECEPTION for visiting dignitaries, the mayor of Stockholm surprised his guests by serving them glasses of a clear liquid that turned out to be water. It came, he explained, from the water surrounding this island city, and the purpose of the tongue-in-cheek gesture was to demonstrate that modern cities can afford clean environments. In fact, Stockholm has won the European Sustainable City Award in competition with 90-odd other cities, and a large swathe of Stockholm, including the vast royal domains, has been declared a national park for the benefit and enjoyment of the populace.

There were sound practical reasons to build Stockholm on the fourteen islands that command access from the Baltic Sea to Lake Mälaren. Back in the 13th century, after the Vikings had retired from plunder and discovery, Estonian pirates had taken to pillaging the shores of the lake, which extends deep into the Swedish heartland. Birger Jarl, the ruler who founded Sweden's first dynasty, put a stop to all that by stockading the islands the pirates had to pass. His effigy lies in gilded splendor at the foot of the city hall tower.

Stockholm without water would be unthinkable. It's the water that gives it beauty, character, life. The north shore and the south are, to be truthful, rather Germanic in character, not too different from, say, Zürich or Berlin. But watch them from across a busy waterway, mirrored in the blue lake, and they become invested with a lively charm.

The pearl in the oyster, however, is the small island known as Gamla Stan, or Old Town, dominated by the tawny colored, massive Royal Palace, designed by Nicodemus Tessin in the 17th century and completed in the 18th. In the Middle Ages, so many German merchants settled here that a law was proclaimed to limit their number on the city council to less than half of the members. The winding streets are lined with old houses in yellow, ochre, and occasional oxblood red. Some of the city's most attractive small hotels, gourmet restaurants,

and lively jazz clubs are here. To many people, the greatest treasure is found inside Storkyrkan, the Stockholm cathedral, next door to the palace: a larger-than-life, polychrome wooden statue of St. George slaying the dragon from 1489.

Skeppsholmen, a smaller island east of Gamla Stan and once the nation's principal navy base, is an idyllic place for a stroll, and great for art lovers. The Museum of Modern Art by the Spanish architect Rafael Moneo opened in 1998 and is one of the great contemporary museums. It blends in well with other structures, such as the "old" modern museum, a former armory and a trendsetter since its opening in 1958; it is now becoming the Museum of Architecture. Also on Skeppsholmen is the exquisite East Asiatic Museum, another Tessin creation, which houses one of the world's finest collections of Chinese art.

After you cross the bridge from Skeppsholmen on your way back to the city center you'll walk past the National Museum and you'll do well to stop there—not just for its Rembrandts and Swedish masters of centuries past but also for its new atrium restaurant, one of the city's best, in the piazzalike inner courtyard.

The piers of Stockholm's islands are lined with so many vessels of every category, from cruise ships and seagoing roll-on/roll-off vessels to island-hopping steamboats and pocket-size ferries, that it would seem impossible to squeeze in another motorboat, sailboat, or sloop. There were more than 100,000 of them at last count, and still the number keeps growing. The waterborne traffic jam when they return on a Sunday night in summer after a weekend at sea is something to behold.

Most of the Stockholm sailors travel no further than to one of the 25,000 islands and skerries that make up the Stockholm archipelago, extending 73 km (45 mi) east into the Baltic Sea. A red timbered cottage on one of these islands in the Baltic is most Swedes' idea of ultimate bliss, and there they seek to re-create the simple life as they imagine their forefathers to have lived it.

A fair approximation of archipelago life is just a 25-minute ferry ride away from the city center. This is Fjäderholmarna, or Feather Island, an islet that not long ago was a navy munitions dump. The rock is worn smooth by retreating Ice Age glaciers, there's a clump of yellow reeds at the water's edge, and on the rock the inevitable red cottage, windows and corners trimmed with white, against a backdrop of dark green foliage. There's a restaurant serving excellent Swedish specialties and a small colony of craftsmen making high-quality souvenirs.

Take a boat trip west from the city, and you're in a different world, verdant and tranquil. An hour away and you're at Drottningholm Palace, also designed Nicodemus Tessin and now the residence of the royal family. The palace and its formal French garden are impressive and the little Chinese Pavilion enchanting, but the real gem is the 200-year-old and perfectly intact Drottningholm Court Theater, where period performances of operas by Mozart, Gluck, and other 18th-century composers are presented every summer. The orchestra wears wigs, the singers appear in original costumes, and the ingenious old stage machinery produces thunder and storms.

As you wander through the reception areas and dressing rooms you'll be struck by the sparse, cool elegance of the decor and furnishings, a style borrowed from Louis XV but stripped down to the bare essentials. It may strike you, too, that this is not very different from modern Swedish interiors and design. Then you will have discovered a well-hidden truth: the Swedes, who take such pride in being modern, rational, and efficient, are secretly in love with the 18th century.

–Eric Sjogren

Eric Sjogren, a Swedish travel writer based in Brussels, is a frequent contributor to the *New York Times* and other publications.

ASTRID LINDGREN

APPROPRIATELY, the career of Astrid Lindgren, Sweden's best-know children's writer, author of the *Pippi Longstocking* books and many others, has a fairy-tale beginning. Once upon a time, Karin, her seven-year-old daughter, ill in bed with pneumonia, begged her: "Tell me a story . . . tell me the story of Pippi Longstocking."

"Neither she nor I know where on earth she got that name from," says Lindgren. "That was the first time I ever heard it. I made up the character right there and then, told her a story, and only wrote it down much later."

Thus was born one of the most memorable characters in children's fiction, her adventures translated from Lindgren's native Swedish into more than 50 languages.

"A few years later, I was awarded a prize for the stories and offered to share it with Karin," recalls Lindgren, "but by then she decided that she was too old. She said she was bored with Pippi."

With younger children all over the world, however, Pippi continues to strike a responsive chord: a little girl of indeterminate age with a gap-toothed smile, freckle face, and a wild mop of ginger hair from which a braid juts lopsidedly out over each ear.

Phenomenally strong, irrepressibly cheeky, she lives, independent of adults, with a horse and monkey in a tumbledown house, supporting herself from a hoard of gold coins. She has no table manners and doesn't go to school. She does just what she likes, when she feels like doing it.

"Bertrand Russell once said that children dream of power the way that adults dream of sex," says Lindgren. "I was very impressed with that at the time, and I think I must have had it in mind when I created Pippi."

Despite vociferous protests from educationalists and child psychologists, Pippi won immediate favor with kids. Lindgren has since created several other memorable characters, but Pippi remains the basis of her enormous popularity in her home country.

It would be well-nigh impossible to find a Swede who has not heard of Lindgren. She is *Tant Astrid*, Aunty Astrid, a gray-haired, short-sighted little old lady who is a symbol of hearth and home, of faith in traditional values and love of rural Sweden, with its deep, dark pine forests, wide blue lakes and meadows dotted with red-painted wood houses.

The independent spirit that created such an unconventional character as Pippi Longstocking still exists within this grandmother, however, and, using her awesome popularity, Lindgren has been partly responsible for the fall of one Swedish government and for forcing a second one in 1989 to draft radical new legislation protecting the rights of pets and farm animals, about which she has a bee in her bonnet.

She remains refreshingly unspoiled by all the adulation and attention she receives.

"When I go out, people come up to me in the street and tell me how much they've enjoyed my books, and children will hug and kiss me," she says. "Of course, that's very nice, but you know somehow I always feel it's not happening to *me*.

"It's as though someone else had all that celebrity and I am standing alongside her."

The mere suggestion that she wields power brings a steely glint to her blue eyes. "Power? I have only the power of the word," she says. "I wouldn't want power in the real sense. That's the worst thing I know. People always abuse it."

Yet there is more than a suspicion that, Pippilike, she revels in the influence she, an ordinary (or perhaps one should say, extraordinary) citizen can use to inject rebellious ideas into the heads of her youthful public and bend Sweden's rulers to her will.

One of her characters is *The World's Best Karlson*. Lovable figment of a little boy's imagination, Karlson is a jovial type who laughs at reality and flies around the house aided by a propeller set in the middle of his back. The Karlson books have become particularly popular in Russia, where *Literaturnaja Gaseta,* a literary review, has described the character as "the symbol of innocent, uncorrupted childhood, the childhood we as adults find so difficult to remember and accept."

The Satirical Theater in Moscow staged a play based on the character in the 1960s, and Lindgren says that when she visits Russia, taxi drivers always talk to her about Karlson.

When former Swedish Prime Minister Ingvar Carlsson visited Moscow, she was delighted to hear that many Russians were disappointed because he wasn't the *real* Karlson.

HOWEVER, SAYS LINDGREN, it is the stories of the Bullerby children that most closely approximate her own childhood. These feature the adventures of children from three families in a little village somewhere in Sweden and eulogize rural life set against a fondly painted picture of seasonal contrast. The Bullerby children are Lindgren's *nicest* characters: playful but, unlike Pippi, unwilling to overstep the line.

Bullerby is based on the little village of Sevedstorp, set amid the dense pine-and-spruce forests that cover the southern Swedish province of Småland, birthplace of her father, Samuel August Ericsson, who by the time Astrid was born, in 1907, had moved to the nearby town of Vimmerby.

Home was a simple clapboard house, painted red and with a glassed-in porch, surrounded by well-tended flower beds, daisy-strewn lawns, and apple trees. Her father had started life as a hired hand but wound up running his own farm. The family was reasonably well off, though there was rarely money left over for luxuries. Samuel Ericsson was an excellent storyteller, and many of the anecdotes he told his children surfaced later in Lindgren's books. Her mother, Hanna, wrote poetry in her youth and at one time dreamed of becoming a schoolteacher.

Lindgren was one of four children. She had an elder brother, Gunnar (born 1906), and two younger sisters, Stina (born 1911) and Ingegerd (born 1916). All displayed literary talents of some kind or another: Gunnar became a member of parliament

renowned for his political satires; Stina a translator; and Ingegerd a journalist.

The innocent childhood fun and games described in the Bullerby books are, by and large, those of Astrid herself and her brother and sisters. "We played the whole time from morning to night, just like the children in the Bullerby stories," she says.

She enjoyed a warm relationship with Samuel August, a fact that is reflected time and again in her books, peopled in the main with warm, understanding, though often gruff fathers. She describes her mother, on the other hand, as a rather distant person, recalling that as a child Hanna hugged her only once. It was from her that she inherited her willpower, energy, and stubbornness, she says.

The creator of Pippi Longstocking rebelled against Hanna's authority just once as a child: "I was quite young—perhaps three or four—and one day I thought she was stupid so I decided to run away and hide in the outside toilet. I wasn't there for too long, and when I came back in my brother and sisters had been given sweets. I thought this was so unfair that I kicked out in mother's direction. I was taken into the front room and beaten."

When she started at the local school at the age of seven, in 1914, she was overcome with shyness (a traditional Swedish handicap) when the teacher called out her name and, instead of answering "yes," burst into tears.

The priest in charge of registering the new arrivals told her she could go and sit down instead of standing with the other children. "I wanted to be with the others," she says. "I absolutely didn't want to go and sit down." The tears subsided, and she now sees the incident as the day she broke through her "wall of shyness."

She was a conscientious pupil, remembered by classmate Anne-Marie Fries, the model for Madicken, another of her characters, as "unbelievably nimble. I remember her in the gym; she could climb from floor to ceiling like a monkey."

Astrid also began to show evidence of literary talents. Her essays were frequently read to the rest of the class, and, when she was 13, one of them was even published in *Wimmerby Tidning,* Vimmerby's local newspaper. This was titled "Life in Our

Backyard" and described two small girls and the games they played. "They joked and called me Vimmerby's answer to Selma Lagerlöf, and I decided that if there was one thing I would never be it was an author."

She recalls her teens as a melancholy episode. "Like most teenagers, I thought I was ugly," she says, "and I just *never* fell in love. Everyone else was in love."

She left school at 16 and was given a job on *Wimmerby Tidning*, reading proofs and even covering some local events such as weddings and funerals as a reporter.

In 1926 Astrid's blissful childhood came to a very definite end, when, at the age of 18, she had an affair with a man and became pregnant. In recent years Sweden has developed a reputation for liberality in such matters, but in those days, pregnant and unmarried, she created a huge scandal in Vimmerby, a small town steeped in traditional Lutheran values.

Astrid left home and traveled to the capital, Stockholm. "Of course, my parents weren't pleased, but I wasn't thrown out or anything like that," she explains; "wild horses wouldn't have kept me there."

She knew nobody in Stockholm. "I was terribly alone at first," she says. "I had left behind all my friends. I was very unhappy. Childhood is one thing," she says philosophically; "youth is something else."

She took solace in reading the works of Norwegian author Knut Hamsun. Hamsun's book *Hunger* made a deep impression on her. She still names it as her principal literary influence. Lonely and poor herself, she identified strongly with Hamsun's graphic descriptions of the life of a starving young writer in Norway.

In an essay for the mass-circulation Stockholm evening newspaper *Expressen* in 1974, she recalled sitting under a bird-cherry tree outside a church, reading *Hunger*. "That was the greatest literary experience I've ever had," she said.

She gave birth to a son, Lars, whom she handed over to foster parents in Copenhagen, returning to Stockholm to study shorthand and typing and to land a job at a local firm working for the father of Viveca Lindfors, the Swedish actress.

"I soon started to make friends in Stockholm, and I went to Copenhagen as often as I could to see Lars. There was never any question of his being adopted. He was my son and I loved him deeply," she says.

On one occasion she left her job during working hours to take the train to Copenhagen, only to be spotted by her boss. She was sacked.

However, her luck seemed to have turned. Astrid found an editorial job with KAK, the Swedish automobile association. There she met Sture Lindgren, whom she married in the spring of 1931. Her son came to live with them, and in 1934 she gave birth to her daughter, Karin.

THE FAMILY LIVED IN the part of Stockholm known as Vasastan, at first in a small apartment close to the main railway line to the north of Sweden, later in a spacious, light apartment overlooking a park. Lindgren still lives there today, surrounded by her books and memorabilia of her lifetime as an author.

It was in the winter of 1941 that Karin asked her to tell the story of Pippi Longstocking. "Much later I was out walking in the park when I slipped and sprained my ankle," she recalls. "I was forced to lie in bed, so I began to write down the stories I had told to Karin."

She typed a manuscript and sent it to Bonniers, one of Sweden's leading publishing houses. It was refused. Undaunted, she wrote a girl's story, *The Confidences of Britt-Mari*, which she entered for a contest organized by another, much smaller, publishing house, Rabén and Sjögren. She won second prize, and in 1944 the story was published. Lindgren also began working for the company as an editor.

The following year Rabén and Sjögren published her follow-up, titled *Kerstin and I*. Then in 1945 the company announced a new contest for books aimed at children age 6–10.

Lindgren revised her Pippi Longstocking manuscript and entered it for the contest, along with a new effort, *All About the Bullerby Children*, in which she lovingly recreated her childhood in Vimmerby. *Pippi Longstocking* won first prize. *All About the Bullerby Children* failed to take an award but was bought for publication.

The first Pippi Longstocking book was well received by both critics and public and soon sold out. However, a year later, the follow-up, *Pippi Goes Aboard,* caused a furor, with Lindgren accused of undermining the authority of parents and teachers.

Professor John Landquist, writing in the evening newspaper *Aftonbladet,* accused Lindgren of "crazed fantasy" and said Pippi's adventures were "something disagreeable that scratches at the soul."

Today there is a different perspective. Viví Edström, professor of literature at the University of Stockholm, has described Pippi as "a child's projection of everything that is desirable" and claims her as a major influence on Swedish literature.

"In the still prim and moralizing children's literature of the 1940s, Astrid Lindgren's breakthrough meant that children had a literature on their own terms," says Edström.

The third and last Pippi Longstocking book, *Pippi in the South Seas,* was published in 1948. In this, Pippi sails away to a Pacific island for a reunion with her father, returning to Sweden for Christmas, which she spends alone. It could be an allegory on the fate of nonconformists in Sweden, a country where the good of the collective has always been prized above that of the individual.

Physically, the model for Pippi was a red-haired, freckle-faced friend of daughter Karin, Sonja Melin, who today sells vegetables in Hötorgshallen, one of Stockholm's few surviving indoor markets. "I meet her now and again when I go out shopping," says Lindgren. "She was just so lively as a child. As soon as I saw her, I thought, 'That's my Pippi!'"

Lindgren has created many other well-loved and sometimes controversial characters in the 30 books she has written since.

Mio My Son, written in 1954 (perhaps significantly, two years after the death of husband Sture) is one of Lindgren's most ambitious books: a highly advanced fairy story that explores difficult themes such as fear and death.

In 1985 a journalist asked Lindgren on Swedish Radio: "Isn't *Mio My Son* actually a pretty nasty book?"

She replied, "Of course; that's why children love it."

WHILE SHE HAS never attempted a "serious" adult novel ("I never really wanted to. I'm not sure I'd be any good at it."), she has not fought shy of exploring themes considered improper for children. In 1973 controversy raged once more over *The Brothers Lionheart,* in which a dying child dreams of meeting, in another world, the brother he idealizes who has died heroically in a fire. The two boys ride off to fight the forces of evil.

Shortly after this, in 1976, Lindgren, a lifelong voter for the Social Democrats, caused a still greater fuss when she became embroiled in a row with Sweden's Socialist government.

It all started with a demand from the tax authorities, which, she calculated, would, along with her social-insurance contributions, exceed her actual income. She wrote a fairy story for *Expressen,* the Stockholm newspaper. Its main character, Pomperipossa, has always loved her country and respected its rulers. Now she turns against them: " 'O you, the pure and fiery social democracy of my youth, what have they done to you?' thought Pomperipossa, 'How long shall your name be abused to protect a dictatorial, bureaucratic, unjust, authoritarian society?' "

The barb went home, and in the Swedish parliament (*Riksdag*) the then finance minister, Gunnar Sträng (his surname translates into English as "Strict") reprimanded Lindgren. "The article is a combination of inspired fantasy and total ignorance of tax policy," he said. "Astrid Lindgren should stick to what she knows, namely making up stories."

Lindgren hit back: "He may not be good at arithmetic, but he's certainly good at telling fairy-tales. I think we should trade jobs, he and I."

In that year's general election the Social Democrats lost power, after more than 40 years in office. An analysis of the result by the influential Sifo public-opinion research institute named the controversy over Lindgren's story as a major contributory factor.

Ronia, the Robber's Daughter, published in 1981, returned to a "straight" fairy-tale format, the story of a boy and girl from two different, warring bands of robbers, who run away together. This was turned into an award-winning Swedish film by comedian/director Tage Danielsson. Eleven of her books have been filmed, and Lindgren herself still takes an active interest in each project.

She has been positively deluged with prizes, including in 1989 the Albert Schweitzer Award, for her work on behalf of animal rights. At a time in life when most people would be content to wind down, she joined forces with veterinary surgeon Kristina Forslund in a campaign to persuade Sweden to introduce more stringent rules on animal husbandry.

A string of articles and open letters soon brought the government to its knees. Prime Minister Carlsson announced new legislation that he dubbed "Lex Astrid" and called on Lindgren personally to tell her about it.

Despite the fact that the laws are considered the most advanced in the world, Lindgren is not satisfied. She describes them as "toothless." "They are full of loopholes," she says. "Now we have to fight to get them tightened up."

Although hampered by failing eyesight, she began the 1990s with a new children's play written for Stockholm's Royal Dramatic Theater, plans to film *The Brothers Lionheart,* and has thoughts of writing a new book.

"It depends whether I feel inspired. I write quite quickly, in shorthand at first, then I type it. I do a chapter, then re-write until it flows properly. After that I continue with the next one. A word processor? I couldn't use one of those; I'm not a bit technically minded, I'm afraid.

"I really don't know what I would have been if I had not become an author." She smiles, perhaps thinking of her battles with authority, the Pippi Longstocking side of her personality coming to the fore. "Maybe I could have been a lawyer. I might have been rather good at that."

— By Chris Mosey

BOOKS AND VIDEOS

Books

A History of the Vikings (Oxford University Press, 1984) recounts the story of the aggressive warriors and explorers who during the Middle Ages influenced a large portion of the world, extending from Constantinople to America. Gwyn Jones's lively account makes learning the history enjoyable.

One of the easiest and certainly most entertaining ways of finding out about modern Swedish society is to read the Martin Beck detective series of thrillers by Maj Sjöwall and Per Wahlöö, all of which have been translated into English. One of these, *The Terrorists,* was even prophetic, containing a scene in which a Swedish prime minister was shot, a precursor to the murder of Olof Palme in 1986.

Similarly, an entertaining insight into how life was in the bad old days when Sweden was one of the most backward agrarian countries in Europe may be obtained from Vilhelm Moberg's series of novels on poor Swedes who emigrated to America: *The Emigrants, Unto a Good Land,* and *The Last Letter Home.*

The plays of Swedish writer August Strindberg greatly influenced modern European and American drama. Perhaps the most enduringly fascinating of these, *Miss Julie,* mixes the explosive elements of sex and class to stunning effect.

One of the most exhaustive and comprehensive studies in English of the country published in recent years is *Sweden: The Nation's History,* by Franklin D. Scott (University of Minnesota Press). Chris Mosey's *Cruel Awakening, Sweden and the Killing of Olof Palme* (C. Hurst, London 1991) seeks to provide an overview of the country and its recent history seen through the life and assassination of its best-known politician of recent times and the farcical hunt for his killer.

Films of Interest

Of course, Sweden was home to Ingmar Bergman, who produced such classics as *The Virgin Spring* (1959), *Wild Strawberries* (1957), and *Fanny and Alexander* (1982).

SWEDISH VOCABULARY

English	Swedish	Pronunciation
Basics		
Yes/no	Ja/nej	yah/nay
Please	Var snäll; Var vänlig	vahr snehll vahr vehn-leeg
Thank you very much.	Tack så **mee**-keh	tahk soh mycket.
You're welcome.	Var så god.	vahr shoh **goo**
Excuse me. (to get by someone)	Ursäkta.	oor-**shehk**-tah
(to apologize)	Förlåt.	fur-**loht**
Hello	God dag	goo **dahg**
Goodbye	Adjö	ah-**yoo**
Today	I dag	ee **dahg**
Tomorrow	I morgon	ee **mor**-ron
Yesterday	I går	ee **gohr**
Morning	Morgon	**mohr**-on
Afternoon	Eftermiddag	**ehf**-ter-meed-dahg
Night	Natt	naht
Numbers		
1	ett	eht
2	två	tvoh
3	tre	tree
4	fyra	fee-rah
5	fem	fem
6	sex	sex
7	sju	shoo
8	åtta	oht-tah
9	nio	nee
10	tio	tee
Days of the Week		
Monday	måndag	mohn-dahg
Tuesday	tisdag	tees-dahg
Wednesday	onsdag	ohns-dahg
Thursday	torsdag	tohrs-dahg
Friday	fredag	freh-dahg
Saturday	lördag	luhr-dahg
Sunday	söndag	sohn-dahg
Useful Phrases		
Do you speak English?	Talar ni engelska?	tah-lahr nee ehng-ehl-skah
I don't speak . . .	Jag talar inte svenska . . .	yah tah-lahr **een**-teh **sven**-skah
I don't understand.	Jag förstår inte.	yah fuhr-**stohr** **een**-teh
I don't know.	Jag vet inte.	yah **veht een**-teh

I am American/ British.	Jag är amerikan/ engelsman.	yah ay ah-mehr-ee-**kahn**/ **ehng**-ehls-mahn
I am sick.	Jag är sjuk.	yah ay **shyook**
Please call a doctor.	Jag vill skicka efter en läkare.	yah veel **shee**-kah **ehf**-tehr ehn **lay**-kah-reh
Do you have a vacant room?	Har Ni något rum ledigt?	hahr nee noh-goht **room leh**-deekt
How much does it cost?	Vad kostar det?/ Hur mycket kostar det?	vah **kohs**-tahr deh/hor **mee**-keh **kohs**-tahr deh
It's too expensive.	Den är för dyr.	dehn ay foor **deer**
Beautiful	Vacker	**vah**-kehr
Help!	Hjälp	yehlp
Stop!	Stopp, stanna	stop, **stahn**-nah
How do I get to . . .	Kan Ni visa mig vägen till . . .	kahn nee **vee**-sah may **vay**-gehn teel
the train station?	stationen	stah-**shoh**-nehn
the post office?	posten	**pohs**-tehn
the tourist office?	en resebyrå	ehn-**reh**-seh-**bee**-roh
the hospital?	sjukhuset	**shyook**-hoo-seht
Does this bus go to . . . ?	Går den här bussen till . . . ?	gohr dehn hehr **boo**-sehn teel
Where is the W.C.?	Var är toilett/ toaletten	vahr ay twah-**leht** twah-**leht**-en
On the left	Till vänster	teel **vehn**-stur
On the right	Till höger	teel **huh**-gur
Straight ahead	Rakt fram	rahkt **frahm**

Dining Out

Please bring me . . .	Var snäll och hämta åt mig	vahr snehl oh hehm-tah oht may
menu	matsedeln	maht-seh-dehln
fork	en gaffel	ehn gahf-fehl
knife	en kniv	ehn kneev
spoon	en sked	ehn shehd
napkin	en servett	ehn sehr-veht
bread	bröd	bruh(d)
butter	smör	smuhr
milk	mjölk	myoolk
pepper	peppar	pehp-pahr
salt	salt	sahlt
sugar	socker	soh-kehr
water	vatten	vaht-n
The check, please.	Får jag be om notan?	fohr yah beh ohm **noh**-tahn

INDEX

NOTES

NOTES

Fodor's Travel Publications

Available at bookstores everywhere, or call 1–800–533–6478, 24 hours a day.

Gold Guides

U.S.

Alaska	Florida	New Orleans	Seattle & Vancouver
Arizona	Hawai'i	New York City	The South
Boston	Las Vegas, Reno, Tahoe	Pacific North Coast	U.S. & British Virgin Islands
California		Philadelphia & the Pennsylvania Dutch Country	USA
Cape Cod, Martha's Vineyard, Nantucket	Los Angeles		Virginia & Maryland
	Maine, Vermont, New Hampshire	The Rockies	Walt Disney World, Universal Studios and Orlando
The Carolinas & Georgia	Maui & Lāna'i	San Diego	
Chicago	Miami & the Keys	San Francisco	Washington, D.C.
Colorado	New England	Santa Fe, Taos, Albuquerque	

Foreign

Australia	Europe	Montréal & Québec City	Scotland
Austria	Florence, Tuscany & Umbria	Moscow, St. Petersburg, Kiev	Singapore
The Bahamas			South Africa
Belize & Guatemala	France	The Netherlands, Belgium & Luxembourg	South America
Bermuda	Germany		Southeast Asia
Canada	Great Britain	New Zealand	Spain
Cancún, Cozumel, Yucatán Peninsula	Greece	Norway	Sweden
	Hong Kong	Nova Scotia, New Brunswick, Prince Edward Island	Switzerland
Caribbean	India		Thailand
China	Ireland		Toronto
Costa Rica	Israel	Paris	Turkey
Cuba	Italy	Portugal	Vienna & the Danube Valley
The Czech Republic & Slovakia	Japan	Provence & the Riviera	
	London		
Eastern & Central Europe	Madrid & Barcelona	Scandinavia	
	Mexico		

Special-Interest Guides

Adventures to Imagine	Fodor's Gay Guide to the USA	Halliday's New Orleans Food Explorer	Rock & Roll Traveler USA
Alaska Ports of Call	Fodor's How to Pack		
Ballpark Vacations		Healthy Escapes	Sunday in San Francisco
Caribbean Ports of Call	Great American Learning Vacations	Kodak Guide to Shooting Great Travel Pictures	Walt Disney World for Adults
The Complete Guide to America's National Parks	Great American Sports & Adventure Vacations		Weekends in New York
		National Parks and Seashores of the East	
Disney Like a Pro	Great American Vacations	National Parks of the West	Wendy Perrin's Secrets Every Smart Traveler Should Know
Europe Ports of Call	Great American Vacations for Travelers with Disabilities		
Family Adventures		Nights to Imagine	
		Rock & Roll Traveler Great Britain and Ireland	Worldwide Cruises and Ports of Call

Fodor's Special Series

Fodor's Best Bed & Breakfasts

America

California

The Mid-Atlantic

New England

The Pacific Northwest

The South

The Southwest

The Upper Great Lakes

Compass American Guides

Alaska

Arizona

Boston

Chicago

Colorado

Hawaii

Idaho

Hollywood

Las Vegas

Maine

Manhattan

Minnesota

Montana

New Mexico

New Orleans

Oregon

Pacific Northwest

San Francisco

Santa Fe

South Carolina

South Dakota

Southwest

Texas

Utah

Virginia

Washington

Wine Country

Wisconsin

Wyoming

Citypacks

Amsterdam

Atlanta

Berlin

Chicago

Florence

Hong Kong

London

Los Angeles

Montréal

New York City

Paris

Prague

Rome

San Francisco

Tokyo

Venice

Washington, D.C.

Exploring Guides

Australia

Boston & New England

Britain

California

Canada

Caribbean

China

Costa Rica

Egypt

Florence & Tuscany

Florida

France

Germany

Greek Islands

Hawaii

Ireland

Israel

Italy

Japan

London

Mexico

Moscow & St. Petersburg

New York City

Paris

Prague

Provence

Rome

San Francisco

Scotland

Singapore & Malaysia

South Africa

Spain

Thailand

Turkey

Venice

Flashmaps

Boston

New York

San Francisco

Washington, D.C.

Fodor's Gay Guides

Los Angeles & Southern California

New York City

Pacific Northwest

San Francisco and the Bay Area

South Florida

USA

Pocket Guides

Acapulco

Aruba

Atlanta

Barbados

Budapest

Jamaica

London

New York City

Paris

Prague

Puerto Rico

Rome

San Francisco

Washington, D.C.

Languages for Travelers (Cassette & Phrasebook)

French

German

Italian

Spanish

Mobil Travel Guides

America's Best Hotels & Restaurants

California and the West

Major Cities

Great Lakes

Mid-Atlantic

Northeast

Northwest and Great Plains

Southeast

Southwest and South Central

Rivages Guides

Bed and Breakfasts of Character and Charm in France

Hotels and Country Inns of Character and Charm in France

Hotels and Country Inns of Character and Charm in Italy

Hotels and Country Inns of Character and Charm in Paris

Hotels and Country Inns of Character and Charm in Portugal

Hotels and Country Inns of Character and Charm in Spain

Short Escapes

Britain

France

New England

Near New York City

Fodor's Sports

Golf Digest's Places to Play

Skiing USA

USA Today The Complete Four Sport Stadium Guide

WHEREVER YOU TRAVEL, *H*ELP IS NEVER FAR AWAY.

From planning your trip to providing travel assistance along the way, American Express® Travel Service Offices are always there to help you do more.

Sweden

American Express Travel
Service
Birger Jarlsgatan 1
Stockholm
8/679 52 00

Nyman & Schultz (R)
Landvetter Flygplatz (Airport)
Göteborg
31/941 870

American Express TFS
Ostra Hamngatan 35
Göteborg
31/13 07 12

Nyman & Schultz Karlstad
Vaxnasgatan 10 Karolinen
Karlstad
54/14 48 40

do more AMERICAN EXPRESS
Travel

http://www.americanexpress.com/travel
American Express Travel Service Offices are located throughout Sweden.